THE POLITICS
OF DESPAIR

THE
POLITICS
OF DESPAIR

Power and Resistance
in the Tobacco Wars

TRACY CAMPBELL

THE UNIVERSITY PRESS OF KENTUCKY

DB # 1221873

Editorial and Sales Offices: Lexington, Kentucky 40508-4008

Library of Congress Cataloging-in-Publication Data

Campbell, Tracy.
    The politics of despair : power and resistance in the Tobacco Wars
  / Tracy Campbell.
        p.   cm.
    Includes bibliographical references and index.
    ISBN 0-8131-1821-2 :
    1. Tobacco industry—Kentucky—History. 2. Tobacco industry—
Tennessee—History.   3. Tobacco workers—Kentucky—History.
4. Tobacco workers—Tennessee—History.   5. American Tobacco
Company—History.   I. Title.
HD9137.K4C36   1993
331.88'1371'09769—dc20   92-47277

HD
9137
.K4
C36
1993

To Leslie

Contents

Illustrations, Maps, Tables

Illustrations

Maps

Tables

Acknowledgments

In the writing of this book I was financially aided through scholarships provided by the Duke University Graduate School and Department of History. A well-timed dissertation prize from the American Institute of Cooperation in Washington, D.C., proved very helpful. A James Still Fellowship, funded by the Andrew W. Mellon Foundation and administered through the Faculty Scholars Program, University of Kentucky, assisted me in completing the manuscript. I thank Alice Brown and Robin Weinstein of the Faculty Scholars Program for generously making office space and other resources available during my fellowship stay.

Like most historians, I am indebted to a host of diligent and dedicated people working at numerous libraries and archives throughout the country. I wish especially to thank the staffs of the Agriculture Library and the M.I. King Library, University of Kentucky; the Perkins Library, Duke University; the Kentucky Historical Society; the North Carolina Collection, University of North Carolina at Chapel Hill; the Kentucky Department for Libraries and Archives; the Tennessee State Library and Archives; the Filson Club Library; Mars Hill College; the National Archives; and the Library of Congress. I also wish to thank the editors of *Agricultural History* and the *Register of the Kentucky Historical Society* for permission to reprint sections of this book previously published in those journals.

Angela Ray skillfully edited the manuscript and helped me avoid numerous errors. I also thank John Dawahare for compiling the maps contained in the text.

James Bissett, Charles Bolton, Robert Durden, Raymond Gavins, Lawrence Goodwyn, James Klotter, Peter Wood, and George Wright each read various drafts of the manuscript. Although we may not have always agreed, their careful and critical readings made this a better book.

Alex Moorehead and his late wife, Bobbi, were kind friends through the early years of this study and provided me a welcome home away from home. Gene and Helen Crawford were generous and staunch allies. I thank C. Leslie Dawson and Tom Bennett for a unique education in politics. My parents, Alex and Anna Campbell, have been steadfast supporters of this project from the very beginning. Tragically, my father did not live to see the final version in print. My son, Alex, enriched the later stages of this project and has provided the most unique education of all.

Finally, my wife, Leslie, delayed her own education and career so that I could begin graduate study. As only she knows, this was only one of many sacrifices she made on behalf of this book and its author. She has good-naturedly shouldered more than her share of the burdens of daily living in order to free my time for research and writing, yet has also managed to remind me of the proper priorities. She has been a sounding board for every conceptual interpretation contained in the book, as well as a keen critic. The dedication of this book reflects a special and deeply felt bond.

THE POLITICS
OF DESPAIR

Introduction

For most of American history, the bulk of the population has resided on the land. Consequently, the family farm is one of the more revered institutions in American culture. In Jefferson's time the independent smallholder was viewed as the bedrock of democracy, and few ambitious politicians since have neglected to mention their earnest support for the family farm. Endless production statistics and charts combined with Norman Rockwell images shape our collective picture that, despite occasional disturbances, all is well on the land.

This serene tableau is vividly contradicted by the sobering fact that most American farmers have lived in poverty and despair. Two Kentucky tenant farmers, J.T. and Kate Strand of Muhlenberg County, once expressed their response to this reality. Living in the dark tobacco section of western Kentucky in the early 1900s, the young couple had little when they were married. Speaking in a rural dialect that perhaps allowed others to dismiss him, J.T. reasoned, "I had nuthin' but I 'lowed I would work doubly hard, and Kate, she said she would save all she could, and betwixt us we 'lowed we'd come out all right." As the years passed, however, J.T. realized that "the harder we worked the less we had." Farm life took its toll on Kate and her children, who worked alongside J.T. in the tobacco patch. "I have seen bloody tracks in the snow," Kate said, "left there by my shoeless children." After years of diligent effort, J.T. revealed the anguish he felt as a tenant farmer: "There never was a family as hard up as we'uns." Upon reflection, J.T. corrected himself: "I'll take that back. Every one of the tenants lived as hard as we'uns, and they was only samples of how all the tobacco growers lived as didn't own no land." In such grim words, the Strands expressed the underlying human dynamics that fueled the Tobacco Wars of Kentucky and Tennessee.[1]

The Tobacco Wars occurred at a pivotal time when America was being transformed from an agricultural society to an industrial one. All farmers underwent overwhelming economic stress from the financial structure erected in the wake of the Civil War, but southern tobacco farmers were especially hard hit. The tightening of the nation's money supply insured a permanent constriction of credit sources in ways that over time proved crippling to farm families. The emergence in the 1890s of the American Tobacco Company and the corresponding monopolization of the tobacco industry brought the new industrial order squarely into the social and economic fabric of life in America's tobacco regions. Competing buyers for tobacco disappeared as the agents for the American Tobacco Company dictated the prices farmers received. In the early 1900s tobacco prices fell below the cost of production. Farmers in Kentucky and Tennessee who relied on tobacco as their cash crop consequently found themselves up against the world: a debilitating financial system, an unresponsive political structure, and one of the most effective industrial monopolies in American history.

In response, farmers in the tobacco belt of Kentucky and Tennessee desperately tried to save themselves. Meeting in churches, schoolrooms, and courthouses, they created their own institutions to challenge the encroaching order. They formed cooperatives through which farmers could pool their crops and withhold tobacco from the market until a satisfactory price was offered. These self-generated organizations cannot be understood as automatic responses to low prices. Instead, they were brought about by the activity of farmers who had spent years building the foundations for insurgency.

The subsequent events have come to be known as the Black Patch War, a reference to the activities of farmers in the western portions of Kentucky and Tennessee who grew a particular type of dark tobacco. Scholars and writers of the tobacco revolt have virtually ignored the simultaneous insurgent activity of burley growers in central Kentucky. Yet the burley movement in many ways eclipsed that of the better-known effort in the Black Patch. In 1908, when the tobacco trust refused to buy the pooled burley crops of 1906 and 1907, nearly thirty-five thousand burley farmers, residing in over thirty counties, went on strike and did

not grow a tobacco crop. In November 1908 the American Tobacco Company relented under pressure from the strike and
purchased the pooled crops at prices demanded by the burley
growers. The only large-scale agricultural strike in American
history thus came to a dramatic and successful conclusion. The
1908 burley strike subsequently became the high point of agrarian
organizing in Kentucky and Tennessee, and it remains an unprecedented achievement in the annals of agrarian protest movements. This study concerns both insurgent movements: hence
the term *Black Patch War* is replaced by *Tobacco Wars*.

The topic of a strike—an action seemingly reserved exclusively
for industrial workers—occurring among farmers presents a conceptual problem for the historian. Besides the usual barriers confronting those undertaking concerted work stoppages, farmers
are traditionally perceived to possess additional organic problems that preclude such collective attempts. Instead of working
under one roof, farmers are dispersed over vast areas, making
for a much more difficult organizing task. They are also imbued,
we are admonished, with a certain "individualism" or "peasant
mentality," which decreases the likelihood of cooperative activities.[2] These views are undergirded by a cultural presumption
that rural populations are less sophisticated than their urban
counterparts. This idea was perhaps never more vividly represented than in Marx's famous reference to the "idiocy of rural
life."[3] Such powerful assumptions continue to divide our con-
ceptions of producers with wrenches and hammers from those of
producers with plows and hoes.

To the burley farmers in central Kentucky, however, such
distinctions were not so readily apparent. Their confrontation
with industrial America was as significant as that of industrial
laborers. The events in central Kentucky in 1908 provide a unique
opportunity for historians to understand two fundamental
points: rural people can act collectively, and such collective action
necessarily imposes limits for farmers inextricably tied to a cash-
crop economy. The 1908 strike's success, coupled with the eventual failure of the burley cooperative, dramatically illuminates the
human cost of the nation's industrial transformation.

The saga of the Tobacco Wars, however, did not run its course
solely within the framework of cooperatives fighting the Amer-

ican Tobacco Company. In a last effort to save themselves from
economic ruin, desperate members of both Black Patch and Bluegrass communities undertook vigilantism. Armed "night riders"
soon became the most visible and shocking aspect of the tobacco
revolt. When the co-ops failed to mobilize sufficient numbers of
farmers, night riders began a coercive campaign against nonpoolers as well as agents of the tobacco trust. Night riding attempted to accomplish what democratic organizing could not. It
provided an ironic and tragic ending to the organizing activity
that originally gave democratic life to the farmer movement.

Besides investigating the interior organizational dynamics that
created the cooperatives and the subsequent struggles with the
American Tobacco Company, I also seek in this study to clarify
the economic, social, and ideological circumstances from which
the tobacco insurgency emerged. The farmers who gathered in
cooperative meetings and pooled their collective resources were
not aberrant "radicals" far removed from the mainstream of
American life. They were, in fact, a visibly functioning component of the mainstream. They saw firsthand an encroaching
corporate order that threatened some of their most basic assumptions about American society. The values they defended were as
old as the Republic itself.

The farmers adhered to a republican tradition that valued the
independent smallholder and regarded centralized power with
all the fear and suspicion of the old English Whigs from whom
the tradition derived. They rejected a society that subordinated
ancient ideas of the commonweal to the new notions that celebrated corporate power. The Tobacco Wars consequently constituted one of the final defenses in America of the eighteenth-
century republican tradition. The defeat of the farmers in the
tobacco belt, along with the failure of numerous other agrarian
insurgencies in the early twentieth century, further weakened
republicanism as a commonly held ideology among the American people.

Finally, this story is about the people on the land. They were
poorly educated, left few historical tracks, and are understood, in
general terms, to have become "forgotten people." Those at the
bottom of society historically become visible when they engage in
concerted political activity. The moments in which individuals

organize themselves for collective assertion against powerful entrenched interests have been fleeting. Yet these moments permit us a rare glimpse into the underlying social foundations of the countryside. When knowledge of the motives and circumstances of such "forgotten people" as J.T. and Kate Strand is placed alongside our received knowledge of their wealthier contemporaries, a more complete and differentiated picture of America emerges.

1

A Legacy of Peonage

Credit supports agriculture, as the cord supports the hanged.
—Louis XIV

Farmers, by the nature of their occupation, are placed in a position in which they are vulnerable to exploitation. Those who live on the land must have the daily necessities to sustain life from the time seed is planted until the crop is harvested many months later. This circumstance governs agriculture in every region of the globe, in good years and bad. Farmers must necessarily rely on creditors to survive. In this vein, southern farmers after the Civil War were no different than the generations before or after them.

Amid the enormous dilemmas confronting southerners in the aftermath of the war, the "money question" had profound repercussions on the ability of farmers to obtain credit. The debate surrounding the American economy invariably pitted debtors against creditors, or, more specifically, farmers and other laborers against financiers and commercial interests. The financial structure erected in the wake of the debate over the money question inflicted immense economic hardship on most southern farmers. The resulting poverty produced landless tenantry and increasingly desperate economic conditions for America's agricultural population.

The monetary debate began in 1863, when Congress issued over $450 million in greenbacks in order to finance the war. Prior to this time, America's money supply was loosely based on the amount of gold held in the nation's reserves. A dollar bank note could be exchanged for a dollar's worth of gold. In creating new money, the government suspended the reliance on gold as a standard of value. The new money had no intrinsic value and was backed solely by the credit of the nation. Many conservatives criticized such a move, even to pay for the war. Their cries for "sound" money were ignored, at least while the war continued.[1]

After the Civil War, advocates of the gold standard, such as Treasury secretary Hugh McCullough, once again took up the cause. The primary problem with fiat money—so called because it was money created simply by legislative fiat—was price inflation, which had risen 79 percent from 1861 to 1865.[2] Such inflationary figures alarmed financiers, since loans were being repaid to them in currency that was worth considerably less than it had been valued at the time the money was borrowed. According to critics of the greenbacks, the only way to curb such inflation was systematically to remove the greenbacks from circulation and to restore the gold standard. In this line of thinking, greenbacks constituted "financial heresy" and went against even the will of God. But to opponents of currency contraction, like Congressman George H. Pendleton of Ohio, expanding "the currency when the people are incurring a debt, and to contract the currency when they come to pay it, is public robbery."[3]

Proponents of an elastic currency stated that their policy better served the needs of the population at large and would allow debtors to gain an economic foothold. Farmers, constituting the bulk of the nation's debtors, would consequently benefit from an expanding currency. Credit would be easier to obtain, and prices would generally rise. At the same time, bankers lobbied hard in Congress to constrict the money supply. They were buoyed by the certainty that they would also earn windfall profits on bonds they had purchased during the war with inflated currency. The bonds would be repaid in deflated, thus more valuable, money. In essence, the battle between those advocating a rigid currency and those supporting a flexible currency concerned whether debtors or creditors would suffer in the postwar economy.[4]

In the end, the dilemma was resolved dramatically in favor of creditors. The greenbacks were retired, the gold standard was renewed, and the nation's money supply was shrunk to pre-Civil War levels. The subsequent result devastated the nation's farmers. The contraction of currency significantly lowered prices for farm products at the same time that it increased the price farmers and other producers had to pay for credit. As deflation drove prices down, farmers who produced the same amount in successive years received less. Consequently, the only way to avoid a systematic descent into landless peonage was to produce more the following year. As credit became ever more expensive and crops declined in price, farmers worked harder to produce more, but they received less. Millions of sharecroppers, tenants, and landowners confronted this excruciating circumstance yearly. Their critics, blandly overlooking the underlying structural causes, announced that the farmer's ills were caused by overproduction and warmly greeted the politics of "sound" money.

Not only was credit more expensive to obtain, but the financial facilities in which to acquire credit were rare in the South throughout the 1870s and 1880s. The National Banking Act of 1863 had placed restrictions on mortgage lending while taxing nonnational banks, a circumstance that resulted in the establishment of few state banks in the South. Out of a total of 1,545 national banks in 1870, only 69 were located in twelve southern states.[5]

These dynamics were at work in the tobacco belt of Kentucky. Despite its earlier claim as a "border" state and other such geographic semantics, the economic patterns in the Bluegrass State substantiate Kentucky's southern heritage and its rather vulnerable financial situation after the Civil War. Within nineteen tobacco-producing counties of western Kentucky, only two national banks existed outside the urban center of Paducah, in McCracken County (see table 1). While some of the twenty-one banks had capitalizations of $100,000 to $250,000, the cash surpluses of most banks outside Paducah were between $5,000 and $10,000 (table 2). With such meager resources, the few farmers who could receive loans were usually large landowners who possessed significant collateral. Small farmers and tenants who could not offer adequate collateral were thus denied credit by existing banks.[6] Most farmers throughout the South desperately needed other avenues to obtaining credit.

Into this credit vacuum emerged the southern credit merchants, or "furnishing merchants," who operated the thousands of rural stores across the South. The furnishing merchant at the country store did not gain his newfound status as the sole supplier of credit by his own initiative or business savvy. Instead, the machinery by which the furnishing merchant received the finan-

Table 1. Types of Banks in Nineteen Black Patch Counties of Kentucky, 1885

County	Banks			
	National	State	Private	Total
Ballard	—	—	—	—
Caldwell	1	—	—	1
Calloway	—	—	—	—
Carlisle	—	—	—	—
Christian	—	3	—	3
Crittenden	—	—	—	—
Fulton	—	1	—	1
Graves	1	—	1	2
Hickman	—	—	—	—
Hopkins	—	—	1	1
Livingston	—	—	—	—
Logan	—	2	3	5
Lyon	—	—	1	1
McCracken	3	—	—	3
Marshall	—	—	—	—
Muhlenberg	—	—	1	1
Simpson	—	—	2	2
Todd	—	—	1	1
Trigg	—	—	—	—
TOTAL	5	6	10	21

SOURCE: *The Mercantile Agency Reference Book, 1885* (New York: R.G. Dun Mercantile Agency, 1885).

cial backing to supply credit was set in motion by a New York firm, the R.G. Dun Mercantile Agency.

The Dun Agency, beginning in 1866, sent an army of "credit reporters" throughout the South to compile a detailed evaluation of the credit worthiness of every business establishment in every southern county. Northern manufacturers and wholesalers then supplied the furnishing merchants with the necessary capital and goods to pass on to credit-starved farmers. The furnishing mer-

Table 2. Capitalizations and Cash Surpluses of Banks in
Nineteen Black Patch Counties of Kentucky, 1885

	Banks		
	National	State	Private
Capitalization			
$250,000-500,000	—	—	—
$100,000-250,000	2	1	1
$50,000-100,000	2	2	1
$25,000-50,000	1	2	3
$10,000-25,000	—	—	1
$5,000-10,000	—	—	—
No response	—	1	4
Cash Surplus			
$25,000-50,000	1	—	—
$15,000-25,000	1	1	1
$10,000-15,000	—	—	1
$5,000-10,000	1	3	1
$2,000-5,000	1	1	1
Less than $1,000	1	—	1
No response	—	1	5

SOURCE: *The Mercantile Agency Reference Book, 1885* (New York: R.G. Dun
Mercantile Agency, 1885).

chants obtained goods from the northern business community
on consignment. They were spared the obligation to repay their
suppliers until the end of the year. In effect, through the centralized rating scheme of the Dun Agency, the rural store provided the same services as a small bank in lending short-term
credit.[7]

The circumstances by which southern farmers would initiate
credit in a particular store would soon tie them to a usurious
system that sent shock waves through the southern economy.
Every store item had two sets of prices: a cash price and a credit
price. Since many farmers had little or no cash, the credit price
was always much higher. The interest rates thus charged by typi-

cal credit merchants were often usurious. A survey of Georgia credit merchants showed that the price paid for credit purchases was 40 to 70 percent higher than the cash price. The average interest rate charged by Georgia merchants from 1881 to 1889 was a staggering 59.4 percent.[8]

Claims that the furnishing merchant also paid high interest rates are effectively dismissed in an exhaustively documented study by Roger L. Ransom and Richard Sutch. They found that northern wholesalers charged between 3 and 15 percent on consignment loans to southern merchants. Ransom and Sutch concluded that the furnishing merchant possessed a territorial monopoly. Without other means of obtaining credit and prevented by the merchant from seeking credit elsewhere, the farmer was forced to pay whatever rate the merchant charged.[9] Once an account was opened at a store, the debtor was told never to seek credit elsewhere, or risk having loans called in. The farmer would return periodically for more goods, and the merchant would record the mounting debt in his ledger. In this way, the furnishing merchant's control over a farmer and his crop became complete.

The damaging effects of the crop-lien system and the decisive economic leverage it represented for furnishing and supply merchants can be seen by tracing accounts in southern country stores. For example, the Martin and Johnson Store, located in the tobacco-producing area of Earles, Kentucky, in Muhlenberg County, was listed in 1885 by the Dun Agency as one of the retail outlets whose capital was grounded in tobacco. Between 1885 and 1900 the store's credit rating increased to the highest one possible. Within the same period, the store's capital exploded from less than one thousand dollars to between fifty and one hundred thousand dollars. Obviously, the one-crop system was lucrative for southern commerce, if not for the region's agricultural population.[10]

Driven by the furnishing merchant to grow a cash crop, many farmers in Kentucky and Tennessee were forced to rely on tobacco, a crop that often brought little more than the cost of production. After harvest, the farmer came to settle his account with the merchant. In case after case, farmers across the South found that the results of their year's work were not sufficient to "pay out"—to settle all accounts with the merchant and retain enough profit to finance the following year's effort. Thus, the southern farmer became continually dependent on the furnishing merchant for credit. A typical entry in the Martin and Johnson tobacco ledgers in the spring of 1903 reveals the agony structured into the crop-lien system. Nine farmers were loaned cash advances on their upcoming tobacco crop, and following each name in the ledger were words that drove millions of tobacco and cotton farmers into poverty and despair: "Carried to new book." Such was the descriptive terminology of peonage.[11]

The collateral the furnishing merchant demanded was a lien on the new year's crop. For the majority of southern farmers, this collateral was cotton, a crop that was easily stored, had a high yield per acre, and was readily sold. While King Cotton ruled most of the South, tobacco emerged as the cash crop of Kentucky and western Tennessee. Since three to five acres were all one farm family could reasonable tend each year, tobacco could be produced on very small plots, making it ideal for tenant farming. As S.P. Boatman, a farmer in Henderson County, Kentucky, noted, "The majority of people [in the county] depend on tobacco for their support." Boatman added, "All people make debts payable on the first of January when their tobacco crop is cashed in."[12]

The soil of the western regions of the two states was particularly suited for a dark, strong-flavored variety of tobacco, used primarily in the manufacture of snuff, chewing tobacco, and cigars. The area grew virtually the world's entire supply of this type of tobacco and acquired the name Black Patch because of the dark tobacco produced there. In central Kentucky the soil was suited for a new variety of burley introduced in the 1860s. A lighter blend, it was used primarily in smoking tobacco and in a relatively new product, the cigarette. The region's fertile soil lay on a bed of limestone, and the calcium-rich earth thus produced a leaf that smokers found mild and pleasurable.[13]

The extraordinary rise in the number of tenants and sharecroppers between 1880 and 1910 testifies to the inability of the existing southern credit system to enable farmers to retain land. Once made landless, the farmer found it virtually impossible to recoup losses. The tenant, as a contemporary observed, "does not rise to ownership in the South because, as his affairs are managed, he

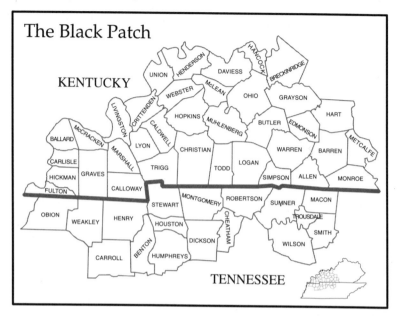

The Black Patch

KENTUCKY

TENNESSEE

can not acquire ownership."[14] Those who owned land often saw it disappear as the mounting debt to the furnishing merchant required all the owner possessed. Many store owners became large landowners because of the defaults of their customers, and likewise, many landowners in time became store owners and credit merchants as a means of further increasing their rather substantial holdings.[15]

Between 1880 and 1910 the number of farms operated by tenants grew from 36 percent to over 50 percent in some southern states. In fact, by 1910 tenant farms constituted half of all farms in the South.[16] In Kentucky the statistics were not as stark as they were in parts of the Deep South. The percentage of farms in the state operated by tenants increased from 26.5 percent in 1880 to 33.9 percent in 1910. The actual number of tenant farms in Kentucky, however, increased from 44, 027 in 1880 to 87, 860 in 1910, a staggering increase of 99.6 percent. In Tennessee the number of farms operated by tenants rose from 57,196 in 1880 to 101,061 in 1910, and 41.1 percent of all Tennessee farmers in 1910 were tenants.[17]

These were the statistical realities. In human terms, as perceived by Lee Baskett, a farmer in Henderson County, Kentucky, "the tenants are in a bad shape. They are pretty near starved to death." Joseph Wilson, another farmer in Henderson County, noted that the drop in farm prices "is much harder on the tenant, as he seldom has anything else to sell except his tobacco. He depends on it solely, and that is not only the case here, but over the whole of the tobacco belt."[18]

The tobacco tenants on Wessyngton, the estate of Joseph E. Washington in Robertson County, Tennessee, were typical. In September 1900 Bose Adams entered into an agreement with Washington: in exchange for living quarters plus a team of animals, feed for the team, tools, and the use of six acres of land, Adams agreed to consign to Washington title to half of his tobacco crop. Another tenant, Tillman Williams, agreed to give Washington half of his tobacco and corn crops. All tenants on Wessyngton agreed to work at Washington's behest anywhere on the farm for sixty-five cents a day. Administrative control in this relationship resided with Washington. His contracts reserved the right for him to sell the crop, "collect the proceeds, and account to party of the second part for his portion." The degree of social control acquired by men like Washington was breathtaking. His contracts read: "Should party of the second part at any time be guilty of bad or immoral conduct, get drunk, or in any manner give good and sufficient cause, said Washington reserves the absolute right to immediately terminate this contract."[19]

Another landlord in the tobacco country, Ben Kimsey of Henderson County, Kentucky, had little regard for his tenants. While acknowledging that the crop lien was a "bad system," he projected upon his tenants a childlike mentality: "The cropper only wants a place to live, and something to eat and hardly any clothes. He has no further interest in the crop and often leaves himself in debt to the farmer." The only way out of this impasse, Kimsey believed, in an interpretive leap uncommon among rural philosophers, was for a farmer to work his own land. "He can then see that it is properly done, but when it is let out to croppers, they do the land no good and go from place to place every year, caring for nothing but a shelter and a little something to eat. Such people are no good to a country." While Kimsey witnessed the poverty of tenantry, he could not understand the economic forces that reduced millions to eking out a living as tenant farmers. Kimsey correctly knew, however, that such a system offered little hope for southern agriculture.[20]

Tobacco is a labor-intensive crop, requiring, in the folk saying, thirteen months a year to raise. This was particularly true in 1900, before the introduction of labor-saving machinery and chemicals. Tobacco seeds are so small that they cannot be sown into the soil immediately. Instead, small "plant beds" are erected. These beds of pulverized soil must be carefully prepared in order for the seedlings to grow. During this time the ground soil must be mounded in parallel rows. The transplantation of the small plants from the bed to the soil begins in late spring.

Constant attention must be given to weeding the soil and guarding against such devastating insects as the flea beetle, the hornworm, and the bud worm. These worms are very large and emit streams of tobacco juice when provoked, making "worming" a particularly loathsome job. As the plant matures, the top buds are pulled in order to concentrate the strength into fewer and stronger leaves. Any sprouts, or "suckers," must also be removed by hand. In late summer the ripe leaves are cut, and the delicate process of curing begins.

Leaves are strung, tied to a stick, and hung in a specially built tobacco barn. Curing is accomplished by using a heat source placed in the barn: with many types of burley, the curing is done by a sheet-iron flue (flue cured), and with dark tobacco, the heat is produced by a direct fire (fire cured). A constant vigil must attend the fire, in order to maintain it and to guard against any sparks that might ignite the barn itself.

After curing, the leaf absorbs moisture from the air and becomes more pliable. At this point the farmer must evaluate each leaf, determine its grade, and sort the leaves into groups, such as prime leaf, good leaf, and lugs. The leaf can be packed into a half-ton "hogshead" or kept in the loose-leaf state. Then the leaf is ready for market. Few crops required as much painstaking care, and few provided so little financial reward.[21]

The tobacco market usually consisted of a local warehouse, where buyers for manufacturers bid on the crops. This occurred in the autumn, and for most tobacco towns and communities, it was a time of high anxiety. As Emma Wilson related in her novel *Under One Roof*, entire communities were grounded in the price tobacco received: "Time itself waited to see how tobacco was selling. If it was selling well, church assessments and doctor bills were paid, merchants beamed. . . . Life limped or cakewalked to the tune of the tobacco market."[22] Unlike cotton farmers, who had a "lay-by" season and other times of enforced "leisure," the tobacco farmers had a never-ending routine. Most growers simply spent what time they had left on growing other crops or on tending their own gardens.[23]

Throughout Kentucky and Tennessee, families of tenant farmers provided the necessary labor to produce a tobacco crop. The lives of J.T. and Kate Strand and their seven children revolved around a four-acre plot of land located on Joel Badall's farm in Muhlenberg County, Kentucky. All the members of the family were needed to attend the crop. For Kate Strand, the worst moment was worming. She related what occurred at the end of a typical day:

I don't suppose the Lord ever permitted a harder, hotter, dirtier, filthier, or more nauseating work than that of worming tobacco. . . . I have seen my husband at the close of the day take off his overalls and stand them alone, so stiff they would be with tobacco juice. Worming tobacco is bad enough for men, but when women and children have to engage in it human torture reaches its climax. My children have toddled along through tobacco rows at my side crying with pain as their eyes were filled with tobacco juice shot into them by tobacco worms.

For tenant families like the Strands, the task of working this four-acre plot year-round produced plenty of physical misery. The essential irony, as Kate Strand understood, was "the thought that half that we and other tenants produced went to the landowners." Their labor, she knew, "consisted chiefly in receiving the rents and spending them. Their families lived well, while ours verged constantly on starvation."[24]

Children were essential to a farm family's labor. Many children in the tobacco regions spent a good portion of their young lives tending the crop. In the 1920s the Children's Bureau discovered through a survey of 563 children in rural Kentucky that one-third worked over three full months in the tobacco fields. In Christian County, Kentucky, 36 percent of boys aged seven through fifteen worked over four months a year tending tobacco. A typical working day in this county found over 48 percent of the children, boys and girls, working over ten hours a day. Because children were so vital to the success of the tobacco crop, their attendance in school suffered. The average yearly absence of children in Christian County was nineteen days, or one school month out of seven. Severe absenteeism kept many students from progressing at the normal rate. Over half the school-age children in the county were classified as "retarded," meaning that they were at least one school year behind other children their age. Of African-American children in Christian County, over one-third were three full years behind in their schooling. Unfortunately, inadequate educational opportunities were not the only human toll inflicted by the culture of tobacco.[25]

The regions in Kentucky and Tennessee devoted to tobacco also displayed extremely low standards of health. Over 32 percent of Kentucky children examined by the Rockefeller Sanitary Commission had hookworm; the rate in Tennessee was over 40 percent. In the highland counties of middle Tennessee, the infection rate was between 48 and 73 percent of the rural children tested. Hookworm infection ultimately caused irreparable damage to a child's physical and mental development.[26]

In 1911 so many cases of pellagra were diagnosed in Tennessee that the state appointed a pellagra commission to investigate. Caused by a vitamin deficiency resulting from poor diets, approximately 2,500 cases of pellagra were reported in Tennessee, with a much larger number doubtless remaining unreported. The illness rapidly became known as the disease of the four *d*'s: diarrhea, dermatitis, dementia, and death. The fear of pellagra in Kentucky was so great in 1910 that pressure for a quarantine was urged and patients suspected of having the disease at the Western Kentucky Asylum for the Insane were isolated. The death rate for children with the disease was over 42 percent in Kentucky. In 1913 Christian County alone reported fourteen deaths resulting from pellagra. To the historian of pellagra in the South, an unmistakable connection existed between such health stan-

Table 3. Average Prices Received for Tobacco, 1866-1905

	Prices (cents per pound)		
Year	United States	Kentucky	Tennessee
1866	11.6	9.2	20.4
1867	11.6	9.5	13.7
1868	12.2	12.7	16.5
1869	10.9	8.9	12.8
1870	9.7	8.2	8.3
1871	10.2	7.6	10.9
1872	10.7	8.3	11.6
1873	8.6	7.2	6.0
1874	13.7	12.4	10.0
1875	7.7	6.6	7.2
1876	7.3	6.9	7.9
1877	5.4	4.6	5.2
1878	5.8	5.0	6.0
1879	6.1	5.0	5.0
1880	8.1	7.0	9.0
1881	9.6	8.8	7.6
1882	8.5	8.0	6.7
1883	8.8	8.6	6.0
1884	8.1	7.5	7.0
1885	7.5	6.5	7.0
1886	7.2	6.0	6.0
1887	10.5	12.0	10.5

dards and the declining rural economy: "To tenant farmers," Elizabeth W. Etheridge writes, "tight credit was but a prelude to illness the next spring."[27]

As the currency contracted in the long cyclical decline that followed specie resumption in the 1870s, the inevitable year-by-year drop in all agricultural prices placed unbearable strain on southern farmers. Corn prices fell from 40.9 cents per bushel in 1874 to 29.7 cents in 1894; cotton prices declined from 11.1 cents per pound in 1874 to 5.8 cents in 1894. In short, over a twenty-year

Table 3. Average Prices Received for Tobacco, 1866-1905, *cont.*

	Prices (cents per pound)		
Year	United States	Kentucky	Tennessee
1888	7.9	8.0	8.0
1889	6.6	5.1	5.2
1890	8.0	6.5	6.3
1891	8.2	7.3	6.7
1892	8.9	8.3	10.4
1893	7.9	7.6	8.8
1894	6.6	5.5	9.0
1895	6.8	5.3	7.0
1896	5.5	4.2	7.0
1897	7.4	8.0	11.0
1898	6.1	4.0	7.0
1899	7.1	6.1	11.0
1900	6.7	6.0	6.0
1901	7.2	6.0	6.0
1902	6.9	6.0	6.0
1903	6.7	6.2	7.5
1904	7.8	6.4	5.8
1905	8.2	7.0	7.5

SOURCE: U.S. Department of Agriculture, Bureau of Agricultural Economics, *Tobaccos of the United States: Acreage, Yield per Acre, Production, Price, and Value, by States, 1866-1945, and by Types and Classes, 1919-1945* (Washington, D.C., 1948), 6-7.

period corn prices fell 27 percent, while cotton prices fell 48 percent.[28] For tobacco, the prices during the same period fell from a record high of 13.7 cents per pound to 6.6 cents per pound, a 52-percent drop (see table 3). The estimated cost of production for dark tobacco was 6 cents per pound, while burley cost 7-8 cents per pound to produce.[29] The rapid drop in prices meant that farmers had to produce more to receive the same total income. Farmers had to purchase more goods, obtaining even more credit, while worrying about all the dangers associated with tobacco culture, such as insects and rainfall. Kentucky tobacco farmers had to produce 171 million pounds in 1879 to equal the income that 88 million pounds had produced in 1867.[30]

The structural effects of the postwar financial system were consequently devastating for southern farmers. While the money supply decreased, population and crop production increased, and the yearly struggle to survive was intensified. Contemporary and later analysts casually dismissed the agony of the countryside by assigning the blame to the farmers themselves. They offered the explanation of overproduction or other market explanations, thereby ignoring the complex mechanisms that worked against the financial needs of agriculturalists. The social costs affecting the countryside in the aftermath of Reconstruction were in full display in the ever-rising rates of landless tenantry, accompanied by increasing rates of disease and lower educational attainments. As ominous as this was, however, one more hazard was about to be added to the picture.

2

Monopoly Comes to the Tobacco Belt

> From the plant in the ground to the finished product, no man can engage in the tobacco business without doing fealty in money and in manhood to James B. Duke.
> —A.O. Stanley, 1906, in
> U.S. House of Representatives

The financial conditions governing southern agriculture after Reconstruction—monetary constriction, the rise of the crop-lien system, and permanent indebtedness—were symptomatic of the ever-expanding role played by industrialism in the American economy. For farmers residing in the tobacco belt, the emerging corporate culture was no mere abstraction. In 1889 an industrial organization was born in New York City that would further compound the problems confronting tobacco farmers: lower prices and increasing flight into landless tenantry. Over the next decade the American Tobacco Company acquired virtually complete control over the nation's tobacco industry. The ATC's dominance soon extended well beyond the bounds of Wall Street and exerted a direct influence on the economic and social life of hundreds of Kentucky and Tennessee farm communities.

At the heart of the tobacco trust was the Durham, North Carolina, firm of W. Duke and Sons. After the Civil War this firm had grown into one of the country's leading tobacco manufacturers under the leadership of its founder, Washington Duke. By the time Duke's son James Buchanan had attained sufficient age and experience to take over the company from his father in the 1880s, the profits from plug and chewing tobacco that the firm earned did not impress the young executive. In the mind of

James B. Duke, president of the
American Tobacco Company.
North Carolina Collection,
University of North Carolina at
Chapel Hill Library.

James B. Duke, the future of the industry was in a new product,
the cigarette.

Cigarettes in the 1870s and 1880s had been of the "roll your
own" variety, and to produce them in mass quantity required
hundreds of workers to roll each cigarette by hand. Similar in
many ways to cotton manufacturing before Eli Whitney, cigarette
production was too time-consuming to be considered profitable
on a large scale. A machine invented by James A. Bonsack in 1880
that could mass-produce cigarettes, however, soon revolution-
ized the industry.

The methods by which Duke approached the Bonsack machine offer instructive evidence about his success in obtaining
dominance over the industry. Duke immediately bought two
Bonsack machines and began mass-producing cigarettes. In order to insure his company's dominance in the burgeoning cigarette industry, Duke negotiated a contract with the Bonsack
Machine Company that stipulated that for a royalty fee the Bonsack company agreed not to distribute the machine to any company except the five major tobacco enterprises: W. Duke and
Sons, Kinney Tobacco Company, Allen and Ginter, William S.

Kimball, and Goodwin and Company. With such a contract in hand, Duke was assured that no fledgling company could emerge and encroach upon the "Big Five's" control of the tobacco market. By 1888 the five companies controlling the Bonsack patent also controlled 86 percent of the nation's cigarette industry.[1]

Duke then moved to deal with his existing competition within the Big Five. His philosophy was straightforward: "To the man that is going to run the business I say go ahead and run it any way you like so you can make profits, that is all I care."[2] By 1889 competition among Duke and his cohorts was intense. Increasing advertising expenses cut deeply into Duke's profits. Yet even at this stage, Duke possessed enormous advantages over his four competitors through another secret deal he had made with the Bonsack company—a guarantee that Duke's company would be charged 25 percent less in royalty fees than the other companies within the Big Five. Through other means such as eliminating middlemen from the purchase of the leaf and unique distribution techniques, Duke acquired economic leverage over the remaining competition within the industry. Thus when Duke approached his peers about consolidating the Big Five into one major concern, which would then reap the benefits of a controlled market, he received a hearty reception. The alternative of increased competition, everyone knew, could only damage even the strongest companies. In no uncertain terms, Duke threatened to wipe out the other cigarette companies if an agreement was not reached. Not surprisingly, in October 1889 an agreement was settled merging the five companies into one, the American Tobacco Company.[3]

In the accord, the five major companies agreed to sell out in exchange for stock in the new enterprise. Capitalized at $25 million, the ATC was headed by none other than James B. Duke. The financial arrangements surrounding this pact are also helpful in understanding the new company's manipulative business methods. The real value of the new enterprise, based on the merged companies' combined real assets, was only $3.1 million. Of the $25 million issued in stock, almost 86 percent was based on such intangible assets as patents, trademarks, and an estimate of potential earning power, referred to as "good will." The monetary value of these items could not be established, and such capitalization produced stock that was commonly termed "watered." With such creative capitalization arrangements behind him, Duke possessed the financial power to buy or drive out of business over 250 separate tobacco manufacturers over the next few years, essentially exchanging "good will" for real assets in the process. The American Tobacco Company gained control of all tobacco products except cigars. A perceptive student of the ATC notes, "The competitive advantages created by the cigarette monopoly proved more than enough to adequately compensate stockholders." Indeed, between 1905 and 1908 the respective common stock dividends of the ATC were 20 percent, 22.5 percent, and 32.5 percent. Thus, in less than four years the holders of common stock in the ATC received approximately $40 million in dividends. By 1907 the American Tobacco Company produced 79.7 percent of all plug and twist products, 71.2 percent of all smoking tobaccos, and 96.1 percent of all snuff products (see table 4). In 1907 the company was estimated to control a capitalization of $450 million, making it one of the largest and most powerful companies in America.[4]

The ATC's methods, according to some observers, bordered on the sinister. Josephus Daniels, a Raleigh, North Carolina, newspaper editor and a future cabinet member in Woodrow Wilson's administration, was particularly outspoken: "If the crop was small one year, [the ATC] paid a good price to increase production; if the crop was large, they took it at less than the cost of production. By this vicious circle, they sought to make the country believe that the law of supply and demand was at work, but it was a law which they controlled."[5]

The ATC's rise coincided, incidentally, with the passage of the Sherman Antitrust Act of 1890. Emerging from a Congress anxious to assuage popular worries about the sudden increase in industrial monopolies, the act seemed, at first, a barrier to the ruthless tactics of men such as Duke. A revealing episode demonstrating how the Sherman Act functioned occurred in 1895, when North Carolina district attorney R.B. Glenn informed U.S. attorney general Richard Olney that the ATC should be indicted on antitrust charges. Glenn wrote Olney in passionate language: "If you only knew how this vast monopoly has oppressed our People, you would more readily excuse my seeming persistency in asking to indict them." Olney never replied.[6]

Table 4. The American Tobacco Company's Share of U.S. Tobacco Output, 1891-1907

Year	Percentage of Production		
	Plug and twist	Snuff	Smoking tobacco
1891	2.6	2.9	13.5
1892	3.5	5.4	21.7
1893	5.9	3.8	21.4
1894	5.6	4.3	20.5
1895	12.4	5.7	22.5
1896	20.4	5.7	20.7
1897	20.5	4.8	24.2
1898	22.5	6.0	26.9
1899	56.2	33.1	54.1
1900	62.8	67.5	61.2
1901	69.8	79.5	60.8
1902	72.5	86.0	66.8
1903	76.0	85.9	66.8
1904	73.4	91.1	68.0
1905	80.3	91.7	67.3
1906	81.4	95.8	70.0
1907	79.7	96.1	71.2

SOURCE: *United States* v. *American Tobacco Company*, 221 U.S. 106 (1911), pp. 259, 260, 263.

The vague language of the act itself reduced reformers to challenging potential monopolists in court. Throughout the 1890s court decisions concerning the implications of the Sherman Act did more to harm labor unions than industrial monopolies. In the notorious E.C. Knight case of 1895, the Supreme Court ruled that the act did not even apply to the activities of manufacturing companies. Considering these actions as well as timid Gilded Age administrations, Duke and the American Tobacco Company proceeded with the drive to monopolize the industry unthreatened and unimpeded by antitrust laws.[7]

The American Tobacco Company's dominion had become international in scope by 1901. In order to gain control of the export tobacco trade, the ATC agreed to relinquish the entire business in

Great Britain to the British tobacco interest, the Imperial Tobacco Company. In exchange, the Imperial agreed not to manufacture or sell tobacco in the United States. The interests of the Imperial and the ATC were thus combined into the British-American Tobacco Company, and no further competition arose between them.[8] The Imperial could purchase its leaf in America without worrying about competition from the American Tobacco Company. To the dark-fired tobacco farmers of Kentucky and Tennessee, who produced tobacco primarily for the export market, the consequences of the American Tobacco Company's control over the worldwide tobacco industry soon hit home. The burley growers of central Kentucky, whose leaf was essential to the cigarette industry, also felt the power of Duke's monopoly firsthand.

By 1906 the ATC, in the words of one authority on American business, "was strategically in a better position to maintain control over tobacco than Standard was to dominate the oil industry." Indeed, that year the Justice Department began investigating the ATC's business methods. Heading this attack was James C. McReynolds, a special assistant to the attorney general, who would later be appointed to the Supreme Court by Wilson. With Secretary of State Elihu Root adamantly defending the ATC within the Roosevelt administration, McReynolds's more drastic proposals—including placing the ATC into receivership and pursuing criminal action against James B. Duke—were quickly tabled. The administration's response was merely to have the Bureau of Corporations launch an investigation of the ATC in 1907, as McReynolds pursued antitrust charges against the company.[9] The case made its way to the Supreme Court in 1911, but not before events in Kentucky and Tennessee had played themselves out.

Before 1900 tobacco farmers in Kentucky and Tennessee sold their crops in a variety of ways. At the Martin and Johnson Store, for example, the crop could be taken directly to the furnishing merchant, who would then ship it to major warehouses in Louisville or Hopkinsville. Alternately, a farmer could sell his crop directly to buyers, either at a local warehouse or from his own barn. If the grower's lien was flexible, he could refuse an unsatisfactory first offer.[10]

By the early 1900s, as Duke consolidated the ATC's control of the industry, competition among tobacco buyers in Kentucky and Tennessee disappeared. In each tobacco-producing county, one buyer was assigned to a particular district, which was usually bounded by roads, streams, or other significant landmarks. The American Tobacco Company and the Italian Regie Tobacco Company, for example, had a working agreement. The Regie, led by Joseph Ferigo, had separate agents in each county, mirroring the ATC's strategy. The ATC and the Regie agreed not to compete with each other in purchasing tobacco. Charles Fort, who would later occupy a key post within the Black Patch tobacco movement, described the Regie as "the ones that were hurting us more than anything else." A.O. Dority, a buyer for the Regie, described the details of monopolistic formations at the social level: "I had a territory, and I was instructed not to go out of my allotted territory, and no other Italian man bought in my district, and nobody else until I got through, and the American Snuff Co. did not buy in my territory while I was working for the Italian Regie." [11]

The price offer of the buyer was the only one a farmer would receive. W.H. Hook, of Montgomery County, Tennessee, stated that in 1903 he had been approached by a buyer for the Regie. Hook was offered seven cents a pound, but the deal was not closed until the buyer checked to see if Hook's land lay within the buyer's allotted territory. Hook learned that his land was outside the buyer's district, and he was referred to the official buyer within his area.[12] Buyers respected buyers' territories, as J.E. Justice of Cheatham County, Tennessee, related:

In 1904 . . . John A. Hunter, one of the Regie buyers, went to the tobacco barn of one Mr. Allen and examined the tobacco in that barn with a view to buying the same. This barn was on the Ashland City and Thomasville Rd., the said road running through Mr. Allen's farm. After looking at the tobacco in that barn, Mr. Allen invited Mr. Hunter to step across the road and look at the tobacco in another barn, which Mr. Hunter declined to do, saying that the Ashland City and Thomasville Rd. was the boundary line of his territory and he could not cross it for that purpose.[13]

Not all farmers saw the district drawn by trust buyers in the same light. J.B. Ferguson, a large landowner in Trenton, Kentucky, in Todd County, elected to consider the careful district arrangements trust buyers followed as a sensible measure to "prevent confusion and to keep the different types separate." Ferguson refused to believe that trust buyers colluded with one another to keep prices down. "The farmers' grievance is of his own allowing," concluded Ferguson. The notion that competition for leaf had vanished was not restricted to stunned farmers. Arthur Jarvis, a leaf dealer in Henderson County, Kentucky, noted, "Formerly the tobacco was bought by dealers here who sold to the English trade." Since the formation of the Imperial Tobacco Company, Jarvis said, "competition in England has been practically wiped out." The entire industry, as Jarvis properly understood, was a monopoly, "and the American Tobacco Company controls it."[14]

The price that trust buyer A.O. Dority offered for the 1903 crop was less than four cents per pound—a price below the cost of production. Another episode reveals the latent power such market conditions held for buyers. W.S. Waller of Trenton, Kentucky, refused a buyer's first offer of five and a half cents in 1905. After hearing from no other potential customers, Waller was again approached by the same buyer, this time offering only five and a fourth cents per pound. Before he could refuse the offer, Waller was warned that if he did not accept the new bid, the next offer would be five cents per pound. Waller reluctantly agreed to five and a fourth cents. After the deal was closed, Waller said that the buyer casually remarked that the crop was worth at least seven cents per pound. Though the exact machinations of the trust may not have been clear to all observers, Lee Baskett, a farmer in Henderson County, Kentucky, well knew that "we have no competition." He added, "I don't think we have but one buyer, that is, the American." Baskett knew one essential truth about small farmers like himself: "The trust has got us."[15]

Considering Duke's substantial economic clout, historians have devoted little attention to his life or his company, especially in comparison with the treatments his Gilded Age contemporaries such as John D. Rockefeller or Andrew Carnegie have received. Matthew Josephson's sweeping study of American "robber barons," for example, virtually ignored the American Tobacco Company and never even mentioned James B. Duke.

Major accounts of Duke's life have the essential quality of authorized biographies. In a 1927 work titled *Master Builder*, John W.
Jenkins wrote that the cornerstone of Duke's business and philanthropic enterprises was "stimulating ambition, providing
work for the energetic," and "inspiring men to make the most of
themselves." While other writers have duly noted that Duke's
American Tobacco Company functioned in direct contradiction
to the mechanics of a free market economy, some scholars remain
ambivalent. Sociologist Dwight B. Billings, in describing the "social origins of southern industry," acknowledges that Duke
adopted a "ruthless labor policy," yet he concludes that the
tobacco industry was "progressive" for its time considering that
southern mill workers earned even lower wages and had worse
working conditions than workers in tobacco plants. He finds that
the "tobacco money" generated by the ATC was later "rein-
vested" in other industrial outlets and given for numerous chari-
table purposes. Billings even concludes that the Duke family had
"Populist connections."[16] Such interpretations provide a profound misreading of the origins of the American Tobacco Company and the dynamics involved in agrarian insurgencies. In order to properly understand the functioning social foundations of
Duke's "tobacco money"—which was later used to build much-
needed hospitals and universities and to support other philanthropic undertakings—one should not forget that the origins of
such well-intentioned activities can be located in the ATC's systematic exploitation and impoverishment of the nation's tobacco
farmers.

3

Organizing the Black Patch

> Human beings do not react to the goad of hunger and op-
> pression by some automatic and standard response of re-
> volt. What they do, or fail to do, depends on their situation
> among other human beings, on their environment, culture,
> tradition, and experience.
>
> —E.J. Hobsbawm and George Rudé

On September 24, 1904, more than five thousand tobacco farmers
gathered on the grounds of the Guthrie Fair Association in the
tiny town of Guthrie, Kentucky, near the Tennessee border. The
grandstand, which held four thousand, was quickly filled to
capacity, and the speaker's stage was soon engulfed by the
throng. The farmers' announced intention was to organize formally to combat the low price of tobacco, which they perceived
directly resulted from the monopolization of the nation's tobacco
industry by the American Tobacco Company. Speakers exhorted
the growers to unite for self-protection, and by afternoon's end,
the Clarksville District Planters' Protective Association (PPA) had
been formed. As a local newspaper remarked: "It was one of the
spectacles of a lifetime, this coming together of so vast a number
of the solid yeomanry. . . . the farmers were never more united
than on this occasion, which marks the beginning of the struggle
for their homes, for life itself."[1]

The spectacle of so many farmers in a single location dedicated
to a unified purpose is extraordinary, not only to the contemporary observer but to the historian as well. The highly visible and
rather dramatic gathering at Guthrie has understandably been
interpreted by many writers as the birth of the farmer insurgency
in Kentucky and Tennessee.[2] The standard account finds the
Guthrie meeting a collective response to low prices, where farm-

ers spontaneously organized themselves in a single afternoon, after decades of silence and general prosperity.

Such causalities are rather common in interpretations of the origins of social movements. When faced with explaining the birth of a particular insurgency, social scientists routinely venture back as far as possible to the earliest moment when an enthusiastic leader first spoke or a sizable crowd first met. Armed with this information, the researcher can easily propose explanations to account for the perceived "spontaneous" eruption of popular agitation: economic difficulties exceeded certain acceptable levels, the "time" had somehow "arrived" for a cause to be brought to the political agenda of a region, or perhaps even the sheer power of one individual energized usually "passive" individuals into acting. The Guthrie event therefore might be seen in this manner: by the autumn of 1904 prices had reached such low levels that a wealthy planter named Felix Ewing, along with other regional growers, decided that something "needed to be done." They subsequently called together the farmers of the Black Patch to meet. Convinced by Ewing of the need for activity, the farmers "rose up" or "acquired a new consciousness" and then recognized the need for immediate organization. In a single paragraph, the ways in which the Black Patch tobacco movement organized is explained.

Insurgent movements such as the one that occurred in western Kentucky and Tennessee at the turn of the century, however, do not begin with five thousand people. More important, economic adversity does not necessarily produce protest movements. To explain social movements by reciting evidence such as low prices, declining wages, spiraling inflation, or charismatic leadership—traits common to virtually all social movements—does not introduce the causal element describing how movements are converted from an abstract notion into reality. Such analyses bypass the crucial ingredient of sustained movements—the daily organizational tasks that must take place well before five thousand people meet.

Sustained organizational forms, distinct from unplanned street riots, are not spontaneous activities. Events such as the Guthrie meeting are the deliberate results of careful planning, usually undertaken by a handful of obscure people who build upon the experiences of previous insurgent activity.[3] In order to properly understand the extraordinary events that occurred after the Guthrie meeting, it is necessary to examine the historical context and the concrete steps that organizers took in making the meeting a reality. As such, Guthrie may be interpreted as the culmination, rather than the beginning, of the organizational phase.

In the Black Patch, the legacy of dissent had begun years before with the Greenback Party. The Greenback-Labor Party had formed in the late 1870s, primarily as a response to the resumption of the gold standard. Greenbackers, forerunning the People's Party of the 1880s and 1890s, advocated a flexible money supply. Candidates on the Greenback ticket were usually unable to generate much support nationally, and they produced only a small ripple on the sea of Kentucky politics. That small billow, however, was felt in the western part of the state, mostly among Black Patch tobacco farmers. In a congressional election in 1879, of thirty-four Kentucky counties in which Greenback candidates polled more than 15 percent of the vote, twenty-six were located in the heart of the Black Patch.[4] While third-party exhortations concerning such seemingly innocuous matters as the money supply were ignored throughout most of the state, Greenbackerism did manage to find fertile ground among Black Patch tobacco farmers.

The core of the Greenback program was an attempt to restructure America's economy in order to relieve the tremendous financial burden placed on debtors and to provide easier access to credit. The short-lived attempt by the Greenbackers was soon followed by a system of cooperative stores that tried another approach to the problem of agriculture credit in the South. The Patrons of Husbandry, or Grangers, built local stores in which farmers could purchase necessary items at lower prices, based on the principle that in buying in large volumes, Grangers could obtain goods at cheaper prices and pass the savings on to the farmer. Patterned after the English Rochdale system, the Grange stores used a "cash only" method that was incapable of aiding the farmers' credit crunch. No matter how inexpensive an item might be, farmers could not afford to pay cash, and this alone doomed any hope of the Grange being able to fundamentally solve the credit problem plaguing southern agriculture.[5]

The Grange did, however, make its presence known in the Black Patch. In Montgomery County, Tennessee, the local Grange studied the feasibility of building a fertilizer factory that could produce cheaper products for farmers. In Hopkinsville, Kentucky, some tobacco growers attempted to sell their crop through the local Grange. The Grange solicited propositions from local warehouses, and the highest bidder received all of the Grangers' business. By 1883, Hopkinsville warehousemen combined to refuse further dealings with the Grange, and the organization soon collapsed. A Grange store located in Robertson County, Tennessee, experienced some typical problems. From 1875 to 1878 the store received $11,300 in orders, but it closed in 1878, according to its manager, because of "severe competition of rival houses." The secretary of this store, Joseph E. Washington, who later became a key figure within the PPA, learned some of the pitfalls of agrarian organizing by the experiences gained through the Grange.[6]

Tobacco farmers in Kentucky and Tennessee were very similar to cotton growers throughout the South. Both were trapped in producing a cash crop that promised little but continued debt and poverty. While tobacco growers searched in vain for relief in the Greenback and Grange schemes, the most serious insurgent attempt began among cotton farmers in Texas. The Farmers' Alliance, which produced the movement known today as populism, was formed in Texas in 1877 and sought to reconstruct the American economy and relieve the agriculture debt crisis. As Alliance "lecturers" organized suballiances throughout the South and West, the Populist movement ultimately threatened the hegemony of the two major political parties and became the largest democratic movement in American history.

Experiments in cooperative efforts proved to Alliance members that farmers could escape the credit trap only by erecting "subtreasuries"—government-backed holding stations that would advance low-interest loans to farmers as they pooled their resources and waited for higher prices. Through the agency of the subtreasury, Alliance members proposed a means by which farmers could finally escape the structural problem of continual indebtedness. The apex of the Alliance was reached in the 1890s, as the movement gave way to the People's Party and its attempt to gain national political power. Before its death in 1896, the

People's Party became a substantial political force across the South and West.[7]

The Texas Alliance dispatched Kentuckian F.T. Rogers to his home state late in 1886, where he organized the first suballiance in Trigg County. Concurrent with the development of the Alliance, a similar organization known as the Agricultural Wheel had been forming and had found great support in Henderson County, Kentucky. By August 1889 the Wheel and the Alliance of Kentucky consolidated their interests and combined their efforts. In Tennessee the first Alliance organizers appeared in 1887, and the first suballiance was created in March 1888. By September, over 308 suballiances had been formed in the state. The Farmers' Alliance gained strong support in both states among the same farmers who had participated in the Greenback and Granger experiments.[8]

To the tobacco growers in the Black Patch, the organizing core of the Alliance program was a self-help formation known as the Tobacco Congress. The congress was convened in July 1888 in Clarksville, Tennessee. There, farmers met to discuss marketing the crop in order to increase prices. Throughout the summer the congress debated several marketing methods. In October, the congress discussed the radical step of not planting a crop ("cutting out") in 1889 in order to increase demand for the current crop. Not surprisingly, the members of the congress, fully recognizing the unprecedented nature of such a tactic and the enormous organizational network required to sustain it, deferred action.[9]

The Alliance did more, however, than simply provide a way for large growers to debate new marketing strategies. It also fostered an environment in which people could gather and discuss, in a democratc manner, their most pressing concerns. African-American farmers of the area found the meetings of the Colored Alliance of Montgomery County a forum where open and honest discussion could occur—a remarkable event considering the southern racial environment of the 1890s. Concerning the cutout of the 1889 crop, members of the Colored Alliance candidly stated that they disliked the idea of allowing manufacturers and speculators "to dictate to us as to whether or not we shall raise tobacco." Such emphatic public statements made by powerless and vulnerable people revealed how the Alliance meetings altered some traditional cultural habits of social control.[10]

Between January and May 1889, as the cooperative idea spread, Kentucky's suballiances doubled their membership. By the end of the year Kentucky could boast of more than one thousand suballiances in the state. In January 1889 Tennessee claimed more than seventy-eight thousand Alliance members, a total second only to that of Texas. In the fall of 1889 the Tobacco Congress met to discuss a plan "to rescue our tobacco growers from the clutches of middlemen" and other speculators in tobacco. Tobacco farmers were generally not fond of warehousemen, or "middlemen," who charged stout fees to store crops and often graded crops too low, which resulted in lower market prices for the producer. Harry Tracy, a national Alliance organizer and one of the founding theoreticians of American populism, recognized the importance of the congress in organizing Alliance members on a recruiting trip in 1889. In order to reach the largest audience, Tracy addressed the Tobacco Congress on the step-by-step process of achieving effective cooperatives. The Alliance organ of Tennessee, the *Weekly-Toiler*, commented: "We never heard a better Alliance speech."[11]

The eventual result of the Clarksville Tobacco Congress was a plan to build an Alliance warehouse in that city. The warehouse was planned as a joint-stock company, selling shares of five dollars each. Throughout the Black Patch, more Alliance warehouses were constructed. By building and maintaining Alliance warehouses, growers hoped to receive fairer treatment from warehousemen and better prices. During the first year of the Clarksville warehouse, the Alliance chose C.P. Warfield as manager. Another young Alliance man noted for his organizing skill was John B. Allen. Warfield and Allen, along with many other tobacco growers, gained valuable experience in organizing insurgencies during the high tide of populism, and they later took this knowledge on to the Planters' Protective Association.[12]

While the more radical aspects of the Farmers' Alliance never gained a serious hearing in most parts of Kentucky, one section of the state consistently advocated less conventional political stances. Not surprisingly, the Alliance gained its staunchest following in the same region that had earlier expressed approval of the Greenback party. The strongest loyalty to the Alliance platform articulated at a convention in Ocala, Florida, in 1890, which advocated a fundamental reordering of the American economy centered on the subtreasury, came from western Kentucky and Tennessee. Alliances throughout the Black Patch departed from the rather conservative politics of Kentucky Alliance president Thomas Gardner and demanded passage of a subtreasury bill. In Springfield, Tennessee, Alliance meetings produced strong resolutions in support of the bill. These farmers recognized that the subtreasury was the core component of populism, and they refused to allow the movement's central strategy for addressing the agricultural debt crisis to be co-opted. In such ways, tobacco growers in the Black Patch became increasingly politicized.[13]

The height of populism in Kentucky and Tennessee extended from 1890 to 1892. Ben Terrell, a national lecturer for the Farmers' Alliance, visited Kentucky in April 1890 and found the Kentucky Alliance movement to be "in good shape and spreading rapidly." Terrell could also see something else occurring among the members of the Kentucky Alliance: "No one could go with me through Kentucky and not see and feel that a great revolution is taking place in the minds of the people." During state and national elections in the early 1890s, the "revolution" that Terrell mentioned came home to Democratic and Republican candidates, as the new independent movement began to sink political as well as economic roots throughout the South and West. The network of cooperative organizations revealed itself in a series of stunning victories achieved by the third party in Kentucky and Tennessee. In 1890 the Alliance elected a governor, fourteen state senators, and forty state representatives in Tennessee. In the same year a constitutional convention was called in Kentucky, with Alliance men in a clear majority. In the 1892 presidential election, twelve Kentucky counties cast more than 20 percent of their total vote for the Populist candidate, James B. Weaver. All twelve counties were located in the Black Patch.[14]

The cooperative movement had come to Kentucky and Tennessee comparatively late, however, and it had not had time to sink roots of the kind that sustained the third-party movement in some other areas. Nevertheless, the idea of cooperative marketing and purchasing had been given wings, and concepts that were to become the basis of the Black Patch War had been set in place in the tobacco region. Quite simply, the agrarian movements of the 1880s and 1890s provided area growers the experiential knowledge in insurgent politics necessary for the movement of the early 1900s.

Historian Richard Hofstadter wrote that after 1896 the American farmer entered "upon the longest sustained period of peacetime prosperity he has ever enjoyed."[15] Prosperity, however, managed to evade the multitude of tobacco farmers residing in the Black Patch. As the trust consolidated, prices for tobacco continued to decline. The average price for all tobacco in Kentucky fell from 8.3 cents in 1892 to 4.0 cents in 1898, while the average price for dark tobacco in one town in Christian County, Kentucky, fell from 8.0 cents in 1884 to 4.0 cents in 1894 (see table 5).[16]

In October 1901 growers representing over sixteen Black Patch counties met in Clarksville, Tennessee, to discuss ways of combating the damaging effects of the monopolization of the tobacco industry. Vital to the interests of the farmers at this meeting was the cooperation of local banks. One farmer stated: "If the trade will not come to the help, then the banks will be forced to lend assistance, or keep their money and live on the big trust deposits of three per cent money, and have the pleasure of paying out on five cent tobacco, instead of lending their own capital of seven and eight cent tobacco." This appeal for financial support from area bankers rested on the shrewd assumption that tobacco was the foundation of the regional economy. Higher prices ultimately meant more money for area banks. This crucial component of Black Patch insurgency developed as bankers and farmers viewed their condition as one. The meeting also witnessed the conjunction of past and future insurgent movements: the growers at this meeting included William Elliott, John W. Jones, John Childress, William Browder, and M.V. Ingram, all former local Alliance leaders; and Felix Ewing, W.C. Warfield, Joel Fort, and J.B. Ferguson, who would later play central roles in organizing the Planters' Protective Association.[17]

The meeting heard a healthy mixture of opinions. G.M. Brockman stated that little change in the method of selling tobacco had

Table 5. Average Price per Pound Received for Dark Tobacco in
Pembroke, Kentucky, 1849-1894

Year	Price	Year	Price
1849	4.5	1872	6.0
1850	10.0	1873	5.5
1851	4.0	1874	11.0
1852	5.5	1875	9.0
1853	6.5	1876	7.2
1854	8.0	1877	8.0
1855	7.7	1878	5.5
1856	15.0	1879	5.5
1857	10.0	1880	5.0
1858	7.7	1881	6.0
1859	8.0	1882	5.7
1860	7.5	1883	8.0
1861	10.0	1884	8.0
1862	20.0	1885	4.5
1863	20.0	1886	4.2
1864	20.0	1887	9.0
1865	10.0	1888	5.0
1866	11.2	1889	4.5
1867	12.0	1890	6.0
1868	12.0	1891	6.2
1869	10.0	1892	5.7
1870	6.0	1893	4.2
1871	6.0	1894	4.0

SOURCE: *Western Tobacco Journal*, March 2, 1896.

occurred in the past few years. He felt that any insurgent movement against buyers was therefore unwarranted. M.V. Ingram,
who as an Alliance member had advocated the cutout of the 1889
crop, remarked that the idea was not to prevent anyone from
buying but simply to increase competition among buyers.[18] The
committee on organization, however, failed to generate an effective recruiting plan. By December, the cooperative idea in the
Black Patch had achieved no clear outline. Since most sharecrop-

pers and tenants needed money to pay liens and to prepare for Christmas, the organizing drive found few willing to sign contracts to curtail acreage or to pool their crops. One thoroughly pessimistic observer felt that "the farmers have no more chance of making a successful fight against this well organized and magnificently commanded body of buyers than an unarmed, straggling mob has against a battalion of U.S. regulars." The committee decided to postpone any organizing activity until 1902.[19]

Throughout 1902 this self-selected group of incipient insurgents, calling themselves the Tobacco Growers Association, struggled to find a plan of action that could recruit the bulk of the region's tobacco farmers. Meanwhile, sporadic experiments continued. In October 1902 a group of local farmers gathered in Mayfield, Kentucky, and demanded a one-cent-per-pound price increase from buyers. The farmers at this meeting soon discovered the cost of insurgency: trust buyers refused to come to these farmers' barns after the meeting was held. Blacklisted farmers learned in a direct way that the tobacco trust and its buyers did not look favorably upon cooperative organizing.[20]

While the Growers Association groped for a workable plan, a crucial organization came into existence on December 12, 1902. At the county courthouse in Springfield, Tennessee, the Robertson County Tobacco Growers Association was launched by an organizer named John M. Foster. This organization ultimately gave the larger Growers Association a definite plan of action and was instrumental in later making the PPA a reality throughout the Black Patch.

While the singular role of Felix Ewing in forming the Black Patch movement has been long accepted, the role of Foster has been virtually unknown. After receiving a law degree from Vanderbilt University in 1879, Foster had practiced law in Nashville. In 1890, with Alliance ideas of agricultural cooperation filling the rural air, Foster moved to Springfield and became a tobacco farmer. In the spring of 1894 Foster proposed a plan for organizing area growers to Ewing in a livery stable in Nashville. Ewing, the son-in-law of Joseph E. Washington, raised over 260 acres of tobacco. Ewing wished Foster well but felt that farmers were not yet "ripe" for organization. Washington soon gave Foster the

same reply. While Ewing and Washington dismissed such cooperative ideas during the era of the Farmers' Alliance and returned
to their spacious farms, Foster was left on his own to find a means
to organize tobacco growers.[21]

Writing in the *Black Patch Tobacco Journal* in 1907, Foster displayed his loquacious prose and his affirmation of Jeffersonian-
ism in describing the democratic legitimacy of the tobacco movement. "We believe that among the unalienable rights of man are
Life, Liberty, and the Pursuit of Happiness," Foster proclaimed.
Then he proceeded to list the grievances and rights of agricultural
people:

Every farmer who toils industriously is entitled in due season to an
unencumbered home; his wife and children are entitled to food and
raiment; these children are entitled to the God-given pleasures of youth
and the State to have them grow up useful citizens. And we believe they
have been deprived of all this without their consent but over the solemn
protest by the American Tobacco Company. . . . and we say that it were
better that the unhallowed bones of these cold-hearted men would
bleach on the deserts scorching waste, if their living would blight the life
of a single child; it were better that their gold be condemned and sunk to
the bottom of the sea if it blasted the happiness of a single home; and that
their factories be dismantled and piled in the scrap-heap to be eaten by
corroding rust than they should flavor a single plug with the tears of
innocence and prize it in the groans of the oppressed.[22]

In 1897 Foster sold the principles of cooperation to three of his
neighbors in an instructive way. Foster received the agreement of
James Draughon, Arch Cohea, and Perry Cohea that the three of
them would pool their 1898 crops (because of poor health, Foster
no longer raised tobacco himself). The three agreed to fix a price
on their respective crops. Unless all three received the prices they
asked, no single member of this cooperative trio would sell. In
1898 the three successfully sold their crops to an Adairville, Kentucky, buyer after other local buyers had refused to meet their
demands.

In 1900 Draughon and the Coheas again agreed to pool their
crops. One buyer offered Perry Cohea fourteen cents a pound for
his crop but refused to take the others. Perry Cohea rejected the
offer and waited. Two weeks later, the same buyer agreed to take

all three crops at the prices all three found satisfactory. Through the success afforded by this unique example of the power of cooperation, Foster was convinced that farmers throughout the Black Patch could realize higher prices.[23]

In December 1902 Foster called together prominent tobacco growers in Robertson County.[24] The growers agreed to incorporate their new organization into the Tobacco Growers Association, and they established eighteen districts within the county that would each be led by appointed delegates, responsible for organizing the districts. In essence, the Robertson County association gave the larger tobacco body a concrete plan of action combined with an excellent organizational structure.

The initial program decided upon by the Tobacco Growers Association in December 1902 was a traditional appeal for legislative action. The TGA wanted Congress to remove a tax placed on all manufactured tobacco, which was perceived by some growers to be a hindrance to their obtaining better prices. Cries for the revocation of the tobacco tax were strong, especially since no similar tax was levied on other agricultural products. The tax had been briefly removed in 1890, but then it was renewed in 1897 by Congress at the rate of twelve cents per pound. While the public explanation of increased revenue was offered by supporters of the tax, some critics charged that the tax was inspired by the tobacco trust to eliminate the grower-to-consumer market. Sellers of tobacco were required by law to post a five-thousand-dollar bond—a menial sum to the trust, but one that kept growers from selling directly to consumers. The tax also meant that smaller manufacturers had to pass on the burden of the tax to consumers. In 1902 the tax was reduced to six cents per pound, a sum still sufficient to eradicate any chance of growers' selling their crop directly to consumers.[25] To thoughtful observers, however, the expressed goal of the tobacco movement at this stage was rather palliative: the removal of a federal tax that had arguable consequences. Such an approach did not essentially disturb the marketing mechanisms established by the ATC, nor did it address the underlying problem of credit.

Organizers tried various ways to reach the rank and file. In January 1903 Charles Fort, president of the TGA, sent an open letter to a Louisville newspaper: "Knowing your paper to have a wide circulation in Logan, Todd, Christian, and Trigg Counties, I wish to reach the farmers in these counties through the medium of the *Courier-Journal*. An association will meet in Clarksville on January 24, and I earnestly urge that these counties be represented that day." Fort added that "the Association wants a systematic and thorough canvass carried into each civil district . . . to get every man in the district to sign a petition to Congress asking that the tax be taken off tobacco." Similar letters were sent to various newspapers throughout the Black Patch in an effort to get the word out to the region's farmers.[26]

Meanwhile, growers from four Kentucky counties gathered in Henderson in January 1902 to propose yet another plan of action. More than four hundred farmers from Webster, Union, Henderson, and Hopkins counties agreed that limiting acreage and thus curtailing the supply of tobacco would increase the demand for their product. Organizers were nominated to go into these counties and begin signing farmers to an acreage-reduction contract.[27] Such evidence illustrates that self-organization, designed along somewhat different lines than those proposed by some of the region's wealthier growers, was beginning to take firm root in the Black Patch.

This was reflected in 1903, when the TGA sent its organizers throughout Black Patch counties. The immediate work was to collect signatures on the petition appealing to Congress to remove the tax on manufactured tobacco. On a more fundamental level, however, organizers hoped to educate farmers and solicit their support to organize a new system of marketing. In the opinion of some organizers, only through the cooperative pooling of tobacco could farmers significantly raise the price for their product.[28]

Yet the issue of the tobacco tax remained highest on the agenda of others. The fight to repeal the tax began in earnest in early 1904. After a meeting held at the opera house in Clarksville, a committee was chosen to testify before a congressional subcommittee concerning the tax. Those chosen were Felix Ewing, R.E. Cooper, F.W. Dabney, W.F. Flowers, C.C. Reynolds, J.W. Dunn, and C.P. Warfield. During their testimony before a House subcommittee on internal revenue of the Committee of Ways and Means, Tennessee representative John W. Gaines described the cumulative effect of the tax: "It prevents the neighbors of the tobacco grower from purchasing it. It bars trade." Ultimately, Gaines warned, the tax "destroys the liberty of the grower."[29]

R.E. Cooper of Hopkinsville, Kentucky, felt that the tax hindered farmers from attempting to lift themselves from debt. Cooper stated: "If the farmer owes the supply store that furnishes him his supplies for the year, he can take this tobacco in a box and deliver it to the proprietor of the store and let him give it to his wholesaler and pay his debts."[30] While the tax was invoked, therefore, the producer had no choice but to sell directly to the trust buyer. The farmer could not even allow the furnishing merchant to bid on the crop.

Other advocates invoked conventional ideas of white supremacy to confuse the issue further. Said Charles Fort: "In our country we have an ignorant class of laborers who know nothing except what they learn from us. We white people teach them all they know and take care of them." Fort added, "These negroes are afraid of the revenue law. . . . they are afraid that they will be sent off out of the country where there are no white people." Although the bill passed the House, the efforts of the delegation failed when the bill was tabled in a Senate committee by a notable representative of the nation's financial sector, Rhode Island senator Nelson W. Aldrich.[31] A Clarksville *Leaf-Chronicle* editorial asked: "Isn't it an outrage that this trust-bossed Senator should possess the power to prevent an enactment of so righteous a measure, giving the relief so urgently needed by our struggling farmers?"[32]

Throughout the Black Patch, tobacco farmers struggled to find alternative answers to their economic misery. Growers in areas such as Corena, Kentucky, in Logan County, and Weakley County, Tennessee, held their own meetings to form voluntary associations. As many as three thousand farmers from Mayfield, Kentucky, met to resolve the dilemma of no competition among buyers and low prices. After the failure of the repeal of the tobacco tax, farmers sought to use legal channels to indict the American Tobacco Company on antitrust charges. The TGA formed a committee chaired by Felix Ewing to collect evidence that competition among tobacco buyers had been eliminated by the trust. Ewing's committee solicited responses from area farmers, and the findings were presented to Congressman Gaines, who was content to forward the files on to the U.S. Justice Department for further review.[33]

After waging such futile battles in the realm of traditional politics through petitions, appeals to elected leaders, and legal challenges, Black Patch farmers in the summer of 1904 renewed their efforts to address more directly the underlying economic problems they confronted. An alternative tactic undertaken, in the spirit of the earlier Alliance effort, was to organize cooperatives. Within the TGA, the center of Black Patch organizational efforts continued to be the Robertson County Tobacco Growers Association. Long before the Guthrie meeting, the organ of the PPA later stated, the Robertson County association "had been doing good work in enlisting the planters to think and grow interested."[34]

Organizers like John M. Foster, Felix Ewing, and M.V. Ingram utilized local newspapers such as the Clarksville *Leaf-Chronicle* and even the Cincinnati trade paper, the *Western Tobacco Journal*, as mediums for spreading the cooperative message. From Ingram's experienced pen came loquacious pleas: "The first and great command is 'to till the soil and make it blossom as the rose.' This covers the greatest of God's laws. When agriculture is prosperous every other avocation is sure to blossom as the rose." Ingram said, "Therefore it behooves all honest men to look first to the prosperity of agriculture, expel the obnoxious drones and give the bees a chance and gather in the fruits of their labor that all may enjoy the milk and honey of the land."[35]

The metaphor of the drone implied that certain sectors of society were expropriating the righteous rewards earned by the labor of the workers. In other words, in the minds of tobacco organizers the emergence of the tobacco trust threatened the entire society by draining the profits earned by farmers. As this challenged the common good of the entire region, only by cooperative action could farmers hope to bring greater equity to the region's economy. The idea of agrarian organization, in the opinion of a local farmer, crystallized "the many virtues that constitute the brotherhood of man." The movement was grounded in "Divine law and the principles of Christianity—help one another." The binding force of the farmers was simply "that of honor, which characterizes every true, manly man and good citizen who cherishes virtue."[36] In their early efforts, organizers thus drew upon a legacy of republicanism—an ideological strain that stressed the central importance of the common good and assailed private accumulation. Spoken in the tobacco belt, such pleas struck responsive chords.

In a series of articles written under the name Cactus, Ewing urged cooperative efforts among tobacco growers. By 1904 Ewing had emerged as a central player in the tobacco movement, and this development had fateful consequences. Ewing was not endowed with the usual accoutrements of agrarian radicalism. For one thing, he was extremely well-off financially. A balding, square-faced man, Ewing lived in a large three-story mansion in Robertson County, Tennessee. Ewing's daily surroundings were not those common to the bulk of the region's growers. A dinner guest at Ewing's home was once startled when Ewing ordered one of his black servants to pray before the meal. The guest later told Ewing that such a request was prayer "by proxy." Ewing responded that such activities were "a good influence on the negro's life." The owner of a three-thousand acre farm, Ewing required thirty-one tobacco barns to house his crop, the region's largest. Ewing felt that future organizations should learn lessons from the Grange and the Farmers' Alliance, which "were cumbersome and unwieldy . . . having politics, the monetary system of the country, and diverse other things injected into them." Ewing believed that these institutions "died of their own weight." He concluded that in the Black Patch "there should be an association with but one end in view, the better price of tobacco."[37] Self-evidently, Ewing was something less than an agrarian radical.

Ewing's views, in fact, displayed a fundamental innocence about the structural problems tobacco farmers faced. But his approach also had one strength. Most farmers were so disheartened by the failure of the agrarian movements of the previous decades that cautious plans seemed to be the only ones that stood a chance of success. This was their point of contact with men like Ewing, who were cautious for much more deeply rooted social and cultural reasons. Emerging on the heels of the earlier failed agricultural movements, Ewing and the PPA were determined to focus their efforts solely on raising prices in the short term. Ardent Ewing supporters such as Charles Fort remarked that Ewing's plan was "a complete solution" to the problems gripping tobacco farmers.[38] Yet, though neither Ewing nor his potential farmer recruits could know as much at the time, without long-term structural solutions to the problems of agricultural credit, the fight to achieve a higher standard of living for all tobacco producers rested on shaky ground.

Ewing soon drafted a report stating that a committee had been established to submit a plan of organization to the farmers of the Black Patch. In February 1904 more than sixty prominent growers in Robertson County were invited to a meeting at Ewing's home, and they decided to organize farmers into a crop-withholding cooperative. The committee on organization consisted of Ewing, A.B. Porter, Sterling Fort, V.A. Bradley, and Neel Glenn. The committee's plan was to pool the year's crop and withhold it until the price was satisfactory. This plan was suggested to farmers by organizers in the summer of 1904 in every major tobacco-producing county of the Black Patch. To conclude the plan, a culminating meeting was proposed. The site selected was Guthrie, Kentucky, located on the Kentucky-Tennessee border and served by the L&N Railroad. The fairgrounds in Guthrie provided an appropriate location for the meeting. Circulars were passed, and announcements were given to local newspapers telling of the "great meeting" that was imminent.[39]

Foster heartily supported Ewing's plan for cooperation. As the Guthrie meeting approached, Foster made a desperate appeal to Black Patch farmers who remained unconvinced of the necessity of cooperation to organize collectively, else they "deserve the name of cowards, and the very women and children will crook the finger of scorn at you."[40]

Ewing's general plan was a narrow one: there was no intention to implement anything approaching a subtreasury system, and most emphatically, no third parties were envisioned. The plan was simply an attempt to raise tobacco prices within the Black Patch. In the beginning, the organization that Foster had designated the Tobacco Planters' Protective Association was to include thirteen counties in the Black Patch. Charles Fort indicated the hope generated by this early organization: "With proper protection from our own Government, and a thorough organization on the growers' part, we can 'stand pat' and demand a profit. Whenever the growers educate themselves to a thorough knowledge of the existing evils, and their causes, then will they be ready to apply the remedy, which, as Mr. Ewing says, is 'concentration by organization.'"[41] As the September 24 meeting approached, local congressmen John W. Gaines, Ollie James, and A.O. Stanley agreed to attend and address the gathering. Reports from various county agents promised that the meeting would find thousands of farmers in attendance and in earnest support of the organization.

While organizers anticipated the Guthrie meeting, some were more concerned with the long-range aspects of organizing. Former Alliance man M.V. Ingram understood the crucial importance of properly financing a crop-withholding effort. He further knew that in order for the movement to succeed, long-term plans were necessary. He suggested that local businessmen purchase stock in the PPA in twenty-five-dollar shares. If this occurred, Ingram estimated that between fifty and one hundred thousand dollars could be raised to advance to farmers who were pooling their crops. Ingram added: "Deposit the money with the several banks to be paid out on order, every farmer that borrows giving a mortgage on his crop and agreeing to leave one dollar per hundred pounds of tobacco sold with the company as stock, for which he receives a certificate of stock and sharing in the profits. This mortgaged tobacco and stock will furnish collateral on a credit basis as fast as tobacco comes in for all money wanted to carry out the scheme." Ingram fully recognized the dramatic recruiting potential inherent in his proposal: "The farmers will climb over each other to get an interest in a scheme like this, and in two years the company will have two millions paid up capital of its own, paying a nice little profit to every stockholder and thus collect together great banking capital to furnish credit."[42] Ingram's innovative plan, though never realized, not only promised hope for farmers but also offered greater income for the region's economy. Businessmen, bankers, and merchants might contribute to the success of the plan. At this early moment Ingram's plans demonstrated that the PPA did not lack ideas that could alter the economic lives of Black Patch farmers.

Throughout the spring and summer of 1904, organizers, already firmly established in each district as a result of the extensive network built by the Robertson County TGA, spread the word of the cooperative drive to area growers. The underpinnings of the organizing message, however, consisted of more than merely an appeal for higher prices. Organizers stressed that something was occurring on the land that threatened some deeply rooted values. A new social and economic order, represented in clear fashion by the ATC, hovered over the countryside. Organizers reiterated that farmers had little time to react if they wished to defend the republican heritage. A resolution sponsored by the Montgomery County PPA revealed a sense of the ideas undergirding the farmers' movement. The trust, according to the resolution, "has destroyed the 'law of supply and demand'" and consequently "robs the laborer and sharecropper of a just price for his only money crop."[43] Statements about a "just price" and republican warnings of a new corporate order struck exposed nerves.

At the beginning of the insurgent effort, local bankers were naturally somewhat less than eager to lend money to the association.[44] Yet organizers avidly pursued bankers, in the grip of the certain knowledge that the ruinously low prices for tobacco were depressing commerce as well as agriculture throughout Kentucky and Tennessee. Under such circumstances, even bankers were fair game, as the entire region had become subjected to what was essentially a colonial relationship of dependency to the empire of James B. Duke. It is, then, not too surprising to discover that John M. Foster obtained the financial backing of P.P. Pickard, a banker in Ashland City, Tennessee, and an association warehouse was soon erected in that town. While the banking community remained somewhat skeptical of the insurgents, the tobacco warehouse of Warfield and Ladd loaned nearly four hundred thousand dollars to the PPA.[45]

The cooperation of local banks in loaning money while the crops were pooled was deemed essential to the success of the movement by PPA organizers. M.V. Ingram noted: "It is up to our bankers to take an interest in this matter. Can you gentlemen afford to keep money hoarded and idle in your banks? Surely not, and you can't afford to let this opportunity for restoring your trade slip by and be gathered in by some other enterprising town."[46] Sterling Fort, one of the members of the organizing committee, was himself a prominent banker.

In mid-October 1904 Ewing dramatically announced that thirty-two banks in the Black Patch region had pledged their support to the farmers' movement and had promised that funds were available for advancing to association members. This startling announcement, seemingly ignoring the historical tension existing between farmers and bankers, represents one of the more extraordinary ingredients distinguishing the Tobacco Wars from other agrarian insurgencies in America or in any other country. The question arises: Why did local bankers come to the aid of the agrarian insurgents in Kentucky and Tennessee?[47]

With such local luminaries as Ewing and Washington heading the movement, bankers could take comfort in the political reliability of the nascent organization. After all, Ewing was the region's largest tobacco grower, and Washington had once served as an adviser to that staunch defender of the gold standard, President Grover Cleveland. Also, the conservative nature of the farmer's expressed desires—higher prices, with no talk of third parties or government-owned railroads or utilities—provided bankers with conclusive evidence that they were not dealing with anything that smacked of neopopulism. Yet these relationships do not reveal the essential reason why financing the tobacco movement served the best interests of bankers.

A keen insight into the world of commercial bankers was offered by the bankers themselves in an open pledge of support to Ewing: "Believing that if the planters are organized, tobacco will bring better prices and therefore will be better security, we will loan such sums of money as may be necessary to enable the planter of limited means to hold his tobacco."[48] Since tobacco fueled the local economy, low prices hurt the entire community. With the pooled tobacco serving as collateral, bankers were assured that they could receive, at the very least, the already low prices then being offered by the tobacco trust. Additionally, the loans were not free: farmers were charged interest that accrued throughout the duration of the withholding period. If the movement succeeded, the bankers would receive greater income, and the entire local economy, upon which the banks depended would be strengthened.

Only with all these organizational imperatives in mind can the Guthrie meeting be coherently interpreted. After years of futile effort, farmers in the Black Patch embarked on an organizing strategy in early 1904 that mobilized segments of the entire community. Building upon the organizational structure of the Robertson County Tobacco Growers Association established by its founder, John M. Foster, the crop-withholding campaign began to sink roots among Black Patch farmers, as organizers ventured into every county spreading the cooperative message. To conclude plans and to provide visible public evidence of the vitality of the movement, the culminating meeting at Guthrie was considered an imperative organizing step. It is essential to note that the road to Guthrie was paved with years of organizational development. Guthrie was anything but a spontaneous reaction to low prices.

When the day for the Guthrie meeting arrived, organizers were heartened by the enthusiastic turnout of over five thousand farmers. The Louisville *Courier-Journal* noted: "The rafters overhead each had its quota of eager listeners, and so great was the crush that the planters overran the speaker's stand, and it was never cleared during the course of the convention." An array of speeches traced the rise of monopolistic customs in the tobacco trade. Ewing, Charles Fort, Joel Fort, and congressmen John W. Gaines, Ollie James, and A.O. Stanley each spoke of the disastrous situation created by the American Tobacco Company. Delegates from each county were selected to continue organizing the tobacco growers for sustained and coordinated action during the coming season. Felix Ewing was elected chairman of the new organization, and a constitution of the PPA was adopted, which emphasized that a county could not become a member of the PPA unless 70 percent of its acreage was pledged to the association. This provision strikingly illustrated the enlarged sense of purpose and confidence that previous efforts had instilled in the organizers.[49]

After the Guthrie meeting, Felix Ewing assumed command of the Black Patch movement. While his role in the developments of the PPA was crucial, one cannot ignore or dismiss the pivotal roles played by John M. Foster and M.V. Ingram. In the late 1890s, while Ewing brushed aside the possibility of organizing Black Patch farmers, Foster remained committed. His central role in organizing the Robertson County Tobacco Growers Association, which provided the essential early core of organizers, was of vital importance. In the crucial months after the Guthrie meeting, the roles of Foster and former Alliance men Ingram and John B. Allen were important in giving coherent organizational shape to the cooperative attempt. Ewing himself said about Foster, "He is the ablest writer and best read man in the Association, and knows more about it than I do." [50]

The events that ultimately led to the gathering of five thousand farmers in Guthrie thus provide a window through which we can view the war in the Black Patch. A complete organizational structure was firmly in place well before the historic meeting occurred, and the organizers of this movement drew upon the cooperative experiences embedded in the agrarian heritage. Their message not only stressed the harm low prices were causing the entire local economy but also asserted that something was very wrong in a society that sanctioned industrial monopoly over the commonwealth.

Yet close inspection reveals that even in the seeming glory of the Guthrie meeting, the foundations of cooperation were less than robust. The financing strategy, involving the unique alliance of bankers and farmers, often placed the farmer in the same debilitating economic condition as before. In addition, many local growers could not afford bank loans, which became increasingly expensive. Such a financing strategy appealed principally to larger, wealthier growers.

Yet there was a far deeper reason why the involvement of bankers in the PPA would prove more damaging than constructive. With bankers as allies, the PPA hierarchy necessarily adopted a rather limited approach, which left intact the ominous economic barriers that threatened the region's agricultural economy. Specifically, the PPA chose to ignore the principal issue of continual indebtedness, which produced the regional reliance on tobacco in the first place. Without an appeal that addressed the crippling burden of agricultural credit—an appeal that promised hope to small growers, tenants, and sharecroppers, while threatening the financial well-being of the region's farm creditors—recruiting at the local level would not be easy.

Ewing's conservative approach to the economic ills affecting rural America obviously did not correspond to the agenda of all farmers in the region. Some growers, who had earlier supported the subtreasury program of the Farmers' Alliance and were responsive to republican warnings of corporate intrusion and the subsequent loss of autonomous social and economic relations, initially supported the PPA for far different reasons than Ewing. How this division between the various segments of the PPA would be settled would determine the parameters of democratic forms within this self-help formation.

At this early juncture, the Planters' Protective Association had no clear plan for addressing the fundamental problems confronting farmers, neither the age-old problem of credit nor the more recent appearance of the American Tobacco Company's monopoly. The tobacco cooperatives were structured to raise prices and nothing more. Yet it became increasingly clear that without structural solutions to some overriding problems, the cooperatives were ill prepared to meet the challenge they had created for themselves.[51]

4

Rumors of War

The prime organizing period of the cooperative movement in the dark tobacco regions of Kentucky and Tennessee only lasted five years. By 1909 the Planters' Protective Association was in rapid decline. While the tobacco trust certainly did its share to break the cooperative effort, internal problems within the organization itself as well as a national financial crisis also caused considerable damage. The development of the tobacco cooperatives in the Black Patch, nevertheless, provides an excellent example of how insurgencies evolve—how they are created and how they endeavor to develop a workable strategy to address their problems.

In the autumn and winter of 1904 PPA organizers continued the crucial work of recruiting area farmers. To lead this organizing campaign, Ewing, not surprisingly, called upon John M. Foster, the man instrumental in organizing the Robertson County Tobacco Growers Association. For fifty-three consecutive days, Foster worked in fifteen counties, feverishly urging farmers to join the PPA. Foster worked through all conditions, and the *Black Patch Tobacco Journal* later remarked: "Foster was laughed at for walking miles through the snows of Calloway County, Kentucky to organize the people." Such persistent efforts paid off, however. As the paper noted, Foster resoundingly "made a hit" among local farmers.[1]

Other chief organizers at this time were John E. Garner and the old Alliance organizer and former Texas Ranger John B. Allen. Even at this early moment, organizers saw how the trust would react to a farmers' organization designed simply to achieve better prices. When Allen and Garner made an appearance in Calloway County, an unusual thing happened. Prices on the western Kentucky market, which had been reaching as low as two to three cents per pound, suddenly advanced to five cents. Thus while organizers asked farmers to join the tobacco pool and withhold the crop from the market until higher prices could be obtained, farmers in one Kentucky county were offered high prices for their crop immediately. As Allen and Garner continued to recruit, the price advanced again to seven cents. To counter this move at killing the recruiting effort, Allen and Garner stressed that the trust had a short supply of tobacco on hand and was desperate to obtain more. If seven cents per pound was being offered, the growers reasoned, those pooling their crops could expect more, if only they waited.[2] As seen in microcosm in one county, the battle lines between the association and the trust were being carefully drawn.

Throughout the Black Patch, scores of organizers continued to recruit farmers. In January 1905 more than seven hundred farmers came to the Fulton, Kentucky, courthouse to hear John B. Allen. The farmers reacted with enthusiasm, believing that the PPA, according to a local newspaper, "is their only hope." Allen alone canvassed thirty-one counties in six months.[3] Garner and Allen received help from Ewing's father-in-law, Joseph E. Washington, in organizing several districts in Tennessee. In Mayfield, Kentucky, Allen, along with one of the most energetic organizers in the PPA, Joel Fort, spoke before five hundred farmers in January 1905. That session alone ended with farmers signing almost 440,000 new pounds of tobacco to the PPA pool. Fort affirmed that he had never seen such crowds as those that came to hear his recruiting speeches. Allen, meanwhile, remained in Mayfield for the next week, making two recruiting speeches daily at different locales in the continuing effort to enlarge the grassroots base of the PPA movement. The results of such activity were best expressed by J.W. Usher of Graves County: "The seeds that were sown by J.E. Garner, John Foster, F.G. Ewing, J.B. Allen and Joel Fort are germinating rapidly." These daily chores of creating agrarian audiences, informing them of the specific details of the new cooperative effort, and recruiting them into the fold constitute, in the aggregate, the political process that is the cornerstone of movement building. This is a process that is essentially oral: it consists of recruiting speeches and one-on-one conversations. Thus, historians have little written evidence to use in reconstructing the dynamics that are, in fact, busily at work. Yet tapping this often obscured evidence is essential to understanding the sequential steps involved in constructing a movement.[4]

For example, organizers such as W.P. ("Old Shanks") Anderson and C.P. Warfield went together to places like Adairville, Kentucky, and Orlinda, Tennessee, to recruit. Reporters in Orlinda noted only that the town had never seen such a gathering as the one that greeted Warfield.[5] The experiences Old Shanks and Warfield gained from their recruiting activities shaped their understanding of how democratic movements occur. Later, at the precise moment other PPA leaders sought to impose some rather authoritarian forms on the farmers' movement, the two alerted their fellow growers of the danger that such designs posed on the ability of the PPA to sustain its struggle.

While organizers such as Foster, Fort, Warfield, and Allen peformed the necessary task of recruiting, Felix Ewing's self-assigned role during this critical early phase was revealing. Instead of focusing his political attention on increasing PPA membership by actively joining his organizers in the field, Ewing directed his attention to the affluent members of society by appealing to the nation's elected leaders for help. In early February 1905 Ewing met in Washington with U.S. Secretary of Agriculture James Wilson, who, in Ewing's opinion, was "very much in favor of the bill" lowering the tax on tobacco. Wilson then took Ewing to see President Theodore Roosevelt, who, Ewing believed, listened "thoughtfully" to his views on the tobacco tax. Ewing left these meetings "most encouraged" by the reception afforded him by the president and the agriculture secretary.[6] What this line of approach revealed about Ewing had profound long-term ramifications. He saw politics as existing in the form of a palliative bill that needed to be "sold" to presidents and agriculture secretaries. In short, he saw politics primarily as a legislative process rather than a complex democratic organizing challenge in which the first task on the agenda was recruiting farmers into a substantial force that would give him political clout. The administration undoubtedly would have been more receptive to serious approaches from Ewing concerning the issues facing farmers had he supported his claims with a constituency of thousands of farmers. At this early stage, Ewing's agenda for building an insurgent movement was already rather different than that of his organizers.

As counties were organized, the growers selected district chairmen. These chairmen reported to a county chairman, who represented the county before the Executive Committee, also elected by the rank and file. Meetings were established in the districts twice monthly at which members could air and discuss concerns. In the beginning, these meetings were primarily occupied with the enormous task of recruiting.[7]

The Montgomery County association met in Clarksville, Tennessee. Local meetings usually began with a roll call of district chairmen, who reported how recruiting was progressing within their areas. The roll call in March 1905 gathered these reports:

District No. 2.—Mr. Anderson: "Have seen 27 men all signed. Will get others."
District No. 3—Mr. Smith: "Have 30 signers. Some refused."
District No. 13.—Mr. Heggie: "All have signed but one man, who says he has 15 boys and is obliged to raise tobacco."

The ties that naturally grew among the farmers who met in these gatherings were displayed in sometimes dramatic and poignant ways. Some meetings engendered prolonged and earnest discussions that transcended immediate problems concerning tobacco prices. In April 1905 the Montgomery County district came to the aid of one of its members, J.W. Pollard. Pollard had recently seen his home destroyed by fire, and his wife was badly injured. M.V. Ingram moved that a collection be taken up for Pollard and his family. Pollard tried to stop the collection, but as the *Leaf-Chronicle* noted, "that did not stop the boys; dollars, halves, quarters and dimes came spontaneously until every man had put in a mite. It was just simply a heart offering and Mr. Pollard broke down with emotion under this double demonstration of regard for him."[8] What is interesting about such a phenomenon is that it provides evidence—to be arrayed alongside and against Ewing's preoccupations at the top of society—of a growing communitarian ethos among the rank and file of this voluntary association.

In these meetings held all over the region, farmers could gather and shape their own movement as it formed before them.

District chairmen, men who worked and lived within their districts, personally knew most of those whom they attempted to recruit. After the initial recruiting, these meetings were crucial in sustaining the life of the farmers' effort. The PPA grew, but not merely as a result of low prices. Instead, the work of men like Allen, Foster, Garner, and Fort produced local organizers like Mr. Smith and Mr. Heggie, who were largely responsible for the early success of the Black Patch tobacco movement.[9]

In early 1905, as the tobacco movement gained strength, one national trade newspaper, the *Western Tobacco Journal*, was less than sympathetic with the farmers' cause. An article that appeared at this time, in fact, even celebrated the tenancy system that characterized the tobacco region. In the *Journal's* estimation, tobacco tenants received sixteen cents per pound for their crops, lived in "comfortable circumstances," and often developed into "substantial and influential businessmen." One angry local farmer responded by noting that prices were closer to five cents, and thus five acres of tobacco garnered two hundred dollars for a tenant family. Since landowners usually received half of the renter's crop, the tenant was left with only one hundred dollars for his year's work. With bitter sarcasm, the farmer responded, "Here is the income the professional man would be proud of." He further wrote, "Let this tenant buy a little flour, and some sugar, coffee and his wife and children a pair of shoes, pay his taxes and doctor's bills." After this, the tenant "has to start in for another crop without a dollar in sight until he has another crop ready."[10]

Leaders of the movement stressed more than higher prices. They warned farmers of an ominous new force: industrialism. In 1906 organizer Joel Fort told a gathering: "We are now in the midst of an age of money madness, an age in which the beast of greed and corruption races with impetuous speed over our fair land, trampling under its cruel feet the weaker and less fortunate laboring people of the county." The new industrial corporation, according to Fort, "yields not to the imprecations and the prayers of the poor and needy. It hears no cries or wails which come from the valley of misery." The tobacco trust was nothing more than "a cruel master, and whenever it fixes its grasp upon the throat of labor, it will not voluntarily turn loose or quit its hold."[11]

County organizers often used local newspapers to recruit.

J.W. Usher pleaded in one newspaper: "I most earnestly urge
you to join the PPA and get good prices for your tobacco.
. . . F.G. Ewing has about concluded the negotiations with a
powerful syndicate to dispose of the entire crop now owned by
the membership of this Association." In an attempt to portray the
power of the PPA, Usher exaggerated, saying that twenty thousand farmers had joined by December 1904.[12]

In considering the decision to join the co-op, most farmers in
Graves County, Kentucky, like those throughout the region,
were in a bind. While large landowners could afford to wait
months, even years, for their crop's returns, a crop-withholding
campaign placed immediate burdens upon smallholders, tenants, and sharecroppers. J. Frank Boyd of Boaz candidly stated
the situation: "The small farmers and tenant farmers have got to
live somehow and tobacco is about all he has to look to for money.
. . . if the organization don't finance the thing, this class of men
will convert their tobacco into cash whenever the pinch gets hard
enough."[13] Financing "the thing" was a matter of great concern
to PPA organizers. Without affordable credit, farmers would find
trust offers too high to refuse or the waiting involved in a withholding campaign too arduous. While the PPA held the crop off
the market, children still needed to be fed, and bills needed to be
paid. Unless adequate credit was obtained, the tobacco movement seemed imperiled.

The responsibility for advancing loans fell to the counties, and
each county worked out different ways of administering ad-
vancements. In Graves County, for example, warehousemen
advanced half of the value of a crop brought in by a cooperating
farmer in exchange for a loan at 8-percent interest, with the
money being provided by local bankers. In Springfield, Tennessee, three banks agreed to lend advances to cooperating farmers
at 6-percent interest. In Hopkins County, Kentucky, the local
PPA made a public request for bankers to aid the cooperative.
Within hours, presidents of two local banks agreed to loan ten
thousand dollars to the Hopkins County PPA. In Montgomery
County, Tennessee, bankers were willing to help, since they
estimated that a higher price for tobacco could inject at least two
million dollars into local circulation.[14]

This method of financing, however, could only help farmers in the short term. While some local banks provided loans, they were only offered for half a farmer's estimated crop and at interest rates of usually 6 percent and higher. When the withholding effort produced long waiting periods, the meager loans were not sufficient.[15] The PPA's great challenge was to find alternative financing schemes that could address structural agricultural needs. Without long-term, low-interest advances covering the entire crop, the PPA could never expect to recruit a majority of Black Patch farmers.

By the winter of 1904 the PPA had successfully pooled twenty-five thousand hogsheads of the 1904 crop of dark tobacco, from an estimated seventy-five thousand hogshead produced.[16] As the PPA sought to enlarge its constituency and dispose of the 1904 crop at a satisfactory price, the association found itself the target of a boycott by the American Tobacco Company. Trust buyers refused to buy association tobacco and instead offered high prices to those growers declining PPA recruiters. Ewing was able to sell part of the 1904 crop to foreign buyers in Germany: 155 hogshead were sold for eight and a half cents per pound, and 300 hogshead were later bought for seven and a fourth cents. After expenses, however, these sales brought prices barely above the four cents offered by trust buyers in 1904 and were certainly lower than the ten-to-twelve-cent prices offered to noncooperators by trust buyers. By November 1905 less than half of the PPA's holdings had been sold, and organizers discovered dissatisfaction brewing among some members. In Trigg County, Kentucky, organizer C.P. Warfield found that "a few of our farmers who were members last year are not joining this year because their tobacco has not been sold."[17]

Nevertheless, after the first full year of cooperation, the PPA successfully pooled over 34,600 hogshead, or 55 million pounds, of the 1905 crop. Another Guthrie celebration was planned for September. The second meeting far surpassed the initial 1904 meeting. Between 15,000 and 20,000 people gathered to celebrate the efforts of the first year and to renew their collective confidence in the movement. The highlight of the day was a massive parade, in which thousands of farmers marched, four abreast. Proud wives marched alongside their husbands. The wagon of PPA chairman Felix Ewing was drawn by four horses. Seated

The annual rally of the Planters' Protective Association, Guthrie, Kentucky, 1905. J. Winston Coleman Kentuckiana Collection, Transylvania University Library.

next to him were the men who were, in Ewing's estimation, the first "to enter the fight," including organizers John B. Allen and M.V. Ingram.[18]

These meetings also provided an appropriate arena for local politicians to denounce the American Tobacco Company and to pledge their support for the farmers' cooperative attempt. Many of the congressmen in attendance, such as A.O. Stanley, John W. Gaines, and Ollie James, gave their explicit support for the battle on the nominal issue of repealing the tobacco tax. One contemporary observer correctly noted that the bill actually did little for the financial situation farmers faced and was instead "a shrewd political expedient for currying favor with the agricultural multitudes." Politicians naturally sought the official endorsements of the large tobacco cooperative. Yet it was the avowed policy of the PPA, specifically Felix Ewing, not to become "involved" in party politics by endorsing particular candidates for office. This was not unusual in the aftermath of the Farmers' Alliance, as many agricultural organizations vowed to remain aloof from party politics. Ewing made it clear that "this Association never has and never will, as far as those in charge of it can prevent, lend its aid as an organization to further or defeat the political aspirations of any man."[19]

This removal from political activity was heartily supported by PPA members, who felt that the tobacco movement transcended party politics. An example of how opponents of this policy were treated was provided in Trigg County, where Dr. J.H. Lackey took issue with PPA policy and moved that the co-op should "take a hand in all the political contests." The chairman of the Trigg chapter, E.E. Wash, arose immediately to disapprove Lackey's motion, and several hundred farmers loudly applauded Wash's action.[20]

This remoteness from political participation by the PPA, however, revealed the extent to which Ewing wanted the tobacco movement to remain no threat to established political interests. Ambitious politicians, including E.E. Wash himself, could thus exploit the movement by using their well-known attendance at association rallies and their expressed support of "progressive" legislative measures to their political advantage. The PPA, nonetheless, rendered itself impotent to assert its own political agenda.[21]

During the early years of the PPA, the rank and file discovered various undemocratic elements steadily seeping into official PPA policy. Within the hierarchy of the association itself, a perception emerged in the first year of cooperation that the PPA was becoming dominated solely by Ewing. An exploration of the interior structure of the PPA, in fact, reveals steadily growing dissent and anger at the autocratic methods employed by the leadership of the farmers' organization. The movement, at its apex, was increasingly losing sight of democratic presumptions and aspirations.

The smoldering displeasure was evident in a local meeting of the Montgomery County association in December 1905. A district chairman, Mr. Chapman, reported great uneasiness among farmers within the district because of the low prices that PPA members had received. Chapman urged an immediate advance of two cents per pound to help farmers during the waiting period. After Chapman took his seat, the *Leaf-Chronicle* reported: "Mr. Chapman stirred up a veritable hornet's nest. . . . complaints more or less vigorous and numerous came from all parts of the house concerning excessive warehouse charges and other alleged irregularities."[22] An even more telling criticism came from John M. Foster himself. Concerning tobacco sales, Foster asked: "How do we planters know today what our crops sold for, except by the returns made to us?" While cautiously warning of "future fraud" by unscrupulous PPA employees, Foster was also directing his charge against Ewing's policy of secret sales. Such heavy-handed decisions alarmed the movement's original founder, who ceased his participation in the PPA shortly thereafter.[23]

Ewing initiated the policy of secret sales to cover all purchases of PPA tobacco. Prospective buyers of PPA tobacco thus conducted their business with co-op officials in private, and the individual grower never had a voice in the sale of his crop. Consequently, many farmers wished to see "open sales," in which buyers and sellers negotiated in public, using PPA prices as a minimum standard. Profound disagreement with this aspect of PPA policy was provided in December 1905, when a committee was appointed in Montgomery County, Tennessee, to investigate precisely how the PPA went about its business in selling tobacco.[24] When the committee asked to see the books of the PPA, the request was rejected. "Is there anything wrong," asked a local editor, "in allowing a farmer to see his tobacco sold, and to accept or reject the bid as he may see proper, settle with his agent, the warehousemen, and leave no room for complaint against the Association or grounds for suspicion of wrong doing?"[25]

Ewing further angered many within the PPA in March 1906, when he ordered the association's headquarters moved from Clarksville, Tennessee to Guthrie, Kentucky. Ewing cited the ninth clause in the PPA's charter as the principal reason for abandoning the large Clarksville market. The clause prohibited association warehouses from handling any business other than that from the PPA. Clarksville warehousemen found the policy impossible to follow, since they could not keep track of the ownership of all incoming leaf. Additionally, warehousemen were too financially hard-pressed to ban all incoming tobacco except PPA leaf. To the local farmers, many of whom composed the essential early constituency of the Robertson County Tobacco Growers Association, Ewing's decision also meant that their tobacco had to be hauled dozens of miles away to smaller markets.[26]

One of the more vocal critics of this policy was Clarksville warehouseman and early PPA organizer C.P. Warfield, who told Ewing that he could not "acquiesce in the warfare being made by the Executive Committee in Clarksville." A local grower sided with Warfield and asked why "Mr. Ewing wants to impose hardships on Clarksville," adding that Ewing had "departed from first principles and had turned to splitting hairs."[27]

A revealing episode occurred in April 1906, when Joel Fort came to Clarksville to try to settle the dispute. Much to everyone's pleasure, Fort worked out an agreement by which Clarksville warehousemen pledged to store PPA tobacco separately from nonpooled tobacco. Despite the open and candid way in which the agreement was reached, Ewing simply vetoed the measure. This dictatorial display was dismaying not only to Fort personally but also to thousands of Clarksville farmers. The basic issue was clear: To what extent did the popular base of the movement have a voice in the organization's policy?[28]

The Clarksville *Leaf-Chronicle*, an initial supporter of Ewing and the PPA, nonetheless warned of the ominous effects that Ewing's actions were having on the health of the tobacco movement. "Do you mean to breed dissension, disrupt and pull down all you have labored a year to build?" the paper inquired. Fully alert to potential disaster, Joel Fort visited Clarksville a second time, only to see another agreement fashioned between himself and the warehousemen vetoed by Ewing.[29]

Disgusted by Ewing's high-handed methods, the *Leaf-Chronicle* then reported that "one close to the throne" stated that Ewing and the Executive Committee of the PPA had essentially tired of criticism over the Clarksville matter and would not compromise: the issue was settled. No more questions from the rank and file, in essence, would be answered. Ewing was quick to respond that such a claim was "a malicious falsehood." In a stunning journalistic move, the *Leaf-Chronicle* responded openly: "We are sorry for this because some good friend's head will have to come off for daring to utter opinions different than the lawgiver." The paper then proceeded to reveal its source: "The Honorable Joel B. Fort is authority for the statement." Whether Fort agreed to this remarkable disclosure is unknown. In any case, it revealed not only the increasingly dictatorial manner of

Ewing but also the deep fissures his rule had created among the movement's most committed activists.[30]

Members in local county meetings continued to speak out against secret sales and the removal of the Clarksville headquarters. When James H. Ferguson of Franklin, Kentucky, noted that when he mentioned some of the "miserable blunders" committed by Ewing and the PPA, he was accused by the local leadership of being a "traitor" to the farmers' efforts, which effectively quieted critics in the crowd. Ferguson nonetheless felt that three-fourths of the farmers in his region fully supported open sales but were relatively invisible because they were "denied the right to discuss these matters in our meetings."[31]

In meetings in Montgomery County, Tennessee, in August 1906, the discontent among the rank and file increased. J.W. Hunt spoke of a certain "restlessness" pervading the membership of the local PPA, which he felt was "brought about by the management refusing to take the people into their confidence." J.T. Morrison then rose and addressed a component of the organizing process that, he felt, produced such dissension. Believing in organization, Morrison nevertheless made a crucial qualification: "The organization should consist alone of farmers. Instead, we reach out and take in everybody." Morrison's observations raised a central question: Who should compose the membership of the farmer's organization? Indeed, this aspect of insurgency has historically caused deep concern for many in agrarian movements in America. It is noteworthy, for example, that a movement among farmers in Oklahoma at this same time approached the issues of class and constituency far differently. In organizing the Farmers' Union in Oklahoma, large landholders like Ewing were perceived by tenants and smallholders as "farmers by proxy," who thus held different economic interests than the bulk of the region's farmers. The smallholders consequently denied membership in the union to larger growers and businessmen. In Kentucky and Tennessee, such issues never received such careful consideration. Instead, smallholders and tenants in the Black Patch who joined the PPA found their movement led by wealthy landowners in alliance with local bankers, whose interests ultimately differed from those of members like Morrison.[32]

Morrison's simple but profound question identified one of the decisive limitations of the agrarian movement in Kentucky and Tennessee. In the formative phase of the PPA, wealthy land-owners constituting the leadership of the organization naturally assumed that a movement directed by themselves in conjunction with bankers offered the best hope for the region's tobacco growers to achieve higher prices. At this promising yet vulnerable point in the Black Patch effort, the leadership did not respond to the rumblings from below, which questioned the basic premises of Ewing and the PPA hierarchy. Such rumblings revealed the certain knowledge that a movement sanctioned by bankers and the local gentry was organically incapable of alleviating the structural problems of credit and land ownership that brought bankers and large farmers like Ewing increased wealth while impoverishing the region's smallholders.

Despite their best efforts, farmers in the Black Patch were further shocked by events that Ewing precipitated in June 1906. Though several months would pass before the implications of what he had done would be fully realized, Ewing had PPA attorneys draw up a new charter for the organization. While the first charter explicitly gave ownership of the association to member farmers, who elected their officials each year, the new charter introduced some startling changes. First, the officers were to be elected not by the farmers themselves but by the PPA's Board of Directors. Second, the new charter issued 200 shares of stock in the new corporation, of which Ewing owned 191, purchased at the astonishing "price" of one dollar each. Through the new charter, the PPA thus became a closed corporation, one in which future profits belonged to its new major stockholder, Felix Ewing.[33] Even members of the Executive Committee were unaware of the new charter and its implications until the document was printed in the Clarksville Leaf-Chronicle months later. The newspaper summarized: in addition to secret sales and the arbitrary moving of the headquarters to Guthrie, "this new charter changes the whole situation, leaving farmers out as only coerced patrons."[34]

Reactions to Ewing's latest move met with swift reprisal in county meetings. J.W. Hunt spoke in defiance of the new arrangement: "This new charter was not obtained by consent of the stockholders," claimed Hunt, adding, "I do not propose to have a collar out on my neck that I cannot take off." His comments, according to reports, were greeted with frequent applause from his fellow farmers, reflecting an increasingly precise focus upon the source of the organizational problem. I.G. Sallee, of Trigg County, called on all growers not "to desert the ship, but court martial her officers." C.P. Warfield sustained the growing clamor with a crucial observation: "The present methods of secrecy, denying the planter any voice in the sale of his tobacco, cannot inspire confidence." Unless corrections were implemented to alter PPA policy, Warfield warned, the results of Ewing's actions were "bound to destroy the organization." [35]

Perhaps of all the issues dividing the PPA, one that revealed the true extent of Ewing's haughty conduct toward his constituency concerned salaries. In the original charter, PPA officials were prohibited from receiving any compensation for their services. The proceeds from PPA sales were to return to the member farmers. In August 1907 W.P. ("Old Shanks") Anderson made a speech in Keysburg, Kentucky, in Logan County, that created a stir among association members. Anderson claimed that the forecasts of association enemies, much to his regret, had come true. PPA officials had voted themselves high salaries, which were not commensurate with the services provided. These salaries, for administrators, prizers, graders, and others ranged from $1,500 to $2,100 yearly. Joel Fort, meanwhile, who in Anderson's opinion "had done more real good for the Association than any other man, had received only $1,200 and paid his own expenses." Anderson exhorted all members to express their indignation over this new development to their district chairmen and thereby begin to reclaim their movement. To many within the association, it seemed clear that the needs of the rank and file were being submerged under those of the PPA leadership. "This structure was built by the labors, sacrifices, and devotion of the people," Anderson stated, "and we don't propose to give up our right of suggesting reforms. . . . let the power remain with the people and not be centralized anywhere." [36]

In response to such remarks, Ewing's defenders, unable to mobilize persuasive arguments on the specific issues at hand, spoke only in allusive generalities. G.B. Bingham felt that Anderson's comments reflected "a spirit greatly disturbed." In the opinion of the increasingly skeptical Clarksville *Leaf-Chronicle*, however, Anderson "was exactly right and he has the backing of every right thinking member of the Association." When claims that association officials deserved high salaries because of their hard work surfaced, Anderson responded emphatically: "They do not take into account the hundreds and thousands of poor people who went half clothed and half fed for years and refused to sell their tobacco to the Trust for perhaps twice as much as they got for it out of the Association."[37]

The extent to which "poor people" such as tenants and share-croppers felt that their interests were not well served by the PPA was illustrated by an extraordinary event in 1906. Tenant farmers in Logan County, Kentucky, and Robertson County, Tennessee, formed their own protective union, distinct from the PPA, and compiled a list of demands to landowners. The tenants demanded the right to keep half of all tobacco raised, the right to raise two acres of corn for every acre of tobacco, $1.25 per day for threshing, $15.00 per month for room and board, and a horse to help them tend their private gardens. This local group, which lasted for only a few weeks, constituted a truly remarkable example of very poor people, the poorest of the agrarian poor, organizing themselves for collective action. As James B. Walker, a tobacco tenant in Daviess County, Kentucky, noted: "The owners are oppressive to the tobacco tenant in a majority of cases. They aim to get it all. There is no doubt of this fact and this feeling among the tenants. They have too much rent to pay and no competition in the tobacco market." While both tenants and owners faced low prices, Walker observed a distinction: "When the price goes down, it is much harder on the tenant, as the crop is his sole reliance." Tenants and sharecroppers would be more likely to join the PPA, according to Walker, if "better terms were given so the tenant would not be so hard up he could afford to hold his tobacco." Instead, the situation, aggravated by PPA policies, had become unbearable for tenants. Walker summarized: "With the landlord on one side crushing us down and the trust on the other controlling the market, we have no show whatever."[38]

Felix Ewing was now in a highly exposed position. To erect a barrier between himself and his many critics, Ewing exploited a cultural battle whose origins rested, in many ways, within the economic realities of the Black Patch. Having established an organization that two-thirds of the region's farmers either had no confidence in or were financially unable to join, Ewing turned to even greater undemocratic methods to recruit members and to deflect criticism of his leadership. An easy target in this process was the nonpooler. W.S. Waller, a farmer in Todd County, Kentucky, noted that trust buyers were "offering $10.00 and $12.00 per hundred for tobacco outside of the Association," almost three times the price offered in 1904. These offers, according to Waller, were obviously an effort "to break up the Association."[39] Employing a tactic that struck at both trust agents and nonpoolers in one swoop, Ewing suggested in 1905 that a campaign of ostracism be undertaken against all who refused to join the co-op. When PPA members were confronted with a nonpooler or a PPA critic, "side track him," advised Ewing. "Do not know him when you see him." Merchants were not to tend to the business of such outcasts, and doctors were not to treat their illnesses. District chairmen kept detailed lists of all those within their districts who refused to sign cooperative contracts. The ostracism extended to all spheres of social relations. In church, a minister requested that one nonpooler lead in prayer. Afterward the minister was asked not to call on that particular parishioner again. "He is not one of us," the minister was told, "and we will not follow him anywhere, not even in prayer."[40]

For tenants and smallholders, the choice was obviously painful. They could choose either to join the co-op and further impoverish themselves while awaiting better prices or to remain outside the pool and financially benefit at their neighbor's expense. The central task of the PPA subsequently became one of creating a way to recruit these reluctant farmers. Thus a cultural war of ridicule and coercion came to characterize the Tobacco Wars.

The lines were sharply drawn between PPA members and those outside the fold. The label *hillbilly* was affixed to all nonpoolers. Urbanites widely used the word to dismiss rural Americans, as they used other terms such as *redneck* or *hoetoter*. When *hillbilly* was used by an association member, however, the term was one of dishonor among farmers.[41] To some such as PPA member Jewell Lyle, hillbillies were "back-sliding farmers" who, in resisting the cooperative movement, were "casting their lot with the degrading thieves and other miserable and misguided creatures of humanity." Another member claimed that a man who "would not become a pledged member was a traitor." He was a traitor "not only to his country but to the whole race of soil workers." The *Black Patch Tobacco Journal* revealed the opprobrium the term held when one writer remarked, "call me Benedict Arnold, call me Judas Iscariot, but don't call me hillbilly." [42] In the heat of combat within the cooperative movement, resolve and tempers were transparently heightening.

By far the most dramatic definition of a hillbilly was given by the president of the tobacco division of the American Society of Equity, E.L. Davenport: "Ashamed to look manliness in the eye, he skulks and avoids contact with honorable association men whom he has betrayed. Despised by man, forgotten by God, unwept by women, and unmourned by the living—he passes on, and, stumbling through life, finally falls into a dishonored and soon-forgotten grave. And it was written on his tombstone: 'He was a hillbilly.'" [43]

Hillbillies were not confined to one particular economic or social group. Everyone from large planters to tenants belonged to this collection of outcasts in the tobacco fields. Limited evidence about hillbillies in Montgomery County, Tennessee, offers some clues about these social pariahs. There, the PPA published a list of 105 hillbillies living within the county.

One of the few social measurements provided by the 1910 manuscript census concerns the housing situations of individuals. Of 3,854 farmers listed as heads of households in Montgomery County, 1,602 owned their residences, 1,030 owed mortgages, and 1,222 rented. Thus, 58.4 percent of the county's farmers were indebted for their homes or lived in homes owned by others. Although this does not necessarily mean that 58.4 percent of farmers were tenants and sharecroppers, it is certain that the indebtedness confronting these workers influenced their economic independence. The task of recruiting in a county divided so clearly by debt lay at the heart of the problems that culminated in the Black Patch War. Unfortunately, only 48 of the 105 hillbillies in Montgomery County can be identified in the manuscript census. Of the 48, 18 owned their homes, 7 owed mortgages, and 23 rented.[44] Hillbillies thus were not confined to the rural poor: over one-third of the known nonpoolers in the county owned their own homes and had attained some measure of financial independence. This is not to suggest, however, that these growers were necessarily self-sufficient, independent yeoman farmers. The farmers who owned their own houses were, in part, smallholders not yet trapped in administrative peonage. Those remaining, who either paid mortgages or rented, were no doubt familiar, in clear fashion, with the crop-lien system. An important dynamic that should be noted when evaluating these data is the relationship between landowners and renters. Landowners' decisions to join the PPA usually carried over to their tenants. Thus, some of the known nonpoolers were probably tenants on the farms of landowners who refused PPA recruiters.

Two factors might explain why more than half of the listed nonpoolers in Montgomery County could not be found in the manuscript census. First, a considerable number of these farmers may have left the county by 1910. Tenants or sharecroppers would have been most likely to leave the area. Second, the census taker may not have located some of the more obscure citizens of the county. Again, these would most likely have been tenants. Thus it is probable that the number of tenants, smallholders, and sharecroppers on the list of hillbillies in Montgomery County was larger than available figures indicate.

African-Americans constituted nearly 40 percent of the population of the county, and ten of the forty-eight hillbillies located in the manuscript census, or roughly 20 percent, were African-American. This remarkable statistic, even considering the Jim Crow age of the early twentieth-century South, fails to adequately depict the enormous risk that African-American farmers took in visibly demonstrating their refusal to join a movement sanctioned by local white elites. In the era of accepted white supremacy, black farmers who directly opposed a sizable number of desperate white farmers could expect even more scorn and abuse than their white counterparts received. Such were the stark racial and class realities of the southern countryside in the early 1900s.[45]

The limited evidence available, however, does not indicate

that anything approaching a class war developed in Montgomery County. This pattern reveals that whether farmers were rich or poor, white or black, the economic costs in a withholding campaign proved too much for many in the Black Patch region. With no strategy to alleviate the pivotal problem of agricultural debt, the PPA was generally unsuccessful in persuading many debt-ridden farmers to join the cooperative effort. New methods to accomplish this task, however, were forthcoming.

Despite its many internal problems, the PPA continued to pool tobacco from 1904 to 1907. According to PPA records, the amount of tobacco placed under the control of the PPA doubled during those years. The prices received nearly doubled as well (see table 6). It should be noted, however, that these prices were averages of income received over a considerable period of time. The 1904 crop, for example, brought a price barely above the cost of production, and the wait extended over eighteen months. Included in these figures were also many hidden charges: sundry expenses, fees, and interest charges on cash advances meant that the actual price farmers received for the crop was considerably less than that quoted by the PPA.

The fact that the PPA still enjoyed popularity among many tobacco growers can be seen in the third, and last, Guthrie meeting. Approximately twenty-five thousand people came to the annual gathering in September 1906, five times the number attending just two years earlier. This meeting was a festive occasion, where cooperators could gather and renew confidence in their organization. While Felix Ewing remained conveniently absent amidst all the criticism directed his way, a number of dignitaries and politicians, eager to capitalize on such a collection of the agrarian multitudes, again attended the meeting.[46]

The meeting in Guthrie seemed to signify that the PPA had become a permanent fixture in Black Patch culture. Yet the annual meetings would never again occur, and the organization never enjoyed the "success" it had experienced in its first three years. Not only did internal problems and the actions of the tobacco trust damage the movement, but a financial panic originating in New York City also weakened the PPA at a vulnerable point: in the financing of its poorer members.

Table 6. Yearly Business of the Planters' Protective Association, 1904-1907

Year	Pounds	Hogsheads	Average price (cents per pound)
1904	37,198,500	24,999	5.5
1905	51,957,000	34,638	7.5
1906	59,053,900	39,369	9.5
1907	75,000,000	50,000	10.5

SOURCE: The Tobacco Planters' Yearbook, 1908 (Guthrie, Ky., 1908).

In 1907 New York banks placed restrictions on the conversion of deposits into specie, or payments in hard currency. Runs on various banks in New York meant that withdrawals were quickly restricted, further heightening the sense of panic on Wall Street. U.S. Treasury secretary George Cortelyou deposited twenty-five million dollars into the reserve banks of New York in an attempt to calm the storm. Similar deposits by J.P. Morgan also helped to alleviate the panic, but the sudden contraction sent shock waves through the American economy.[47]

Previous currency crises had taught the nation's country bankers to demand currency as quickly as possible in times of perceived danger, before payments were suspended. This was indeed the inherent nature of a financial panic. Though the New York banks were not depleted of funds and could still extend loans, New York banking houses nevertheless erected strict rules that made converting demands of country banks into currency a difficult chore. People far removed from Wall Street struggled with the mystifying issues surrounding the panic, but one thing was clear. A local newspaper in the burley region announced: "Why is money 'tight' here? Because when New York takes snuff, the rest of the country is compelled to sneeze."[48] The 1907 panic hit at a particularly hard time. Agricultural regions demanded more currency from the larger banks during the harvest season of late autumn and early winter, and the effect of the panic on local banks was felt during the winter of 1907. Some banks in the Black Patch closed, and others that had aided the PPA had no longer made loans available to PPA members.[49]

Table 7. Fifteen Black Patch Banks and Their Suppliers

Local Bank	Louisville Bank	New York Bank
Bank of Allensville	Louisville National	Mechanics
Bank of Elkton	American National	Latham
Bank of Trenton	Bank of Commerce	Latham
City National, Mayfield	First National	Seaboard
Clarksville National	—	Hanover
Exchange Bank, Mayfield	American National	Chase
Farmers and Merchants Elkton	Bank of Commerce	National Park
First National, Clarksville	—	Importer's
First National, Fulton	Union National	Seaboard
First National, Mayfield	Citizen's National	Chase
Graves County Bank	Union National	Hanover
People's, Adairville	Citizen's National	Western
People's Bank, Springfield	—	Hanover
Robertson County National	—	—
Springfield National	—	Importer's

SOURCES: Clarksville *Leaf-Chronicle,* Oct. 17, 1904; *The Mercantile Agency Reference Book, 1885, 1900, 1901* (New York: R.G. Dun Mercantile Agency, 1885, 1900, 1901).

NOTE: Clarksville National, First National of Clarksville, People's Bank of Springfield, Robertson County National, and Springfield National were located in Tennessee. All others were in Kentucky.

A typical reaction to the panic was witnessed in Hopkins County, Kentucky, where banks limited cash withdrawals to ten dollars. As was the case throughout the Black Patch and most of Kentucky, banks in Hopkins County were supplied by major banks in Louisville, which in turn were supplied by banks in Chicago and New York. Fifteen local banks in the Black Patch that offered loans to the PPA were virtually all supplied by larger banks in Louisville and New York (see table 7). When the New York banks refused to make currency shipments to Louisville

during the 1907 panic, the country banks soon suffered. In Mayfield, Kentucky, the local PPA urged those who had money to
deposit all they could in the Exchange Bank of Mayfield, where
the money would be used to extend to warehousemen for PPA
advances to association members. In Paducah, bankers in the
winter of 1907 were not able to loan money to warehousemen for
PPA advances.[50] As the central Kentucky newspaperman had
duly noted, when New York bankers took economic "snuff," the
rest of the country was indeed convulsed.

Graves County PPA chairman J.W. Usher realized the severity
of the financial situation. In December 1907 Usher claimed:
"Everything is going our way except the panic, which has prevented our storage men from advancing 60 percent on tobacco
delivered to the prizers." The local banks, according to Usher,
were severely damaged by the panic: "The banks have been
drained of their cash and are not able to help us much." To relieve
the situation, Usher asked those who were able to deposit one
hundred dollars in local banks to help advance loans to association warehouses.[51]

Felix Ewing moved quickly to lessen the damage of the panic.
He negotiated a deal with American National Bank in Nashville
to provide funds for solvent banks to borrow and loan to the association. To worried and frightened farmers in the Black Patch,
Ewing gave advice on the panic, which did little to lessen their
fears. "Be frugal," Ewing admonished. "Abandon contemplated
expenditures of money . . . and make liberal deposits."[52]

The practical effect of the 1907 panic was to delay markedly the
delivery of tobacco to prizers. Many farmers were thus forced to
wait an additional three to four months before receiving advances. The 1907 panic strained the ability of the PPA to advance
loans to credit-starved farmers, which further weakened the
resolve of cooperators to resist prices offered by trust buyers
intent upon breaking the tobacco movement.[53] Once again, actions among the nation's financial elite in New York City had
agonizing effects on the ability of Kentucky and Tennessee farmers to escape their poverty.

The early years of cooperation in the Black Patch were thus a
time of distress for thousands of tobacco farmers. The prices the
PPA eventually received were not, in some minds, high enough

to justify the long waiting periods. Besides, those outside the PPA received prices were considerably higher than association prices, and "hillbillies" obtained their money immediately. The financial panic of 1907 damaged the local economy—further weakening the ability of the co-op to finance poorer members— while the hierarchy of the insurgent organization continued to alienate even its staunchest supporters by engaging in haughty and undemocratic behavior. In the face of these overwhelming obstacles to altering the living conditions under which farmers labored, the Tobacco Wars soon violently erupted. The politics of hope, which had earlier characterized the tobacco movement, had given way to the politics of frustration and, ultimately, of despair.

5

Night Riders

To hang John Brown was not difficult, but to keep his soul
from marching on proved another matter.
—Mason County Night Rider,
Lexington *Herald*, February 16, 1908

The Tobacco Wars are generally not remembered as a long and
ultimately fruitless effort to achieve effective large-scale marketing cooperatives by Kentucky and Tennessee farmers. The memory, rather, concerns night riding. Beginning in 1905 a new
element began to insinuate itself into the tobacco movement, one
that grew as the times became more desperate: bands of armed,
hooded men on horseback appeared, determined to enforce cooperation by coercion. They primarily targeted farmers who
failed to take part in the crop-withholding program and the
warehouses and agents of the tobacco trust. Though some modern observers might see this development as evidence of the
"militancy" or even the "class-consciousness" generated by the
tobacco movement, it is quite clear that vigilantism emerged out
of the failure of the PPA crusade for cooperation and verified the
limits of the internal democratic forms the farmers endeavored to
create.[1]

Night riding was born of despair. In the Black Patch, the
inability of the Planters' Protective Association to recruit all tobacco farmers and obtain better prices within a short period
fundamentally threatened the entire effort. The resulting sense
of frustration was channeled toward the American Tobacco Company and the noncooperating "hillbillies," both of whom were
seen as the enemies of the PPA. Their continued presence was
perceived as an obstacle to all prospects of the association's
achieving real success. Eventually frustration and anger erupted

in violence. Night riding thus became synonymous with the tobacco movement in Kentucky and Tennessee and raised the conflict to a new and tragic stage. The violent activities of the night
riders serve as a revealing window into the larger issues involved
in the Tobacco Wars.[2]

The culture of violence that fostered night riding did not
appear overnight. Southern life after Reconstruction was marked
by various bloody episodes. C. Vann Woodward described the
New South: "In the place of the code duello, the traditional
expression of violence in the Old South, gunplay, knifing, man-
slaughter, and murder were the bloody accompaniments of the
march of Progress." Violent aggression achieved new levels in
the South by the end of the nineteenth century. In 1890, while
Massachusetts had 16 homicides, Kentucky witnessed 92, and
Tennessee had 115. Indeed, one Kentucky newspaper editor
estimated that between 1879 and 1885 an average of 223 murders
per year occurred in the state.[3]

Violence in the South was not confined to any particular race
or class. Newspapers often reported killings among planters,
lawyers, doctors, and even preachers. The action of vigilantes, in
fact, was not abhorrent to some community leaders. In 1885 the
editor of the Breckinridge, Kentucky, *News* felt that mob violence
was an acceptable alternative to a perceived breakdown in the
jury system. "The law would be preferable to the mob if it could
be depended upon. But it cannot be—no dependence can be
placed in it. It reads well in the books, it sounds admirably in
judges' instructions, but there praise of it must end." According
to the editorial, the mob presented definite advantages: "From its
verdict there is no appeal. The murderer it condemns will find no
friend, no savior, in the court of appeals. It is impartial as the sun
that shines and the rain that falls. It simply does the work the law
should perform."[4]

Lynchings became common regional events in the 1880s as
southern "redeemers" claimed political power after Reconstruction.[5] These murders were usually community affairs, in which
men, women, and children gathered as participant observers.
Some examples from Kentucky reveal that lynch mobs acted for
various reasons and with varying methods. In January 1906 a
mob of over three hundred took Ernest Baker, a young African-

American, from the Trigg County jail and hanged him from the beam of the city scales. His alleged crime was an unsuccessful attempt to rape an eighteen-year-old white woman. In Russellville in 1908, four African-American youths were placed in the city jail, suspected of the high crime of appearing as "trouble makers." A mob subsequently took the four and hanged them. In 1909 another accused rapist named William Miller was hanged by an angry mob in front of a Hopkinsville church.[6]

In such a social climate in which vigilantism had become an acceptable way to adjudicate perceived injustices, night riding was not the bizarre departure from norms it otherwise might have appeared to be. The dynamics through which night riding emerged began with the campaign to ostracize "hillbillies" and was set in motion by the foremost leader of the Planters' Protective Association. Felix Ewing stressed that ostracism was vital to the task either of enlisting the aid of hillbillies or of driving them from the area. District chairmen were ordered to report all names of those refusing to sign PPA contracts. One result of this ostracism can be seen in the fate that befell one of Ewing's neighbors, J.W. Norman.

Norman had originally joined the PPA, hoping he could deliver his crop in a loose-leaf state and have it resold soon afterward. This urgency resulted from the fact that he had recently borrowed money for his farm and was pressed to meet his debts. When he discovered that the association insisted on prizing the tobacco, Norman knew that this development precluded his meeting his loan deadline. He thus decided to sell his crop outside the PPA. At a subsequent association meeting, Ewing denounced Norman as "not fit to live with honest people." Ewing asked that no one within the PPA speak to Norman or help him with farm duties such as threshing his wheat. Because of this decree, Norman was unable to find workers for his farm. He soon sold his holdings and moved from the area.[7]

Within months the cultural war took a new tone. The meeting that launched night riding took place in Robertson County, Tennessee, in October 1905, not long after Norman's departure from the region. In a schoolhouse in the Stainback district, thirty-two PPA members formed the Possum Hunters Committee. The committee announced its intentions to "proclaim to the world that any farmer or other persons who aid the trust in any way by selling to it their tobacco at a high price, is an accomplice to the trust." Morally, such a person was "as good as the trust." The committee resolved that groups of "not less than five nor more than 2,000 Association members" should visit each farmer who is not a co-op member and "offer him an opportunity to become a member." Should any resistance be encountered, "the committee may (without violence) proceed to counsel and instruct said farmer." Since farmers worked during the day, these committees on horseback usually operated at night—hence the name Possum Hunters. In Logan County, Kentucky, a riding committee of over five hundred of the county's leading farmers and church leaders visited noncooperators and local warehousemen, "encouraging" them to join the PPA.[8]

Members of these "visiting" committees, neither hooded nor overtly violent at the outset, soon began to disregard the plans made at the Stainback schoolhouse. Adamant nonpoolers were left warnings threatening them that they must join the association or else face the consequences. One of the first cases of night-rider violence occurred on December 9, 1905, in Trenton, Kentucky. Ten thousand dollars' worth of trust tobacco belonging to James and B.D. Chesnut and Joseph Russell was set on fire by night riders. The owners were independent buyers for the Italian Regie, which had refused to purchase pooled tobacco. The fire was carefully planned. That same morning, over three thousand pounds of non-PPA tobacco had been delivered to the warehouse for storage.[9]

The reaction by the Black Patch community to this attack was similar to reactions afforded many lynch mobs. "This is war," the Clarksville *Leaf-Chronicle* claimed, "and war means fight and fight means kill, and there is no such thing as conquering the hill-billy and Regie devils by taking them into your bosom and feeding them on milk and mush." A letter from Old Shanks, W.P. Anderson, described noncooperators as "poor, puny pieces of men, too cowardly to fight for liberty and too ignoble to be free men." Accordingly, any such citizen deserved to "suffer the consequences of his folly."[10]

While the Trenton warehouse fire was a spectacle, a more conventional form of coercion began in May 1906. As plant beds were being readied for transplanting, night riders began scraping the beds belonging to "hillbilly" farmers. At this especially vulnerable time for the young tobacco plants, a few swipes with a hoe or shovel could destroy a farmer's entire crop. Most of these attacks in 1906 occurred in Robertson and Montgomery counties in Tennessee and Logan and Christian counties in Kentucky (see Appendix). These were the same counties in which "visiting" committees had been formed just months earlier.

In late 1906 the violence spread as two more large raids occurred. On November 11 independent factories in Eddyville and Fredonia, Kentucky, were dynamited. On December 1 more than two hundred night riders rode into Princeton, Kentucky, and burned the stemmeries of Orr and Steger, which handled a great deal of non-PPA tobacco. An estimated 150,000 pounds of tobacco were destroyed.[11]

The fires in Princeton, however, backfired on the PPA. The fallen warehouses were owned by the Imperial and Gallaher tobacco companies, which held deposits of over one million dollars in Princeton banks. After the fire this money was withdrawn, greatly taxing the financial resources of the Princeton banking community. The money was removed during the winter months when banks were most stressed to meet currency demands. With no other resource, the banks were forced to call in some loans. Within one week of the fires, an estimated one hundred thousand dollars in loans to the tobacco growers had been called in by the local banks. In time, more loans were foreclosed, and new loans were not authorized, damaging the local economy and severely lessening the ability of the PPA to finance the crop in the Princeton area. Seeming to be an agent that cemented association solidarity, the night riders in fact destroyed components vital to the life of the tobacco movement.[12]

During the spring of 1907 numerous farmers witnessed attacks on their plant beds and tobacco barns. Night-riding attacks became more militant during the year and spread into many Black Patch counties. The most spectacular night-riding event occurred on December 7, 1907: a band of masked men, numbering from three hundred to five hundred, raided the city of Hopkinsville, Kentucky. The entire town was held at bay as a precisioned attack was made on an Italian Regie tobacco factory. Animosity toward the Regie had existed since 1905, when hopes for a Regie sale were dashed by Joseph Ferigo, head of the Italian syndicate. Having first promised to buy sixteen million pounds at nine and a half cents per pound, Ferigo decided to offer only eight cents, and the deal was refused by the PPA.[13] Attacking late at night, the masked riders converged on the city, claiming, according to one observer, that "the people of Hopkinsville have made their brags that the night riders would never come here, but we are here!" Houses were fired upon at random, and several people were beaten. One black Hopkinsville resident was killed, as well as a white switchman for the L&N Railroad who allegedly disobeyed orders from a night rider. The attack destroyed an estimated two hundred thousand dollars' worth of property.[14]

The American Tobacco Company moved to disclaim any responsibility for inciting the tobacco troubles in the Black Patch. "Where disorder has occurred the so-called tobacco trust is the smallest factor in the purchase of tobacco," said the official company statement. Future years brought to light the numerous agreements the American Tobacco Company had made that effectively limited competition at the producer level. What Black Patch farmers knew firsthand would be disclosed in 1909 with the release of a report on the tobacco industry by the commissioner of corporations. While carefully maintaining a public facade, the American Tobacco Company effectively controlled the purchasing of tobacco in Kentucky and Tennessee.[15]

The night riders, or the Silent Brigade, as they were sometimes called, essentially constituted a centralized and secret army. The man who turned the original "possum hunters" of the Stainback Resolutions into a regional force of vigilantes was a Caldwell County, Kentucky, physician, David Amoss. In his early fifties, Amoss, who had attended the Christian County Military Academy, wore a bushy mustache and possessed deep-set gray eyes that seemed to some "to smile as he talked," disguising the latent anger underneath.[16]

Amoss eventually acquired the reputation as the "Eugene Debs of the farmers' movement." In fact, Amoss revealed that he was interested in more than higher tobacco prices for farmers: "This industrial war has only begun," Amoss said.

A Hopkinsville warehouse burned by night riders. *Metropolitan Magazine.*

"It is a fight between the working classes and the plutocracy." To Amoss, the struggle was between "those who labor and those who exploit labor." It would be, he said, "a fight to the finish." Despite his passionate "concern" for the region's farmers and their economic troubles, Amoss also stated that farmers "were like dogs" and that the "only way to handle them was to drive them into the Association." Amoss later ran unsuccessfully for Congress on the Socialist ticket.[17]

Though he never grew tobacco himself, Amoss was a stalwart member of the PPA. Beginning in early 1906 he structured the vigilantes into "lodges" that were loosely patterned on Ewing's organizational structure of the PPA. Ten to twelve men in a district could constitute a lodge. A captain was appointed by Amoss to preside over three or four lodges. Amoss actually paid four dollars a day to those who would organize night-rider lodges in Calloway County and personally planned and led the December 1907 raid on Hopkinsville. He gave detailed instructions the night before the raid, instructing his men that when "they went after a man to go after him right, whip him and give him a good one, and if he got mad and died about it they couldn't help it." During the attack, Amoss was accidentally shot in the head by a stray bullet fired from the gun of a night rider. He lost a great deal of blood, but his condition was never considered life-threatening. The event testified to the danger of random shootings for which the riders were well known.[18]

Second in command of the Silent Brigade was Guy S. Dunning. A tobacco grower in Trigg County, Kentucky, Dunning was a prominent member of the PPA, serving as general inspector in 1908. Confessed night riders later testified that Amoss depended heavily on Dunning.[19]

The connection between the PPA and the night riders was naturally suspected from the outset. The New York *Times* stated as much: "In point of fact, the membership of the pool and the riders was almost identical." Countering such accusations, Felix Ewing said that the PPA was composed only "of the very 'flower of manhood' of both states." Ignoring his own rhetorical contributions to the situation, he added: "There is not a scintilla of evidence, circumstantial or otherwise, to the effect that our people have been guilty of anything lawless." It could not be denied, however, that intimidation by night riders added new members to the association. Official sanctioning of night riders' methods was provided by PPA president Charles Fort: "I believe that the Lord sent down these fellows to do work that was tending to make the principles of the Association more closely guarded by all." More directly, W.C. Warfield of the PPA asked: "What is the difference between the night riders and the trust agent? The night rider destroys the property of a few in order that the masses may be benefited, while the trust agent robs the masses to enrich a few. Which is the worse of the two?"[20]

Though cooperative leaders wished to portray night riding in its best light, the unmistakable fact emerged that as lawlessness increased, the legitimacy of the tobacco movement was questioned. As the *Kentucky Evening Gazette* remarked in 1908, "It is unfortunate for their cause as well as for the good name of Kentucky that the struggle over the tobacco question should lead to such results. Nothing else can do so much to discredit the movement."[21]

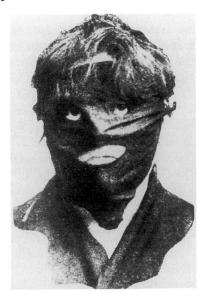

A masked night rider.
J. Winston Coleman
Kentuckiana Collection,
Transylvania University
Library.

A complex set of rituals was created for the night riders, primarily by Amoss. The initiation of new members materialized as a highly somber ceremony. An oath was administered while the new member kneeled before the lodge: "I, in the presence of Almighty God and these witnesses, do solemnly promise and swear to become a member of this order and swear that I will never reveal or cause to be revealed the secrets of this order." The penalty for breaking the oath, similar to that in other traditional secret societies around the world, was death.[22]

Night-rider rituals reportedly made use of Ku Klux Klan examples. Klan members often wore white hoods and robes, not only to disguise themselves but also to intimidate their victims psychologically. While the Klan image was a supernatural one, the night riders were relatively simply adorned. Regalia sometimes consisted of a black mask and a white scarf pinned at the right shoulder and falling to the waist. Amoss also used Klan oaths, grips, and passwords. Before setting out on a planned excursion, night riders sometimes held meetings, complete with many accoutrements of southern culture: in the words of a contemporary commentator, they would "break open a country church, sing songs, hold a prayer meeting, and drink corn whiskey and spit tobacco."[23] Once on horseback, the riders donned their regalia and went about their business in typical Klan-like fashion. Whether or not the customs of the night riders were directly related to Klan examples, the terror for the region's farmers was nonetheless similar.

Just three days after the Hopkinsville raid in December 1907, Kentucky inaugurated a new governor, Republican Augustus E. Willson. During his campaign, Willson was discovered to have once served as a corporate attorney for the American Tobacco Company. At a meeting of PPA growers, J. Morgan Chinn, clerk of the Kentucky Court of Appeals, remarked: "Everyone must know that the closest man to a great corporation is the hired attorney. . . . How can any man vote to place in the high office of Governor of Kentucky a man whom the records of your highest court show to have formed a covenant with the Tobacco Trust?"[24]

Since he had served as an attorney for the ATC, as well as a staunch defender of the gold standard, Willson seemed to have little chance of winning the election, considering the predominantly rural character of the state and the unmistakable air of hatred of the ATC that coincided with the election.[25] The fact that Willson nevertheless won the contest by more than fourteen thousand votes makes the 1907 gubernatorial election worth examining.

Willson's opponent, Democrat Samuel Hager, had been confident of victory since his nomination. Though he proposed no remedies, he spoke of the damaging effects of the tobacco trust on western Kentucky farmers. One issue that emerged during the campaign was Prohibition—a topic on which neither candidate wished to take a strong stand. Even though formidable temperance forces were alive in some rural sections, Kentucky was also the home of some of the nation's largest breweries and distilleries. Both candidates vowed to support a "county option" law that allowed counties to decide individually whether to go "wet" or "dry." In this way, both candidates effectively sidestepped the divisive issue.[26]

Throughout the campaign, Willson hammered away at the Democratic administration of Governor J.C.W. Beckham, charging graft and "machine" politics. Against repeated claims of

Augustus E. Willson, governor
of Kentucky, 1907-1911. Filson
Club, Louisville.

corruption, Hager only responded that "Willson should steal
away to Indiana or some other place where the climate is more
salubrious." Meanwhile, both Willson and Hager repeated
charges that the other was the tool of the elite. Like so many other
campaigns that would occur in the twentieth century, the 1907
Kentucky election boiled down to no single issue and not much
discernible difference in ideology. In fact, Willson answered the
charges made by Chinn that the candidate was an attorney for
the trust by saying that the Democrats had accepted a fifteen-
thousand-dollar campaign donation in 1903 from the American
Tobacco Company while Hager was party chairman. Against
such attacks, William Jennings Bryan came to western Kentucky
and attempted to emphasize Willson's connection to the trust.
"The Bible says a man cannot serve two masters," said Bryan,
"but maybe Willson is an extraordinary man and the Bible does
not apply to him." [27]

For farmers, the choice of candidates in the 1907 race was
scarcely appealing. The incumbent, Governor Beckham, had not
sought any redress against the tobacco trust, much to the disappointment of cooperators. He also had taken no stern measures

against night riders, much to the displeasure of urban voters. Hager, meanwhile, straddled every issue before him, including temperance and night riding. A last-minute charge by the Republicans that Hager had made a deal with whiskey manufacturers seems to have hurt his support with temperance forces.[28]

Willson won the election on his strength among urban voters. He carried Louisville by almost nine thousand votes and also held his own in rural Democratic strongholds. Contributing to Hager's defeat was the fact that twenty thousand fewer people voted in 1907 than in the 1903 gubernatorial election. Rural Kentuckians saw little in Hager to support, while urban voters found much to their liking in Willson. It was in such a manner that a "trust attorney" won the Kentucky governor's office in 1907.[29]

Throughout the campaign, Willson had been careful not to speak disparagingly about the tobacco cooperatives. Since thousands of farmers composed the cooperatives and various businessmen and bankers supported them, it would have been politically foolish for Willson to denounce the insurgents openly. Yet Willson's reaction to the 1907 panic offered an insight into his views about the cooperating farmers. In response to bank failures and tight money, Willson made the unusual move of writing to U.S. Treasury secretary George Cortelyou to request that the Treasury deposit five million dollars in Kentucky banks.[30] The funds could help alleviate the money stringency in the state. "The people," Willson added, "would realize the great help that had been extended to them, treating the West and South just like New York." Willson also asked that the letter be kept secret by the Treasury Department.[31]

The request for funds was denied, and Kentucky voters never knew of Willson's letter. Had the request been granted, no doubt, Willson's correspondence would quickly have become public knowledge. One historian nonetheless views the letter as evidence that Willson "actually sympathized with farmers." Willson's request, however, promised little for cooperating farmers. A one-time governmental deposit would have done little to relieve the enormous financial burden of agricultural debt. Instead, the deposits would have been of greater use to country bankers struggling to meet deposits in a time of financial panic. Considering how these country banks were tied to banks in Louisville, a governmental deposit would certainly have helped stimulate certain cash-flow problems facing large Kentucky bankers. In his letter, Willson further revealed a condescension toward the farmer's role in the "farm problem": "The average grower does not fully understand why he must answer to the ordinary laws of supply and demand and competition. . . . if the present emergency can be bridged over, [he] will be likely in the future to be a little more careful about committing himself as deeply as he has this year."[32]

After his election, Willson, apparently hoping that face-to-face negotiations between the farmers and the American Tobacco Company would produce results, invited James B. Duke, Felix Ewing, and other prominent players in the Tobacco Wars to attend a December 1907 meeting in Frankfort. Duke declined to participate but agreed to send an emissary. Ewing also declined to attend. He felt reluctant to discuss details with other cooperative associations, who, in Ewing's opinion, "are more or less competitive, though sympathetic." Not surprisingly, Willson's summit proved fruitless.[33]

Throughout Willson's administration, many farmers continued to regard him as a tool of the American Tobacco Company.[34] The governor obliged his critics with plenty of ammunition. Willson pardoned growers who had broken cooperative contracts and sold their tobacco to the trust, even in the face of a legislative act prohibiting such sales. The bill had been passed over Willson's veto. When members of the Kentucky legislature wanted Willson to launch an investigation of the American Tobacco Company in order to prove that it was violating the Sherman Antitrust Act, Willson refused. In his State of the Commonwealth message given in January 1908, Willson did little to betray his image as a trust attorney. The governor felt that those who had joined the association had "voluntarily parted with their liberty, right or power to sell as they choose." Willson was also determined to stop lawlessness, and he summoned the Kentucky State Guards to protect Hopkinsville from further attacks by night riders. The *Black Patch Tobacco Journal* summarized: Willson's "every word and action showed that he is not a friend of those who have labored hard to get a living price for their tobacco."[35] In fact, Willson dispatched troops in various areas of

Kentucky in an attempt to curb night riding. Tennessee governor Malcolm Patterson decided against using the state militia and instead offered cash rewards to stop night riding. None were ever claimed.[36] Willson's decision, however, was met with great approval by many. In a letter to the governor, U.S. marshall G.W. Long wished to ease Willson's mind over his extended use of gubernatorial powers: "Nobody contended that Mr. Roosevelt's settlement of the Anthracite Coal Strike was strictly within the limits of his official power; but it worked well and was applauded by the world."[37]

Commanding the troops Willson sent to stop night riding was Major G.N. Albrecht. In the beginning, Albrecht had great confidence, as displayed in a letter to Willson after rumors of a night-rider attack were lifted: "The chief danger of a clash has gone—somewhat to my regret," remarked Albrecht. "I should have dearly loved to have turned loose a few of 'Willson's blue-coated hirelings.'" Albrecht's strategy was "to outwit them and be ahead of them, or to run across them on the road."[38]

Despite Major Albrecht's heady confidence, night riders quickly illustrated the ineffectiveness of state troops in quelling guerrilla warfare. Just days after he planned on running "across them on the road," Albrecht wrote to Willson: "I have the dishonor to have to report that the night riders burned a dwelling within a quarter mile of the western city limits last night." Albrecht added, "I am deeply chagrined at our failure to give chase. . . . If you choose to give me hell for not having horses ready, do so, and I will take my medicine." Recognizing the futility of the troops' presence, Lieutenant Governor William Cox, upon Willson's departure from the state on a trip in June 1908, recalled over one-third of the troops from the tobacco districts.[39]

The statewide frustration found expression in a leading Black Patch newspaper. "Is it not time that something were done to stamp out the 'night rider' evil in Kentucky? When a band of lawless marauders can go through a State, reputed to be a civilized community, and destroy property at will—there must be something radically wrong with the Government of the State." Since Willson was apparently powerless, the *Leaf-Chronicle* said, "Let the Federal Government be asked for aid in putting an end to this modern, 'reign of terror.'"[40]

The *Leaf-Chronicle* did not know that at this time Willson himself was thinking along the same lines. In February 1908 Willson wrote to the U.S. attorney general, testing the possibility of using federal troops. Willson received a reply from President Theodore Roosevelt, who wrote, "Free government can not exist when there is defiance of the law and mob rule." If the lawlessness continued, the president promised, he was prepared to support Willson with the necessary troops.[41]

Federal troops were not dispatched, nor did Willson ever declare martial law. Such actions would probably only have intensified night-rider activity and heightened resentment among the farmers. During the time that night riding generated considerable publicity, attempts were made to portray the reports of violence as exaggerated. Representative A.O. Stanley was the most outspoken adherent of this view. In Washington, Stanley spoke of the "grossly perverted and exaggerated accounts of depredations" that were being spread about the Black Patch. In Ballard County, Kentucky, PPA members accused the tobacco trust of maliciously distributing false reports of night riding. These were, however, futile efforts to cloud the true picture of vigilantism that peaked in 1908.[42]

Interesting and revealing racial dynamics intruded into the issue of night riding in the Black Patch. It is necessary to ask to what extent night riding expressed the collective frustrated aspirations of ordinary farmers and to what extent it merely expressed white supremacy. The complex answer must be traced through several stages of the Tobacco Wars.

During the final Guthrie meeting in 1906, a group of black farmers participated in the great parade, holding a large banner that read: DOWN WITH THE TRUST OR WE NIGGERS BUST! The Planters' Protective Association, in fact, was visibly proud that African-American farmers were, in large part, "loyal" to the association and even held their own local "colored" meetings.

African-American participation in the PPA cannot, however, be viewed in a vaccum but must be considered within its contemporary context. African-Americans in Kentucky and Tennessee, as in the entire South in the early 1900s, lived under excruciating social and political conditions. Successful disfranchisement efforts by white legislators, for example, had reduced black turnout at the polls in Tennessee to virtually nothing after 1896. In an era in which lynchings of African-Americans had become common southern events, black citizens had, as historian Pete Daniel has noted, "little recourse; resistance was suicidal." To resist joining the association, especially since many blacks were tenants and sharecroppers and knew the consequences of rebuking their landlords (those who were PPA members), often meant loss of land and possible violence.[43]

African-American farmers, of course, certainly had fully adequate cause to join the association. Their economic situation was worse than that of white farmers. Black farmers received even lower prices for their tobacco than their white counterparts. Henry Dinwiddie, a black grower in Montgomery County, Tennessee, discovered this when he was once offered $4.75 per one hundred pounds for his crop by a trust buyer. Dinwiddie refused the offer and instead had his white neighbor sell the same crop to the same buyer for $6.75 per hundred.[44]

Even more striking evidence of wanton discrimination—by PPA members as well as by trust agents—exists. Membership in the association, at least for some African-Americans, did not guarantee protection from night riders. In the early stage of the cooperative effort in the Black Patch, refusal to join the PPA often sparked night-rider attacks on African-American farmers. Yet as the conflict ensued, some attacks by vigilantes were not meant to coerce reluctant "hillbillies" into joining the association. Instead, these attacks suddenly evolved into whitecapping episodes, in which blacks were forced from their land in order to enhance white labor opportunities. On March 8, 1908 scores of night riders stormed an African-American community in Birmingham, in Marshall County, Kentucky. The raiders randomly fired into the windows and doors of homes and shops. Six black farmers were wounded, one fatally. The expressed mission of the riders was to force the black farmers from the area completely. On March 23, over two dozen night riders stormed Golden Pond in Trigg County and killed Tom Weaver, an African-American tobacco worker. In May 1908, J.L. Tobin of Braxton received a letter from night riders warning him to fire his black tenants and hire white farm laborers. In Hopkins County, in a display that revealed how some vigilantism had little to do with tobacco, night riders forced black coal miners to leave the region.[45]

One of the more brutal night riding episodes occurred in Golden Pond on October 3, 1908. About fifty riders appeared at the home of David Walker, a farmer described by local whites as a "surly negro." While Walker and his family slept, riders poured coal oil on his house and set it on fire. When Walker came running out of the house, the riders released a volley of gunfire, killing Walker instantly. Mrs. Walker soon appeared, pleading for the life of her infant child. While she clutched the baby in her arms, bullets ripped throught the tiny body, killing the infant and mother. Walker's remaining four children were either shot or burned to death.[46]

These threats and raids were part of wholesale efforts to rid the area of black farmers and, with the resultant shortage of labor, to increase the wages of white farm workers. Whitecapping also extended to other areas of labor. In Franklin County a road constructor was warned by a letter from night riders against "employing negro labor." Simple racial hatred was, no doubt, a factor in these attacks. Sporadic outbreaks against blacks prompted the *Leaf-Chronicle* to note: "There is much uneasiness among farmers in some localities in the dark tobacco district over the antagonism to the employment of negro labor. . . . now come warnings, usually signed 'Night Riders,' and they are being sent to Association and Independent growers." According to some observers, the newspaper reported, the tobacco night riders were at fault, particularly "that class of the band that would expect to succeed the negro laborer on the farms at greatly advanced wages."[47]

Whitecapping became a significant enough issue that the internal organ of the PPA, the *Black Patch Tobacco Journal*, noted that "recent acts of lawlessness have brought back old memories and suggested the idea of giving the negro swift passport." The central cause of such racial tension, according to the paper, "was that the negro was thought to be given the employment the white man should have." The editors of the insurgent paper carefully added, "There is work on the farm for all." Acknowledging that tension existed between poor whites and blacks, the newspaper assured whites that they had nothing to fear from black farm laborers. Socially, the *Journal* reasoned, post-Reconstruction history had taught blacks the essential lesson of white supremacy: "The negro came to realize his proper sphere, and as the Civil War went further and further into the past he recognized every white man as his superior."[48]

There can be no doubt that a number of African-American farmers were reluctant to join the PPA and were subsequently visited by night riders for that reason. In the racial climate of the day, refusal by African-Americans to join the cooperative would have meant violent retribution: white cooperators would not have looked favorably upon black "hillbillies" who received good prices in a time of severe financial deprivation. Evidence of night-rider activity suggests, however, that violence inflicted on blacks did not merely punish noncooperators. In May 1907, for example, the crops of three black sharecroppers on the farm of A.M. Henry of Newstead, in Christian Co., Kentucky, were destroyed by night riders. All of the black croppers, however, were members of the PPA.[49]

Wholesale attacks on black communities were not conducted to defend white women from assaults by black men, a common explanation used throughout this period to defend lynchings. Neither were these attacks a defense of the tobacco cooperatives against traitorous "hillbillies." Instead, attacks by night riders against African-American farmers primarily evolved into an expressed desire to protect or improve opportunities for white laborers. As such, whitecapping became yet another ingredient in the saga of vigilantism in the Black Patch.

As night riding reached its height in 1908, virtually anyone could be attacked. Of course, not all "hillbillies" were victims of night riding. Besides whitecapping instances, did any pattern of attacks emerge that could explain why a particular farmer was chosen as a target? Did some form of class warfare evolve?

In Montgomery County, Tennessee, one of the core counties of the tobacco movement, fifteen victims of night riding are identified in the 1910 manuscript census. Of these fifteen, ten rented their homes, and seven were listed as employing laborers. Thus, evidence in this county reveals no clear-cut economic status of victims of night riders.[50]

In Todd and Trigg counties in Kentucky, detailed tax records

Table 8. Property Listed for Taxation by Victims of Night
Riders, Todd and Trigg Counties, 1906-1907

Name	Total acreage	Total valuation of land	Value of agricultural implements	Tobacco acreage	Tobacco poundage raised
J.W. Barefield	—	—	—	—	—
Nathan Hester	80	$440	$10	6	5,000
S.M. Holland	500	3,500	50	28	20,000
H.C. Merritt	236	4,740	—	—	—
Ben Miller	160	2,000	30	10	8,000
M.B. Penick	239	4,700	50	20	9,000
C.C. Shemwell	250	1,000	60	15	12,000
J.W. Welbourne	137	375	—	1	—
Otis Wilson	274	4,050	—	25	20,000

SOURCES: "Todd County, Kentucky, Tax List, 1906," and "Trigg County,
Kentucky, Tax List, 1907," microfilm, Special Collections, M.I. King
Library, University of Kentucky.

shed light on some other victims of night riding. Nine victims
within these two counties can be found in the tax rolls (see table
8). Except for J.W. Barefield, whose taxable property was either
not reported or nonexistent, the majority of victims in these
counties were men of some means. The nine victims raised
varying amounts of tobacco. J.W. Welbourne had a modest one-
acre plot, and S.M. Holland cultivated twenty-eight acres, so this
list is not composed only of wealthy planters or of penniless
sharecroppers.

The three counties in the heart of the Black Patch thus reveal
no strong pattern. The evidence merely serves to reiterate that
virtually anyone who sold outside the association was a potential
victim. Sometimes even powerful association men were attacked. Guy S. Dunning of Trigg County, Dr. Amoss's protégé in
the Silent Brigade, for example, once had his grain destroyed
by night riders, simply because he patronized a mill owned by
a non-PPA man. The incident also demonstrated that anyone
could become a night rider simply by acquiring a horse and a
mask. He did not necessarily have to join the local lodge formally.
Night riders did not come from any certain economic class, and

neither did their victims. Everyone from a black tenant to a respected white businessman might find himself a night-rider target.[51]

By 1907 some ardent nonpoolers were so threatened by night riding that they formed their own armed protective society. The Law and Order League claimed many law enforcement officials as members. C.H. Branch of the Hopkinsville league quickly recruited twenty-five members within the city. The members of the league made it clear that they did not oppose cooperation. Proclaiming independence from any force, the Law and Order League simply objected to rampant lawlessness. The league, however, like state troops, enjoyed no success in containing vigilantism by force.[52]

In time, some night riders were apprehended and tried. Considering the threat that the Silent Brigade posed, as well as the latent support the tobacco movement commanded from the local community, it is not surprising that few juries were willing to convict accused night riders. Walter Krone, a county attorney in Lyon County, Kentucky, revealed one reason for this: "For the last three courts, running over a period of one year, our grand juries have been dotted with Night Riders to an extent which has precluded the possibility of an indictment." Krone's efforts to indict night riders were not met with community approval. His once thriving law practice in western Kentucky was soon reduced to only four cases in one year, and he lost all four cases because the juries were allegedly packed with night riders. Krone soon needed armed guards to protect his home.[53]

The Socialist newspaper *Appeal to Reason* revealed the unspoken assumptions that many in the area had about the vigilantes. The *Appeal* asked: "If Trust agents were taken in the dead of night and given 40 lashes on their bare backs for opposing the movement for higher prices and better conditions, will any white-livered apologist of capitalism endeavor successfully to prosecute the organized farmers? Not in Kentucky!"[54]

The first successful court case against night riders was a civil suit filed in 1908 by Robert and Mary Hollowell. The Hollowells had been victims of an attack in which their crops were destroyed and both had suffered beatings. They subsequently sued thirty citizens in Caldwell and Lyon counties. The suit was tried in

Paducah, and the plaintiff's case was appreciably strengthened
by the testimony of a confessed night rider, Sanford Hall. Against
Hall's damaging testimony, each defendant had a detailed alibi,
fortified by witnesses testifying to the accuracy of the statements.
The suit was filed ten months after the attack, and the presiding
judge sarcastically mentioned that the accused possessed remarkable memories. In a shocking turn of events, the jury
awarded the Hollowells thirty-five thousand dollars, which was
later compromised to fifteen thousand.[55]

A rather uncommon suit was filed in 1908 by three African-
American men who had been forced to leave Kentucky after the
Birmingham raids. The three identified more than thirty of their
assailants by name. Again, the case was heard in Paducah, and it
soon yielded yet another surprising development: some white
witnesses testified on behalf of the black plaintiffs. The jury
decided against the thirty defendants, awarding the three black
plaintiffs twenty-five thousand dollars each.[56]

Eventually, as the PPA itself declined, other suits were
brought against alleged night riders. In 1911 Dr. David Amoss
himself, along with other leaders of the night riders, was brought
to trial on criminal charges in Hopkinsville. Here, confessed
riders testified in great detail about Amoss's role in organizing
the Hopkinsville raid and other night-riding activities. Even in
the face of such evidence, Amoss was acquitted of all criminal
charges. This outcome testified to the lingering public sympathy
and fear many Black Patch citizens still held for Dr. Amoss and
his defunct vigilante army.[57]

In all its intensity, night riding became a central influence on
the states of Kentucky and Tennessee, especially from 1906 to
1909. In many ways, the activities of night riders contributed to
the strength of the tobacco movement by swelling PPA membership rolls with intimidated farmers. When viewed against the
backdrop of the numerous organizing problems the PPA was
experiencing, it is clear that night riding was a violent attempt to
achieve what democratic organizing could not.

The ability of night riders to supplement the tasks of the
cooperatives diminished in 1909, and their activity declined drastically. The quick demise of night riding, however, did not occur
because of armed troops, unsympathetic juries, or even public

indignation. The end corresponded with the death of the PPA itself. Night riding therefore was nothing more than a secondary ingredient to the failing aspirations of the PPA. The withering organization sapped the energy fueling night riding. Without the tobacco cooperative and the withholding campaign, the night riders had no reason for being.

6

Organizing the Bluegrass

Historians traditionally refer to the struggles of the tobacco farmers of Kentucky and Tennessee as the Black Patch War. While extensive organizing activity and an extended series of night-riding episodes did occur in the Black Patch, the tobacco revolt was not limited to the dark tobacco country. Burley farmers in central Kentucky simultaneously organized themselves to pool and hold their crops in an effort to raise tobacco prices. The central region had its own fair share of night riding and witnessed many of the same dilemmas as did the western region. While Black Patch organizers struggled in their recruiting effort, the burley cooperative ultimately obtained the backing of approximately three-fourths of all burley growers in central Kentucky. In 1908 this solidarity was reflected in one of the most extraordinary insurgent episodes in American history. Few historians have considered the events in central Kentucky as anything more than a postscript to the Planters' Protective Association and the dominating presence of night riders. But to pass over the activities of the movement in the burley region conceals a vital and instructive component of the farmer revolt in Kentucky.[1]

The central organization of the burley growers, the Burley Tobacco Society (BTS), was officially created in 1906. Its rise and development constitutes an essential story within the overall saga of the Tobacco Wars. Like the Planters' Protective Association, the BTS emerged as a result of many years of organizing effort. The initial drive for a viable organization in the burley region began well before the consolidation of the Burley Tobacco Society.

As early as May 1898, tobacco farmers in Carroll County, Kentucky, met to discuss ways of organizing themselves against efforts being undertaken to establish, in their estimation, a

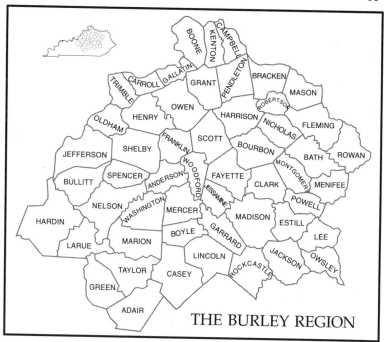

THE BURLEY REGION

"tobacco manufacturing trust." The growers deplored the efforts of "a number of the leading manufacturers of Tobacco to organize a corporation to be known as the Continental Tobacco Company." As the farmers interpreted events, "the plan and aim" of the American Tobacco Company was "to absorb and include all Tobacco manufacturers," such as the Continental, "and thereby form a gigantic monopoly which will have power to fix the prices to producers." Carroll County growers resolved only to call for state and federal legislators to enact more stringent antitrust laws against industrial combinations.[2]

Growers in Bath and Owen counties also brooded over ways to confront the growth of the tobacco trust. They, like tobacco farmers throughout the region in the late 1890s, were placed in an ironic position: though the demand for their product was increasing with the exploding market for cigarettes, the price for their leaf continued to fall. In 1890, 2.5 billion cigarettes were manufactured in the United States, and the number doubled in just ten years. Tobacco production and prices in Kentucky seemed to contradict the economic laws of supply and demand. The 1882 Kentucky tobacco crop of 198 million pounds had been valued at fifteen million dollars, but the 1896 crop of 143 million pounds was worth only six million. Nationally, the price for all tobacco fell from 8.5 cents per pound in 1882 to 5.5 cents per pound in 1896. Burley growers in central Kentucky reasoned that the steadily decreasing tobacco prices were caused by the lack of competition for the purchase of their products.[3]

In July 1898 burley growers from seven Kentucky counties met and agreed that the emerging monopoly threatened to "destroy competition in buying the raw material." The growers sent a petition to Congress and one to the Kentucky legislature, seeking an investigation of the tobacco industry in order to prevent "establishing a degree of servitude far more galling and degrading than African slavery or Russian serfdom." The chairman of this July meeting was a physician, S.E. Hampton of Carroll County.[4]

Like farmers in the Black Patch, burley growers tried both political and economic avenues to relieve the agonizing financial impact the trust had on their daily lives. After attempting to gain political answers through petitions to elected officials, Dr. Hampton began organizing farmers in the burley region to join a crop-withholding company. In a circular sent to farmers in October 1898, Hampton stated the fact as simply as he could: "Tobacco growers do not receive a fair price for their crops." His plan, however, revealed how little he knew about the dynamics of cooperation. "Why not send three of your number to attend the daily sales," Hampton asked, "and whenever the average price is below the cost of production authorize them to stop the sales by refusing to put up your Tobacco until the demand will justify an advance in price?" But Hampton did at least take a step that put the organizing process in motion. He asked farmers: "Will you assemble yourselves on the Third Monday in November next at your county seats and appoint delegates to a State convention to select men to attend to this business for you?"[5]

The call for the November meeting became more complex when a Shelby County organizer, W.L. Brown, revealed a plan to establish a joint-stock company that would erect an independent tobacco manufactory. Each share was priced at ten dollars, and Brown was confident that tenants would buy at least one share each. Brown had approached many growers in Shelby County about his plans and found "an eager willingness to go into it, saying that even if they should get no dividends on their stock they would get a difference in the price of their Tobacco that would justify the investment." Brown added that, if the venture was successful, "we could raise $1 million in a short time, and then you would find $3 to $5 million of capital would be ready to step in behind us." Brown summarized: "All the union and labor classes would use our brands." Such rosy results, flowing so easily from such fanciful plans, were contingent upon raising significant sums among tenant farmers and sharecroppers. As the Grangers had discovered in the 1870s and 1880s, such cash-based cooperative plans could not recruit farmers who had little or no hard currency.[6]

In December 1898 a preliminary meeting to unite twenty-four counties into a cohesive union was held in Lexington.[7] Over eighty delegates at the meeting selected a title for the new organization, the Kentucky League of Tobacco Growers. A committee was established to organize farmers in the counties represented, and W.B. Hawkins, a staunch Democrat and president of the William Jennings Bryan Club in Lexington, was selected to head the committee. Delegates to the Lexington meeting also heard of a shocking new development. Tobias Gibson, a Woodford County farmer, told the assembly of a recent conversation he had with another farmer on an organizing trip in his native county. The grower told Gibson that the key to cooperation was curtailing tobacco output. If the supply of tobacco was lowered, the price for the leaf would rise. Reducing acreage would not only require organization, according to the anonymous farmer, but strict compliance as well. Acreage reduction could be enforced "in the manner the turnpikes were controlled. That is, if a grower insisted upon planting more tobacco than the number of acres agreed upon for each grower by a convention, that the tobacco beds could be destroyed in the same manner that the toll-gates of Kentucky were destroyed, and the output be thus reduced and prices kept up." Gibson's comments stunned the growers, who afterward publicly rejected the enforcing plan and also disclaimed any responsibility for incidents of scraping tobacco beds that had occurred in the spring of 1898.[8]

The turnpike episode to which Gibson referred was fresh in

Tobacco on its way to market, Lexington, early 1900s. J. Winston
Coleman Kentuckiana Collection, Transylvania University Library.

the minds of Kentuckians. The methods used by the tollgate
riders in the late 1890s, in fact, were very similar to those later
employed by the tobacco night riders. The operation of private
toll roads was similar not only to the monopolistic workings of
the tobacco industry but also to the construction and mainte-
nance of southern railroads. Counties subscribed stock to private
turnpike companies in order to construct roads, with the understanding that after completion, all future tolls went directly to the
turnpike companies. County taxpayers thus provided the money
to build the roads and then paid expensive tolls to private concerns in order to use those roads.

In the 1890s the demand for free turnpikes became a statewide
issue in Kentucky. A free turnpike bill was passed by the legislature and signed into law in 1896. It contained provisions permit-
ting every county to condemn and purchase the turnpikes for
public use. For reasons that reeked of collusion between turnpike
companies and politicians, various county leaders simply ignored the new law. County judges and mayors adopted the
public posture that they had no right to raise taxes in order to pay

for the turnpikes, concluding that the roads were better left in the hands of private companies. In the face of such an impasse, Kentucky witnessed in late 1896 the emergence of armed, masked men converging upon and destroying tollgates. In forty-four counties throughout the Bluegrass, more than three hundred tollgates were burned or dynamited within a three-month period. The public uprising was vividly successful. Turnpike companies quickly sold their holdings to county governments. Before the year was out, virtually all turnpikes were made free.[9]

To those at the meeting of the Growers' League in Lexington, many of whom were landowners, Gibson's plan was revealing, since it described what was already in the minds of some tobacco growers in 1898. To insure conformity with a plan to reduce acreage, violence might be used. The culture in which vigilantism could flourish in the early 1900s was alive and well in the 1890s, and such action was already being urged by some tobacco growers in public meetings. This mode of public assertion in the South had become sanctioned practice following Reconstruction.

The Growers' League initiated a two-pronged attack. First, legal action was taken to try to dissolve the tobacco trust and reinstitute competition. Then, the league began recruiting, by designating Claude Thomas of Bourbon County as state lecturer. He was assigned to visit every tobacco county and to organize local leagues. The league was essentially a holding company, comprising farmers who pooled their tobacco and commissioned agents of the league who withheld the crop until an adequate price was forthcoming. The cooperating farmers also hoped to use the proceeds from their effort to build independent warehouses as a step toward autonomy from commercial interests.[10]

Unfortunately for popular morale, the scheme of building independent warehouses failed almost immediately. The simple but sobering fact was that the directors of the league had greatly overestimated the ability of tenants, sharecroppers, and penniless smallholders to buy into a joint-stock company. The league's inability to raise even a modicum of capital was brought home with a certain starkness when the officers of the league had to pay the rent for the headquarters out of their own pockets. Yet long-term gains emerged from the abrupt failure of the 1890s. While the Growers' League proved a quick disappointment, it introduced W.B. Hawkins and future cooperative leaders Clarence Lebus and J. Campbell Cantrill to the tobacco movement and provided crucial lessons on the organizing aspects of the cooperative approach.[11]

Meanwhile, the plight of Kentucky farmers worsened with each growing season. In 1902 burley farmers tried again to organize themselves. In January, they met in Carroll County at the call of James M. Gaunt and formed a company to be known as the Farmers' and Tobacco Growers' Association. Gaunt was named president and chief organizer. By March, farmers from eight counties had joined the new association. Gaunt envisioned a holding company that advanced money to growers upon delivery and would house the crop until a satisfactory price was offered. To finance the crop-withholding plan, Gaunt hoped to raise one million dollars by selling shares of ten dollars each. In March, farmers from thirty-four counties who supported the idea met in Carrollton to write the bylaws of the new association. Contracts between growers and the association were signed: farmers pledged their 1902 crop in exchange for higher prices promised by the association. It was made clear to all that unless forty thousand growers signed the contracts, the association would release all farmers from their contracts and the pool would be cancelled.[12]

In November 1902 the new cooperative group met in Lexington to hear one burley cooperator proclaim: "If the growers knew the power that is in their hands, in place of borrowing money to put in their crop, they would have money to lend."[13] A headquarters for the association was established in Lexington in January 1903, and W.B. Hawkins was made president. While the drive to secure the forty thousand signatures was preeminent in the minds of the members and organizers, Hawkins and an associate, W.B. McChord, attempted another strategy of raising tobacco prices in the burley area.

In September 1903 McChord visited New York to see the president of the American Tobacco Company himself, James B. Duke. McChord offered to sell the pooled crop of 1903 at eight and a half cents per pound to the trust. Profoundly unimpressed, Duke refused the offer and replied, according to McChord, that the association "could not deliver the goods." After a similar visit by Hawkins, Duke replied in writing, blandly offering the thought that "we do not lack any desire to co-operate with the tobacco farmers." Duke explained, somewhat unhelpfully, "the tobacco we have bought, whether at the barn or at the warehouse, has been bought after its price has been agreed upon between the seller and the buyer." While expressing nominal agreement that farmers had a right to organize themselves for self-help, Duke nonetheless refused to purchase any tobacco from the association at an agreed price.[14] With this avenue closed, Hawkins returned from New York and adopted the public stance of quiet confidence. He announced that the association had collected over twenty-five thousand signatures. The figure was encouraging, though still well below the stated goal of forty thousand.

The cooperative vision of independent warehouses soon failed, not because of a weak constituency but because of the inability to obtain adequate financing. To build the warehouses, to maintain personnel and adequate equipment, and, most important, to advance money to farmers while their tobacco was stored all required financial resources beyond the means of organized smallholders and tenants. When the association was unable to raise the needed money, the organizing drive was cancelled. The association officially ended in February 1904. The primary cause of the death of the cooperative drive, as Hawkins assessed matters, was its failure to induce "our city cousins to come to our assistance with money to help ourselves."[15]

Shortly after this venture, Hawkins led yet another pooling attempt, this time for the 1904 burley crop. In June 1904 he launched the Burley Tobacco Growers Company. Projected capitalization was established at five hundred thousand dollars. Hawkins wished to see fifty thousand shares of the company sold in ten-dollar allotments, so that every burley grower in Kentucky could be a stockholder in the new effort. Contracts called for growers to deliver all of their tobacco crop for the next five years to the company, which would hold the crop until at least eight cents per pound was offered.[16]

In his new effort, Hawkins looked other places besides the tobacco fields for financial backing. He sought the support of bankers in New York, Boston, and Philadelphia. All proved unavailing. By October 1904 the inability to secure financing again doomed the cooperative effort. Hawkins's frustration was vented publicly when he blamed the latest cooperative demise on the "apathy" of the farmer: "We advertised for speakings and were met by small audiences," said Hawkins. "I will never again ask any man to sign the contract." This explanation skirted the realities of power functioning in the tobacco industry. The reason farmers had become reluctant to sign pooling contracts in 1904 was grounded in the experience of 1902 and the trust's punitive response in 1903. Those farmers who had signed 1902 contracts only to see the cooperative fail found they were blacklisted by trust buyers when their crop came to market in 1903. No one made bids on their leaf.[17] Thus, behind the apparent "apathy" of growers was a very real threat to their survival. Organizing against Duke and the trust proved no simple matter.

Despite his disclaimer of "never again," Hawkins reasserted his cooperative ambitions in the spring of 1905, when he pushed still another joint-stock company. The new one was a bit more moderate. The capital goal was set at $250,000. Hawkins proposed that the new company purchase the tobacco from farmers at ten cents per pound, then hold the crop until a satisfactory price was offered. The company and the farmer would then share in the profits over ten cents. This plan offered to pay farmers directly with the promise of additional profits later. Obviously, a large amount of capital was necessary to implement such a plan. Hawkins hoped twenty-five thousand farmers in the area would buy ten-dollar shares in cash. This approach to financing, like its predecessors, seemed improbable, if not impossible. After an early sounding proved unpromising, Hawkins decided to go to the Cincinnati banking community.[18]

Hawkins sent an emissary, Archibald Stewart, to Cincinnati seeking the financial backing of the city's financiers. In February 1905 Stewart negotiated a loan of ten million dollars from Cincinnati businessmen and bankers that would supply the cash advances farmers desperately needed. The prospects of the loan made the pooling effort appear a success, and enthusiasm was naturally heightened in the burley region. Suddenly, however, the Cincinnati bankers called the loan off. Considerable speculation arose among growers and association leaders about the reason for the action. Many felt that James B. Duke had spelled out the full implications to John D. Rockefeller of Standard Oil, who controlled the National City Bank of New York as well as many other financial and banking houses.[19] Because of Rockefeller's power within the banking community, growers reasoned that he might have contacted the Cincinnati bankers and interceded on Duke's behalf. Speculation also surfaced about the presence of ATC representative P.B. Gordon in Cincinnati when the loan was under consideration. Gordon dismissed claims that he was in town for the express purpose of blocking the loan, telling reporters that "if the growers land the $10 million capital and corner the burley market, the trust simply will get some other tobacco." In an angry editorial, the Clarksville, Tennessee, *Leaf-Chronicle* asked: "How long can the American people tolerate this trust system of impoverishing the whole country" in order "that a few men, under our money system, may corner the money and lay up enormous fortune?"[20]

The 1905 pooling attempt, like its predecessors, failed because of the lack of access to capital. Organizers announced that an attempt to pool the upcoming 1906 crop would be under way soon after the selling season ended. The 1906 campaign, however, was somewhat different from previous organizing efforts. The new campaign was marked by the presence of a national organization that viewed the tobacco movement in central Kentucky as a test case. It wanted to prove itself as a national union capable of raising prices for all agricultural producers. Known as the American Society of Equity, the new formation was the brainchild of James A. Everitt of Indianapolis. Everitt had no experience in organizing, and he was not even a farmer. Instead, Everitt operated his own feed and seed store and owned his own newspaper. As a rural retail merchant, Everitt seemed genuinely concerned about the impact that low prices had on the family farmers. While urban-oriented reformers were vocal in their concerns over child labor, Everitt found their protests somewhat hypocritical: "While the nation and states cry against female and child labor in factories, not a word of protest is raised against the toil of the farmer's wife and children."[21]

Everitt was personally convinced that farmers could realize higher prices by combining their crops and waiting for satisfactory prices. The concept was not a radical one: Everitt did not address the underlying structural causes of the crisis of agricultural debt. The fact was, as his writings indicate, he did not understand the agricultural crisis in structural terms. In the burley movement, Everitt did not even seek to combat the tobacco trust. Instead, he felt "the American Society of Equity will tame [the trust] and make use of their fine machinery to serve the people in fairness." Essentially, Everitt's sole idea was to raise market prices for all farmers: "The demand is not for government warehouses, free silver, unlimited issues of paper money, loans from the treasury on crops or land, duties on farm products, or even the destruction of trusts and corporations, but simply for the use of the power which the yeomanry have to help themselves." [22]

Everitt's plan was to pool the tobacco crop and to "meet one seller with one buyer." As such, Everitt's ideas were similar to Hawkins's. Both were interested in obtaining higher prices for tobacco and not in directly addressing the problems of agricultural credit or an inadequate supply of currency that depressed prices. The Equity program, then, did not bring innovative ideas in organizing the Bluegrass. Instead, Equity organizers built upon the fragile foundation previously laid by Hawkins and the Growers' League. [23]

Under Everitt's auspices, the American Society of Equity was granted a charter from the state of Indiana on December 24, 1902. Everitt felt confident of organizing large numbers of farmers. After all, he innocently acknowledged, the Grange and the Farmers' Alliance had done so. After an early attempt at organizing midwestern wheat farmers, the Equity came to the burley region of Kentucky. [24] Equity circulars had found their way into Kentucky as early as 1904. Although the Planters' Protective Association did not become part of the Equity, four Equity meetings were held in the Black Patch in 1904. These meetings, however, failed to generate a workable plan among farmers. The Equity doctrine was unable to recruit a substantial constituency. [25]

Nevertheless, the Equity effort had the practical effect of getting people together, and thus it raised the possibility that someone might come up with an organizing agenda containing the kind of substantive promise that the Equity approach itself did not have. In February 1906 growers in New Castle met to hear an explanation of the Equity plan. Out of this conversation came the

Henry County Union. H.E. Swain and G.W. McMillen emerged as the chief organizers of the new venture. The Henry County Union thus engendered the movement that culminated with the Burley Tobacco Society.[26]

The organizing plan again centered on pooling. In March 1906 Swain organized local unions in Bethlehem, Franklinton, New Castle, and Smithfield, all in Henry County. These locals then met in New Castle on March 19 and organized a county union. Throughout the spring and summer, Swain, M.C. Rankin, I.W. McGinnis, and G.W. McMillen urged farmers throughout the burley district to join a pooling program. The core of the new tobacco movement in Kentucky was eight county unions that Swain was instrumental in organizing by the fall of 1906.[27]

The essence of what farmers were told by the organizers in the burley area showed an experiential advance over Hawkins's early agenda. "It is not proposed," said the organizers, "to raise a million of dollars with which to purchase the crop, for this is impossible; it is not proposed to curtail the area, which is equally impossible." The proper course was "by pooling the crop and thus meet the one buyer, the trust, with one seller, the grower's agent." Financing plans had not yet materialized. Instead, farmers were told that organization was the foundation by which farmers could fight to receive "a fair price for the product."[28]

On October 1, 1906, the eight local farmers' organizations of Grant, Henry, Owen, Pendleton, Shelby, Spencer, Trimble, and Washington counties met in New Castle. They called their new organization the Burley Tobacco Society: A Branch of the American Society of Equity. Understandably enough, the farmers whom Swain had organized chose him as chairman. The growers also learned of a "development convention" to be held in Winchester in November. The leaders of the Burley Tobacco Society decided to hold a major meeting of their organization in Winchester to coincide with the convention. M.C. Rankin of the BTS related why this was done: "We would crack the hardest nut first, Clark County having never joined our previous tobacco movements." Also, Rankin added, "the Commercial Club of Winchester was one of the most progressive and enterprising in the whole country and could be depended upon to be most helpful."[29]

At the November meeting of the Commercial Club, the BTS

was officially presented to the convention. Apparently, the commercial and business interests of Winchester saw hope in the farmers' fight. After all, low tobacco prices affected the entire local economy. The Commercial Club provided the burley organization a staff of stenographers and secretaries, who typed and mailed over 3,500 letters to well-known farmers in the region asking them to attend a crucial tobacco conference to be held in Winchester.[30]

When the meeting arrived, an enthusiastic gathering of tobacco growers decided to launch a coordinated campaign to organize the burley region. The atmosphere surrounding these meetings was captured by the Winchester *Democrat*: "No more earnest and determined body of men have ever met here." The tobacco movement, if successful, "means that the grower will be able to get a fair renumeration for his land and labor."[31] H.E. Swain, G.W. McMillen, C.M. Hanna, and M.C. Rankin agreed to lead the organizing campaign. A total of twenty organizers eventually went into the burley counties in a tightly coordinated recruiting effort. The BTS also acquired the services of some organizers working with the Planters' Protective Association in the Black Patch. The growers decided that unless at least 50 percent of the estimated ninety-two thousand acres of the burley in the area had been pledged by January 1, 1907, the pooling effort would be cancelled. While Equity leaders James A. Everitt and H.B. Sherman actively sought credit for the endeavor, the local organizing was conducted by such experienced men as Swain, Hanna, and the venerable W.B. Hawkins.[32]

Burley growers, twenty-five thousand of whom had signed up for Hawkins's previous pooling efforts, were attentive to the new campaign. In Woodford County, farmers met at the county courthouse in December 1906. Each was assigned a district in which he would be responsible for recruiting his neighbors. The organizers also directed their attention to local bankers, realizing that unless the effort was properly financed, the movement would collapse. Before hopes of any success could be realized, the January 1 deadline of signing 50 percent of the crop loomed. The organizing network built by the BTS labored feverishly to recruit during this critical period.[33]

On New Year's Day, 1907, growers from twenty-nine counties

met in Winchester. As each county's representative gave a report
on the amount pooled in the county, the life of the burley cooperative movement was held in the balance. When the totals were
tabulated, 54 percent of the burley acreage seemed to be included
in the pool, while acreage totaling 4 percent more was pledged by
dealers who had already bought tobacco. When the numbers
were announced, county organizers rushed to telephones, in
order to send word back to their counties as soon as possible that
the pool was on.[34]

The meeting also selected Clarence Lebus to lead the BTS. Like
Ewing, Lebus was one of the region's wealthiest growers, owning farms totaling five thousand acres and raising over four
hundred acres of tobacco. Other organizational details were left
for another day. Methods of financing were still incomplete, but
for the moment M.C. Rankin told the assembly that "landlords
should take care of [their] tenants where possible and when not
so that the County Board should finance its own county."[35]

At the organizational birth of the BTS, national Equity
organizer, H.B. Sherman remarked, "Seldom has any campaign
among people, for any purpose, closed in such a blaze of glory.
. . . nothing in our history can run in the same class with the
campaign just closed, for vigor, untiring work, and determination." What Sherman failed to note was that the "untiring work"
had not been conducted by members of the national Equity, but
rather by local organizers. In Woodford County, where local
organizers had recruited their neighbors, over 2,700 acres had
been signed to BTS contracts by February 1907. Sherman and his
highly visible staff did not reach the county in their own recruiting drive until long after the crucial work was finished, in June
1907.[36]

Within weeks of the Lexington meeting, the BTS announced that
it controlled over 65 percent of the burley crop. Who were the first
to join these cooperatives? An insight into the characteristics of
the most committed cooperators—those who joined first—can
be gleaned from Woodford County. In early 1907, 268 growers,
less than one-fourth the number of farmers in the entire county,
had been signed to BTS contracts. Possessing land, capital, and
large crops, landowners were financially much more able to

endure a withholding campaign, and in this county they were generally among the first to enlist. The average acreage of tobacco pledged per signer in Woodford County was 10.3. Since families could only tend three to five acres by themselves, it seems highly likely that most of the early signees were landowners who employed farm laborers. Only thirty-seven farmers, or 13 percent, were listed as pledging five or fewer acres of tobacco.[37]

In order to recruit tenant farmers and sharecroppers, the BTS needed adequate financing to support these farmers through the waiting period. Surprisingly, bankers came to lend their assistance to the cause in the burley region, as they had done in the Black Patch. The reasons for this alliance were grounded in the place tobacco occupied in the local economy. Higher tobacco prices not only alleviated the farmer's plight but also produced two other effects. Increasing the income in farmers' pockets stimulated consumer demand and thus retail trade. Second, an improved tobacco economy also strengthened the loan portfolios of local bankers. An excellent insight into how the financial sector viewed the Burley Tobacco Society is offered by a report issued by fire insurance underwriters evaluating the potential insurability of society warehouses. The report claimed that "the Society should be successful in its purpose, as it is managed by capable businessmen using business methods and commanding the respect, confidence and public sentiment of the general community."[38] The financial community viewed the BTS as a sound organization, led by wealthy, businesslike farmers who merely wanted higher prices. With the pooled tobacco serving as collateral, bankers hoped to realize profits of their own from higher prices. Such an alliance provided a rare moment in American agricultural history—a conjunction of creditors and debtors joined in a common cause.

A more sophisticated analysis of the dynamics of class on the land thus becomes essential to a coherent interpretation of the burley movement. As we have seen, the movement was primarily geared toward the needs of wealthier landowners like Clarence Lebus. In order for the movement to appeal to less affluent growers, leaders had to seek alternative sources of financing in an effort to relieve tenants and sharecroppers from the burden of debt incurred during an extended waiting period. In this way, economic backing from local bankers was introduced. Yet the very genius of this route revealed a fatal weakness. These loans proved no salvation to cooperating farmers. As crops were held in warehouses, only half of the estimated value of the crop was advanced. Meanwhile, the interest accumulated and soon produced even more pressure on farmers of lesser means. The usual advance was five cents per pound, roughly 70 percent of the current offering price. As was the case in the Black Patch, the liaison with bankers in the burley region necessarily meant that the co-ops would not pursue alternative strategies to address economic issues in ways that may not have been in the best interests of bankers. The remarkable alliance might prove helpful in the short run, but it offered no structural solutions.[39]

The plan unfolded. Bankers in Grant County loaned fifty thousand dollars to the BTS. In Washington County, banks loaned ninety-six thousand dollars to the local unit of the society. Owen County bankers agreed to loan one hundred thousand dollars at 8-percent interest. In Clark County, the local Equity warehouse signed contracts with the Cincinnati Warehouse Company, which agreed to finance all tobacco stored by the BTS in the county. The warehouse was to advance half the estimated value of the crop at 6-percent annual interest. Additionally, the warehouse received twenty-five cents per hogshead (approximately 1,200 pounds) while the product was being stored, and it received three dollars per hogshead when the tobacco was sold. By February 1907 Lucien Beckner, secretary of the BTS, issued a circular to growers claiming that each county had arranged to finance its crop. The ever-ambitious W.B. Hawkins hoped to capitalize on the movement's momentum by appealing to organized labor "in the common fight against the trusts." The BTS, in Hawkins's estimation, had "formed a union themselves and desires to affiliate with other branches of organized labor."[40]

By April 1907 the BTS had successfully organized farmers throughout the burley region (see table 9). Predictably, those counties in which organization had taken place before 1907, such as Carroll, Clark, Grant, Harrison, and Henry, had high proportions of signees, whereas those new to organizing had somewhat lower percentages.

The BTS decided to cap its recruiting campaign by hosting a

Table 9. Percentage of Crops Pooled by the Burley Tobacco
Society in Kentucky Counties, April 1907

County	%	County	%	County	%
Anderson	85	Gallatin	75	Pendleton	77
Bath	41	Grant	77	Robertson	80
Boone	40	Harrison	92	Scott	81
Bourbon	63	Henry	73	Shelby	61
Bracken	53	Jessamine	15	Spencer	50
Carroll	100	Mason	50	Trimble	86
Clark	89	Mercer	63	Washington	75
Fayette	23	Montgomery	24	Woodford	59
Franklin	67	Nicholas	57		

SOURCE: "Minutebook of the Burley Tobacco Society," Box 2, pp. 96-97,
Burley Tobacco Cooperative Papers, Special Collections, M.I. King Library, University of Kentucky.

NOTE: In addition, the BTS in Brown and Clermont counties in Ohio and
in Switzerland County, Indiana, pooled 20, 50, and 6 percent of the crop
respectively.

massive barbecue in Lexington in April 1907. To oversee this
event, the BTS logically chose W.B. Hawkins, the area's best-
known organizer. The word went out over the newly generated
organizational network, and when the appointed day arrived,
more than fifteen thousand farmers attended the barbecue at
Woodland Park. The speakers during the day included state
senator J. Campbell Cantrill of Georgetown, who struck a responsive chord with pleas that reached the core of the farmers'
struggle:

> Can the tenant ever hope to become a landowner at seven-cent
> tobacco? Can the farmer under mortgage ever hope to discharge the
> mortgage at seven-cent tobacco? Nothing so demeans a man's hopes and
> throttles his ambitions as the millstone of debt.
> We organize to make our farmers free men; to throw off the burden of
> debt, so that they may stand looking the world in the face—under
> obligation to no man.[41]

Such appeals directly addressed the central need of agriculturists—adequate credit. Tragically, the structural range and implications of the credit problem were never fully understood by burley organizers.

Like the PPA, the BTS entirely abstained from any political endorsements. Yet it is not surprising that various members of the Kentucky legislature at this time were also society members. Equity president J. Campbell Cantrill was a member of the Kentucky Senate from 1901 to 1905, and he was later elected to the Kentucky House of Representatives. Society members C.C. Patrick and W.B. McChord were also elected to the Kentucky legislature in 1908. Area politicians knew that their well-publicized sympathy with the BTS did not hamper their reelection campaigns.

While this visible organizing activity occurred, the tobacco trust did not sit idly by. In June 1907 farmers at a BTS Executive Committee meeting in Lexington discovered that the American Tobacco Company was intent on breaking the new cooperative. Reports asserted that agents of the trust had issued contracts to burley growers promising "to take good care" of those who refused to join the BTS. The prices offered those outside the BTS were usually double the prices offered in 1905. Farmers throughout the region quickly learned that organizing against the trust was a formidable task.[42]

Despite opposition, the conjunction of sound financing mechanisms and local organizers to explain the new system allowed the BTS to overcome considerable resistance. By mid-1907 approximately 75 percent of the region's burley growers were enlisted in the BTS. The Planters' Protective Association may have looked with envy on the quick success of the society in organizing farmers. Though the two organizations seemingly shared a common cause, they were never united. Comparing the BTS and the PPA reveals several features of their efforts. The PPA by 1907 was convulsed in discord and violence, while the BTS was on the verge of its greatest organizational stage. The undemocratic elements present within the PPA severely damaged its ability to recruit initially and then to sustain its constituency. Therefore, farmers in the burley region joined a movement somewhat different from that in the Black Patch. While the PPA struggled in these years with mixed results, no concrete alternatives emerged from Ewing or the PPA hierarchy that could alter economic conditions in the fields. Suggestions from the rank and file were summarily dismissed. By 1907, on the other hand, farmers in the Bluegrass were discussing a bold, unprecedented action that might change the functioning dynamics of the tobacco industry.

The 1906 crop remained unsold, and as the 1907 crop arrived at the warehouse, the outlook for its sale seemed remote. To end this stalemate, major meetings occurred in January and February 1908 in Winchester. Officials of the BTS met with representatives from the American Tobacco Company. Though the rumor quickly spread that a deal was forthcoming, it never materialized. Burley farmers were left with a two-year supply of unsold tobacco, mounting debts, and little hope for an imminent sale.[43]

Considering this imposing predicament, the BTS had some difficult choices to make. To make matters worse, the financial resources with which to pool a third crop simply did not exist. The 1907 Panic had taken its toll in central Kentucky and significantly constricted credit. BTS members thus brooded over ideas for a workable strategy to confront these looming issues. In 1908 the BTS, perceiving no other recourse, embarked on a revolutionary strategy that ultimately became the high point of the Tobacco Wars. The stunning plan the farmers adopted, and its equally stunning success, are unrivaled in American agricultural history.

7

Farmers on Strike

"An assertion of the solidarity of a class."

Despite the Guthrie meetings and the specter of night riding, the most significant development of the Tobacco Wars occurred in the burley district in 1908. Finding the trust unwilling to buy pooled tobacco, the Burley Tobacco Society embarked on an extraordinary strategy in late 1907: no burley tobacco would be grown in 1908. Never before had an agricultural strike on such a massive scale been attempted. As 1908 progressed, the struggle between the BTS and the trust intensified. Despite the collective confidence of the BTS members, however, it is doubtful that any of them was prepared for what occurred in November. To adequately describe this culmination, some contemporary analysts used some revolutionary terminology. In fact, many wondered aloud if the tobacco industry or even American agriculture would ever be the same again. The experience of 1908, it seemed, represented nothing short of a wholesale transformation of the relationship between industrialism and agriculture.

The hope that the events in central Kentucky engendered, however, was short-lived. It quickly became apparent that no revolution had taken place. In fact, the financial straits that tobacco farmers encountered in 1909 were precisely those they had faced in 1906, before the initial pooling effort. Instead of bringing the American Tobacco Company to its knees, the strike seemed to do nothing more than effectively kill the BTS itself. The remarkable events of 1908 offer useful instruction in the dynamics of power that were functioning in the central Kentucky tobacco fields.

The heart of the BTS pooling plan was the demand price of fifteen cents per pound. To farmers accustomed to receiving seven cents per pound, this was a bold plan, indeed. With an adequate financing strategy and an organizational network originally established by the Burley Tobacco Growers Company and W.B. Hawkins, the BTS was successful in pooling the crops of almost three-fourths of the area's growers by 1907. The pooled crops, however, remained in cooperative warehouses, as trust buyers refused BTS prices. One reason advanced to explain why the pooled crops were not being bought was that the American Tobacco Company had a large supply of burley on hand. The trust was therefore willing to wait until the farmers broke ranks before purchasing more. The only way to encourage the trust to buy pooled tobacco, according to some cooperators, was to curtail the supply of burley drastically.[1]

As early as June 1907, the BTS Executive Committee discussed the topic of a tobacco strike in 1908. After this early talk, representatives from eleven counties voted to eliminate the crop. Twelve delegates voted against the plan, and five abstained. The numerous organizational and financial obstacles that might impede such an unprecedented action obviously placed doubt in the minds of many people on the Executive Committee. The discussion of the plan, however, was not limited to the hierarchy of the BTS. In October 1907 ninety of one hundred Fayette County farmers voted not to grow a crop; four days later, fifty-seven of fifty-nine farmers did the same in Bracken County. These local discussions help explain why the BTS was successful in recruiting such majoritarian constituencies, while the PPA plodded along in its organizational drives. Essentially, the local meetings describe how democratic movements are constructed—by the autonomous members of the movement itself. Ewing autocratically decided what was best for Black Patch farmers—as "Moses" leading his children "out of the wilderness"—but the BTS, at this stage, instead responded to the voices emanating from the local level rather than imposing views from the top. By October, the Executive Committee announced that unless the 1906 crop was sold by January 1, 1908, the strike was on. Fifteen district chairmen were absent at this meeting, however, and the possibility of a strike remained uncertain.[2]

On November 4, 1907, the Executive Committee of the BTS, sufficiently emboldened by grass-roots support, decided not to wait until the January 1 deadline. Delegates from thirty-five of thirty-six counties voted to eliminate the burley crop entirely in 1908. The BTS offered two reasons for the decision: since two pooled crops remained unsold, it would be virtually impossible to finance a new crop; also, the cutout would lower burley supplies and no longer allow the trust to cry "overproduction" as a primary cause of low prices. These candid appraisals demonstrated the desperation the BTS felt in battling an uncompromising tobacco trust as well as the enormous financial difficulties the cooperative encountered in the wake of the 1907 panic. The Executive Committee knew that if the campaign stood a chance of success, county organizers would need to recruit large numbers to the effort and convince them of its necessity.[3]

The prospects of the strike's achieving success were naturally viewed skeptically by many observers. A report for fire underwriters summarized the general feeling: "There is a growing sentiment among the members of the Society not to raise any tobacco in 1908." According to the report, "this is practically impossible of accomplishment, and control of the situation to this extent will probably never be attempted."[4] The task confronting BTS organizers in late 1907 was, in every sense of the word, monumental. The very notion of an agricultural strike was a novel idea to Americans in 1908. Labor strikes before 1908 succeeded mainly in demonstrating the costs and apparent futility of such activity. Encouraging hard-pressed farmers to deny planting the region's cash crop, particularly when two years' crops remained unsold, seemed an impossible chore. For the strike to succeed, virtually all of the nearly one hundred thousand acres of burley needed to be eliminated. Of course, those who chose to plant a crop in 1908 could expect high returns from trust buyers in the fall. Those farmers participating in the strike, particularly tenants and smallholders, would face stark deprivation. Any labor organizer would not have envied the job facing BTS organizers as the 1908 planting season approached.[5]

By December, the outlook for the strike seemed mixed. Thirteen County chairmen reported that within their counties little had been done to recruit farmers to the plan. Within a handful of counties, however, the campaign had already achieved results. In Bracken County, 792 farmers had agreed to strike; in Fleming

County, over three thousand acres were pledged to the BTS
effort; 85 percent of the crop would not be planted in Fayette
County; and the chairman of the Owen County BTS reported that
the support for the strike in his county was "almost unanimous."
We can gain an idea of the vast organizational machinery set in
motion by the strike through local evidence. In Nicholas County,
106 farmers were chosen at a local BTS meeting to canvass the
county signing farmers to the cause.[6]

Different tactics were used to increase the effectiveness of the
strike. In Montgomery County, Kentucky, farmers met among
themselves and discussed their situation. The county BTS voted
afterward to support the strike. In Harrison County, growers
responded to a petition circulated at a farmers' rally in support of
the effort. In Henry County, eight hundred interested farmers
listened to a debate between Equity president J. Campbell Cantrill and an anti-BTS advocate, B.F. Hill. Following the discussion, 1,500 more acres were pledged to the strike. The extent to
which the strike was gaining cultural acceptance was seen in
Georgetown, where during a February parade sporadic arguments ensued between farmers in the crowd. The Lexington
Herald reported that "whenever a man who wanted to grow
tobacco this year" began to speak, he was "immediately surrounded by a crowd" of strike supporters, who usually "got the
best of it."[7]

Throughout the winter of 1907-8, before the tobacco planting
season commenced, prospects for a sale of the 1906 and 1907
crops at times seemed hopeful. R.K. Smith, vice president of the
ATC, visited Winchester on January 2 to view the pooled tobacco.
Smith offered to buy the entire holdings at twelve cents per
pound. This price was almost double the price burley farmers
had received in 1905. Yet the offer was refused by the BTS, which
stood firm by its demand price of fifteen cents. In an illustration
of the growing militancy engendered by the strike organization
itself, some BTS members actually considered fifteen cents a
"concession." Another meeting was held in March, but again no
deal was arranged.[8]

Organizers had little time to work, for the strike's effectiveness
would be evident in the early spring, when tobacco beds were
prepared for the upcoming planting. Strike organizers needed to

halt the cultivation of the tiny plants before transplanting began. Their work had significant results. By March 1908 only an estimated 16,250 acres, out of approximately 100,000 acres, was planted. This was still far more than what the organizers had originally envisioned.[9]

For some growers in the burley region, the cooperative spirit was palpable. Earl Ferguson of Bourbon County, for example, owned a large tobacco farm. Three tenant families lived there, and they became members of the BTS along with Ferguson. When the 1908 cutout campaign was under way, Ferguson promised his tenants the free use of their living quarters, as well as all the work he could give them in order to relieve them of the stress placed on them by the elimination of tobacco for an entire year.[10]

One farmer noted that throughout central Kentucky, "consideration for tenants seems the most plausible of all the excuses offered by those who wish to plant in 1908." Such explanations, at least in this farmer's opinion, were not convincing. He advised concerned landowners to "encourage the tenant . . . share with him his burden." He, perhaps, knew what a Mason County farmer observed: "It is not the poor men who insist upon raising tobacco, but rich men who do not work the crop themselves, and who have enough capital invested to live on a small percent of profit."[11]

To those farmers not so enamored with cooperation, J. Campbell Cantrill of the state equity had a simple naked threat: "You who are not in the pool, let me say to you that if you grow tobacco enough to threaten our market, when your crop is almost ready we will dump 175 million pounds of pooled tobacco on the market for what we can get." Cantrill estimated that such a move would produce ruinously low prices, perhaps as low as two cents per pound. The choice for farmers, according to Cantrill, was simple: "Stand idle and help us—or we'll ruin you."[12]

Other appeals were made to the farmer's sense of community. "Shylock had the right to his pound of flesh," an editorial in the *Kentucky Evening Gazette* noted about the legal rights of growers to plant a crop. "But there are moral obligations superior to statutory laws. Intelligent, liberal minded men ought to take into consideration their moral obligations as members of a community and of an industrial class." Jack Chinn, a BTS member, told nonpoolers: "Two years we have gone without money. You have been able to buy dresses for your women folk and toys for your children. We haven't. Now we ask you, as neighbors, not to grow any tobacco this year." Such appeals to "neighbors" and the good of the community were heartfelt. When poorer farmers with hungry families made these pleas, the message was even stronger. On those occasions when large landowners planted crops in 1908, front pages of local newspapers reported the news to dismayed and disgruntled farmers.[13] The words of a striking farmer indicate the growing self-confidence engendered by the burley strike: "The tobacco growers of Kentucky are engaged in an economic movement which is the most significant event of this generation." Another burley grower observed, in language seemingly reserved for industrial labor unionists, that the burley movement, above all, was "an assertion of the solidarity of a class."[14]

By the summer of 1908 the test of the strength of the BTS was at its height. As expected, the movement to grow no burley for the entire year was not met with sympathy from all regional farmers. "It amuses me," said one planter, "how the picture of the poor, shoeless, and starving women and children" was often invoked by BTS organizers. "In fact," at least in this grower's estimation, "I have never seen any such picture and doubt very much whether they ever existed except in the imagination of the speakers." The planter added that his own tenants had refused even to wash his laundry: "Did you ever see one of them who would do a day's work outside of his tobacco crop? No, indeed, they will quickly tell you that they are no negro, and you can do that work yourself. Yet we hear the cry of the poor, oppressed tobacco tenants."[15]

Remarkably, however, little tobacco was grown in the area. By early summer only an estimated 3,500 acres—less than 10 percent of the previous year's crop—was under cultivation in the Bluegrass. Two reasons primarily account for this ability to stop tobacco production: the extensive organizing structure of the Burley Tobacco Society mobilized the majority of burley growers, and the strike's effectiveness was enforced among the holdouts by the introduction of terrorism in the form of night riding.[16] Night riding was not confined to the Black Patch.[17] Besides

"O, Fool, Raise No Tobacco"

NOTICE—Oh, fool: Dare to raise a stalk of tobacco on your land or assist any one else in the raising and ye shall pay the penalty with your home and life. So be ye warned.

"NIGHT RIDERS."

Notice in central Kentucky newspapers during the 1908 strike. J. Winston Coleman Kentuckiana Collection, Transylvania University Library.

sporadic outbreaks in Indiana, Ohio, and West Virginia, concentrated and coordinated attacks also occurred in the Bluegrass region of Kentucky. The number of burley counties in which night riders appeared increased dramatically from 1907 to 1908. It is no coincidence that this increase occurred simultaneously with the 1908 strike.

Early in 1908 the signs of things to come were all too evident. In February, the postmaster in Woodford County found twenty anonymous letters sent to farmers planning to grow a crop. Attached to empty cartridges, the letters read: "Our scouts inform us that you are determined to raise tobacco this year, thereby attempting to starve thousands of poor little children and women to death." The letters concluded: "Sign at once. Signed, Night Rider."[18] The threats turned into violent action shortly thereafter. On March 10, 1908, a group of fifty night riders destroyed fifteen thousand pounds of nonpooled tobacco stored in a warehouse in Brooksville, Kentucky. The next night, two large warehouses, together holding forty-five thousand pounds of tobacco, were destroyed by night riders in New Liberty. Three nights later, a band of sixty riders in Woodford and Scott counties set fire to tobacco barns of expressed nonpoolers. One of the barns belonged to George Graddy, who the day before had published in a local newspaper his determination to defy the strike.[19] While some modern observers may see such developments as manifestations of the "militancy" generated by the burley movement, it is clear that vigilantism emerged out of failure of the crusade for cooperation and verified the limits of internal democratic forms the farmer had earlier endeavored to create.

The cutural sanction given to violence was grounded in majority rule. W.B. Hawkins said in 1908: "The majority has said, 'No crop in 1908!' What will you do? Sow your beds and begin a year of torment? For it will be 365 days of hell for you, sleepless nights, alarm at every noise." In this way, in the thinking of Hawkins, those who chose to grow deserved the consequences.[20] The violence in the burley region was designed primarily to destroy tobacco, not necessarily to intimidate those outside the pool. The number of tobacco beds and barns destroyed was greater than the number of violent acts inflicted on individual farmers (see Appendix). This was a result of the fact that a much higher proportion of growers in the burley area were committed to the BTS than were dark tobacco growers in the Black Patch to the PPA.

Activity of vigilantes in the Bluegrass did not include the episodes of whitecapping or other acts of wholesale racism that occurred in the Black Patch. While the justification of central Kentucky vigilantism was based on enhancing the effectiveness of the strike, another reason for the lack of attacks by night riders on African-American farmers is the fact that relatively few black farmers resided in the region. While black farmers constituted roughly 10 percent of all farmers in the Black Patch in 1910, the corresponding figure for twenty-four central Kentucky counties was only 4.7 percent. In burley counties such as Anderson, Boone, Bracken, Campbell, Carroll, Franklin, Grant, Kenton, and Trimble, African-Americans constituted less than 2 percent of the county's farmers. In a more telling comparison, over seven hundred more black farmers resided in the central Black Patch counties of Robertson and Montgomery in Tennessee and Christian in Kentucky than resided in the twenty-four selected counties of the burley region combined.[21]

During the height of night-riding activity in the Bluegrass, BTS press agent Alice Lloyd felt that a double standard existed among respected members of the local community toward vigilantism. "Burn a tobacco barn or whip a trust buyer," she said, "and the

Members of the state militia stationed outside a tobacco warehouse in Lexington during the burley strike, 1908. J. Winston Coleman Kentuckiana Collection, Transylvania University Library.

press and pulpit are in a frenzy of indignation." On the other hand, Lloyd noted, "systematically in the name of business take away from the laborer the products of his toil, stifle his ambition, quench his aspirations, destroy his hope, reduce him to the minimum wage, and the press and the pulpit have little to say." While the BTS officially denounced the methods of the vigilantes, there was no mistaking the fact that the co-op benefited from Bluegrass night riding.[22]

In the estimation of one local newspaper, the night riders were fully justified in their efforts. "The burley growers have revolted and are now engaged in a death struggle for freedom," claimed the Winchester *Democrat*, which also asserted that BTS members possessed "the moral right to demand that the man on the outside waive a small portion of his legal rights for the common good." The editorial disclaimed support for lawlessness but added, "If lawlessness comes, the outsider, who is faithless to his friends, will not be held guiltless by the imperial public." A respected Fayette County farmer was heard saying that while he would not commit lawless acts himself, he nonetheless sympathized with the methods of the night riders. After all, they were only "looking to free themselves of oppression."[23]

The night-rider campaign of scraping tobacco beds before the crop could be transplanted and destroying full tobacco barns and warehouses enhanced the ability of the 1908 strike to curtail the amount of leaf brought to market that autumn. Night-riding activity in the Bluegrass, however, also became bloody. On the night of March 21, 1908, riders visited the home of Hiram Hedges, a Nicholas County farmer who had set out a tobacco crop. The riders called Hedges from his home and gunned him down in front of his family. Hedges soon died, raising the conflicts to a new, violent level. The obvious threat that night riding posed changed many reluctant minds. Anna and Mary Young of Fayette County were planning to plant a tobacco crop when they received a threatening letter from night riders. "I felt that an owner should be allowed to grow what she pleased on her own land," Anna remarked, but she added, "I should have no option but to obey the commands of the night riders." A.S. Hart of Montgomery County decided not to grow his crop the day after Hedges's murder, because, in his words, of "fear that trouble may occur." The excruciating dilemma facing smallholders and tenants was expressed by one frightened burley farmer, Jessie Taylor. "We don't want to do anything wrong," he said, revealing how refusing to participate in the strike was expressed in moral absolutes. Nonetheless, Taylor pointed to the practical economic consequences the 1908 strike was exacting: "The poor people of this section will suffer if they cannot raise tobacco." [24]

This bizarre conjunction of sound organizing techniques and coercive vigilantism characterized the farmer effort in 1908. The BTS strike consequently achieved great success by the summer of 1908. The results of the elimination of the burley crop were dramatically announced by Kentucky agriculture commissioner M.C. Rankin (a former BTS official). "Where a crop of 135 million pounds of tobacco was grown in 1907," Rankin's report stated, "only five million pounds will be grown in 1908. About 96 percent of the white burley crop is eliminated." [25]

With such a drastic depletion of the central Kentucky tobacco crop, extraordinary steps were needed to insure the survival of approximately thirty-five thousand area farmers. To supplant tobacco, farmers grew corn, wheat, and hemp. Since roughly one hundred thousand acres previously used for tobacco now grew other crops, 1908 should have witnessed bumper crops of these replacement crops in the Bluegrass. Yet that did not occur. While sixty-six thousand more acres were devoted to corn in the state in 1908 than in 1907, for example, the amount produced in 1908 totaled nine million bushels less than the previous year. The reason is that from June 11 to November 10 central Kentucky endured the worst drought since the establishment of weather records in 1871. "Farmers depending on small ponds and streams have suffered, in most, a total loss of water," concluded the Weather Bureau.[26] With the threat of night riding imminent, many burley growers had no other choice but to strike and endure by their own means.

The crucial question in the minds of farmers in 1908 concerned exactly how much burley tobacco the American Tobacco Company already had in its manufactories. Of course, trust officials did not readily provide an answer. As the Lexington *Leader* noted, the question of supply was nearly impossible to discern: "No one knows this except the Lord and President Duke." The ATC, meanwhile, in the opinion of an insurance broker, was "refraining from purchasing [BTS] holdings for so long as possible." The reason for such action was clear to this observer: it was nothing more than a blatant "attempt to wear them out and thus make the movement among the farmers a failure."[27]

While farmers could only guess at the true situation, the fact was that supplies of burley held by the American Tobacco Company were dangerously low in late 1908. A 1909 Bureau of Corporations report noted, "At the end of 1905, the leaf department of the American Tobacco Company had on hand . . . only 42,711,086 pounds of burley leaf." Considering that approximately one billion pounds of burley tobacco was processed by the American Tobacco Company from 1900 to 1907, it is evident that the supplies on hand before the 1906 pool were not abundant. Since burley was a chief ingredient in cigarettes, snuff, and plug products, the American Tobacco Company needed sizable supplies of burley leaf. Complicating matters for the ATC was its own war with an emerging rival within the trust, R.J. Reynolds. Reynolds's Prince Albert brand had emerged between 1904 and 1907 as a chief competitor to the ATC's Bull Durham. The ATC responded by attempting to corner the market on burley in order to choke Reynolds's supply. Since Virginia and other states furnished part of the burley crop, the trust survived without the

central Kentucky crops of 1906 and 1907. Yet supplies continued
to dwindle, and by 1908 company officials began negotiating with
the BTS for the pooled tobacco. Throughout the spring and
summer of 1908 the negotiations stalled. The American Tobacco
Company refused to pay the demand prices of fifteen cents and
upward. The 1908 strike had reached an impasse: eventually the
financial pressure would become so great that one side in this
struggle would yield. Either the trust would need the eighty
million pounds of pooled tobacco for its own financial well-being,
or the BTS members could not endure the hardships of a withholding campaign and a prolonged strike.[28]

The stalemate finally ended in November 1908. Clarence
Lebus, no doubt worried that the co-op might be destroyed
unless an agreement was soon reached, played what the Cincinnati *Enquirer* later called "the great bluff." Early in the month,
some independent tobacco manufacturers agreed to purchase
nominal amounts of the pooled leaf. Lebus cleverly leaked news
of this to the press, quoting amounts purchased that were admit-
tedly "greatly exaggerated." Lebus was then heard "taunting" an
ATC official, saying that the BTS no longer "cared a farthing"
whether the trust purchased any of the crop for the simple reason
that "the independent manufacturers want every hogshead of it
and will take it at our price." The bluff worked. Fearing that large
amounts or perhaps all of the pooled crop might be sold to small
independent companies, the ATC began negotiating with the
BTS in earnest.[29]

By mid-November, early rumors began circulating that a colossal deal was being prepared. On November 13 the ATC offered
to buy the entire 1906 crop for twenty and a half cents per pound
and the 1907 crop at sixteen cents, well above the earlier demand
price of fifteen cents. The BTS accepted the bid for the 1906 crop
but demanded eighteen cents for the 1907 crop. Strong disagreement also rose over another issue. BTS officials were adamant
about offering up to one-fourth of the entire pool to the independents. The American Tobacco Company obviously had no desire
to see fledgling competitors obtain nearly twenty million pounds
of the prized burley leaf. The ATC vigorously sought an agreement to obtain all of the burley pool. On November 19 the
company raised its bid for the 1907 crop to sixteen and three-

fourth cents. The BTS held out and demanded seventeen cents. Facing another potential deadlock, the American Tobacco Company relented and agreed to all BTS demands: twenty and a half cents for the 1906 crop and seventeen cents for the 1907 crop, totaling nearly $12.5 million for the BTS. The BTS also won on the matter of the independent buyers and offered them one-fourth of the pool. This question, in fact, had been the crucial barrier to completing an agreement. One BTS official acknowledged that the trust's refusal to allow other potential buyers to bid on any portion of the BTS pool "had blocked the deal for more than three months." The BTS and the independents reached an agreement by which one-fourth of the pool was sold to the smaller concens at an average price of seventeen cents per pound.[30]

Evidence of the leverage the BTS commanded in the outcome of the strike was revealed the day following the sale. The burley co-op demanded that the trust pay an additional $3.00 per hogshead, or roughly $250,000, in "outage fees." These were expenses for storing and packing the pooled tobacco in warehouses. At first the ATC refused to pay the fees, but after BTS officials threatened to cancel the entire sale, the trust decided, again, to relent and pay the total amount.[31]

After the deal was closed, ATC officials adopted the best public posture they could under the circumstances. Rumors circulating that the ATC had fought to keep independents from the pool were quickly denied. Trust official Thomas J. Ryan assured everyone that the company instead hoped that its decision to restore "peace and harmony" to the central Kentucky tobacco fields would influence the antitrust case then under way against the ATC and prove that no monopoly existed within the tobacco industry. A.J. Carroll, the attorney who represented the American Tobacco Company, further stated that the trust had agreed to BTS demands because the company had the best interests of the state at heart. The Louisville *Courier-Journal* responded: "Everybody knows how much importance to attach to that assertion. The Company accepted the terms of the growers because it needed their tobacco and had not been able to get it on any other terms." Fanciful pleas by ATC officials did not deter other observers from concluding that the trust did not agree to BTS demands because of social concerns over the state's "best interests" or to lessen corporate anxiety over possible antitrust litigation. Rather, the motives of the trust were primarily economic. The Cincinnati *Enquirer* stated that economic self-interest was the only motivation for the company's acquiescence, since it desperately needed "to replenish its stock [of burley] which has been running low." The *Courier-Journal*, alert to trust contentions that the sale was concluded for altruistic reasons, asserted that "it was strictly a business matter on the part of the economy" and that the ATC's efforts all along had been "made from no higher consideration than that of the pocket."[32]

To BTS members, many of whom had not received payment for their crops in three years, news of the sale brought unbridled celebration. Those farmers at the Louisville hotel where the deal was announced were the first to know. Their reaction was typical. One report stated: "They knew not how to contain themselves. They laughed like boys. The suddenness of the announcement that they would no longer have to starve and suffer was too great for even their strong constitutions." The trade paper *Tobacco* noted: "The deal means a godsend to the people in the tobacco belt. Since the fight against the Tobacco Trust began, the families of many of the tobacco growers have been without proper food or clothing. . . . many schools were forced to close for lack of attendance. . . . there was never a time in the history of Kentucky when there had been more mute suffering than in the tobacco belt since the struggle with the Tobacco Trust began." The Cincinnati *Enquirer* added that "no class of men in any state have suffered more hardships or been more debt-ridden" than the BTS strikers. The socialist newspaper *Appeal to Reason* reached the resounding conclusion: "For once in this industrial history of the world farmers went on strike and won!"[33]

News of the deal spread rapidly through the burley region. One of the first to welcome the news was J.T. Wilkerson, president of the Union Bank and Trust Company, who said that the deal would do much for the local economy: "I think the deal is most important as so many farmers as well as other people have felt the recent financial stringency." Wilkerson was especially pleased to note that "much money will flow through Lexington banks."[34]

Louisville bankers, still reeling from the effects of the 1907 panic, were especially heartened when they heard news of the sale. Since many local banks had money tied up in the pooled tobacco, Louisville banks had consequently seen smaller deposits coming in from country banks. Thus the Louisville banks held less reserves with which to obtain loans from New York banks. The flood of millions of dollars from the American Tobacco Company allowed country banks to repay their loans to Louisville bankers, who in turn could obtain more funds from New York. As one Louisville banker stated with relief, "The banks were heavily indebted with loans and there was much apprehension." But with news of the sale, "everything will be in better shape." Another banker said, "While the tobacco deal has been pending, the Louisville banks have been compelled to curtail loans." This was because of "the heavy drain made by the smaller country banks."[35] Counties in the burley region were greatly relieved by the income provided by the sale. Bourbon County received approximately $750,000; Woodford County, about $500,000; Scott County, approximately $900,000; and Bracken County, almost $1,000,000.[36]

For the time being, the word that resounded throughout the tobacco fields was *Victory!* By any estimation, the BTS seemed to have "won." After a three-year battle with the American Tobacco Company, the cooperatives finally received the prices and terms they demanded. The influx of money that soon came to the Bluegrass relieved the pressure on everyone from tenant farmers to Louisville bankers.

This was indeed the high point of farmer organizing during the Tobacco Wars. In fact, the farmers themselves claimed that the strike would usher in a new era in American agriculture, one in which "the growers have established their right to demand a fair price." Amid the jubilation, few within the Burley Tobacco Society doubted that the following year would bring even greater results to farmers. One farmer remarked: "It is scarcely conceivable that intelligent farmers will consider for a moment the destruction or abandonment of a machine which has shown itself to be so powerful for their benefit." BTS officials in Louisville predicted that the following year, "if another pool is formed in Kentucky, every farmer in the state will want to get in. . . . look for prosperous times in Kentucky for some time to come."[37]

The 1908 strike seemed to be a transforming opportunity in the Tobacco Wars, similar, perhaps, to the chance later seized by the sit-down strikers in Flint, Michigan, to transform the labor battles between the United Auto Workers and the automobile industry.[38] After enduring the sacrifices of cooperation, a desperate organization undertook a desperate act that put the life of the BTS on the line. Had the American Tobacco Company held out for a few more months, the question of what to do with the 1909 crop would have dogged the BTS and weakened the strike. Yet that did not occur. The trust simply could no longer hold out for the valued leaf. The strike was an unqualified success that brought instant credibility to the BTS. The cooperative stood before its constituency and the world as the organization that had defeated one of the mightiest industrial combinations in America. This victory seemingly had the potential for mobilizing the entire tobacco-growing population, in not only the burley and Black Patch areas but the entire country as well.

Yet the 1908 strike did not have such a sustained consequence for tobacco farmers or the industry. Understanding why the tobacco strike, unlike the 1936 sit-down strikes, for example, did not produce a transformation in rural America is crucial. The central factor in the 1936 strikes, which forever changed industrial organizing and gave rise to the CIO, was the fact that the strikes in Flint had a structural consequence on management's major weapon in combating strikes—hired strikebreakers or Pinkertons. With workers sitting down at their machines, company owners could not risk the kind of violence so often utilized when picketers struck outside the company gates. The sit-down strike thus not only stopped production but also eliminated strikebreakers from the equation.

Such dynamics are not at work in agriculture, where a strike could not have the same impact. At bottom, the tactic of a crop strike only addressed the issue of surplus reduction: with low supplies (obtained, in human terms, at a brutal cost) available to the trust, the BTS commanded a certain leverage in dealing with the ATC. The strategy of a strike, however, did not address the structural issue of agricultural credit that forced farmers to grow a cash crop, nor did it alter the marketing mechanism set in place by the tobacco industry. The strike had powerful short-term consequences, but it ultimately left intact the machinery that produced the debilitating economic conditions in the tobacco fields. In 1909 tobacco farmers would still rely on tobacco for credit and would still have one buyer for their crop. The 1908 strike verified the limits such tactics necessarily insured for farmers inextricably tied to a cash-crop economy.

The great agrarian strike of 1908 was, therefore, not all that it appeared. As the emergence of night riding testified, the community of thirty-five thousand tobacco growers did not speak as one. Internal dissension beneath the surface throughout the year came to the fore just three days after the announcement of the sale. Farmers in several counties reported that wealthier landowners had bought the warehouse certificates of poorer growers and had earned windfall profits from the sale. Making matters worse was the contention that these wealthier growers were also leaders in their local BTS co-ops.[39] Such class divisions would increase in intensity the following year. For thousands of burley growers, the costs involved in striking proved too much, and pleas by BTS officials to launch successive withholding campaigns fell on deaf ears. Within just eighteen months the BTS essentially no longer existed. The transforming opportunity had been lost, and the chance to change the conditions under which tobacco farmers labored was lost with it.

8

The Demise of Agrarian Cooperation

The cooperative experiment among tobacco growers in Kentucky and Tennessee ended soon after 1908. Diverse reasons help explain this defeat. Overt intervention by the American Tobacco Company weakened the ability of organizers to persuade farmers to join the pool. This disruptive activity by the tobacco trust, however, did not occur in a vacuum. The 1907 panic on Wall Street tightened credit for all Americans, not just for farmers. Adding to the difficulties confronting advocates of agricultural cooperation were internal problems within farmer organizations. Undemocratic features that came to characterize both agrarian cooperatives eventually alienated farmers, especially smallholders and tenants. Without refinements in organizational structure, new cooperative attempts would likely fall prey to dissension. By 1910 it had become obvious that farmers no longer viewed the tobacco cooperatives as an unalloyed vehicle of salvation.

The rapid collapse of the Burley Tobacco Society following its apparent victory in 1908 is one of the more shocking turns of events in the course of the Tobacco Wars. With remarkable suddenness, the subject of most burley farmers' criticisms became not the tobacco trust, but rather the leadership of the BTS and chiefly its president, Clarence Lebus.

Lebus had come to dominate the BTS by 1909 in much the same fashion as Felix Ewing had long controlled the PPA. Of small stature, Lebus had piercing gray eyes, a strong, jutting chin, and a "backbone as big as a telegraph pole." Though he had not yet reached the age of forty, Lebus was already one of the wealthiest landowners in central Kentucky. Even with his large landhold-

ings and considerable wealth, Lebus was committed to the tobacco movement: "Kentuckians are not slaves," he remarked,
"and all the money of Wall Street could not keep them in bond-
age."[1]

The jubilation with which farmers greeted the sale to the ATC
soon passed. A perception emerged among BTS members in
early 1909 that Lebus and other society officials suddenly seemed
more interested in their own personal gain than in the needs of
the rank and file. Specifically, charges of exorbitant expenses and
salaries were heard throughout the burley region. A contemporary observer noted that in addition to suspecting excessive salaries, many BTS members claimed that "the officers have been
allowed too great latitude in their conduct of affairs." Such a
conclusion reflected a far deeper anxiety expressly felt by many
cooperators: "The movement has lost much of its democratic
character."[2] After depriving themselves for three years, farmers
were not likely to accept indulgent officials who used the proceeds from the 1908 sale to enrich themselves. Unless the BTS
returned to the democratic roots that nourished the movement
early on, its quick demise would rapidly approach.

In January 1909 the BTS established a committee to settle a
salary dispute between Lebus and the society. For months, while
the rank and file looked on, Lebus and the committee negotiated
over compensation. The BTS had earlier claimed that "when
salaries are paid they will be so reasonable that no fair-minded
grower will grudge one cent" to officials. In June 1909 the two
sides finally arrived at an agreement. Lebus accepted $12,000 for
each of his first two years of service. Contingent upon the success
of the 1909 pool, he would earn a salary of $25,000. Additionally,
a new BTS secretary was paid $3,500, while members of the
Executive Board were allotted $2,000 each. Sixty county board
members received $500 each, and all officials were given liberal
expense accounts.[3]

The BTS committee therefore affirmed what farmers had long
suspected—that extremely high expenses were depriving the
farmers of their own proceeds. Such figures lent credence to
Governor Willson's earlier pronouncement that the tobacco
movement was composed of nothing more than "shrewd, ambitious leaders" who used the co-op to "satisfy their own greed."[4]

Table 10. Selected Expenses of the Burley Tobacco Society,
1907-1912

Legal expenses, 1908-12	$131,966
Office salaries, 1908-11	107,064
Campaign account, 1907-11	103,440
Executive Board salaries, 1909	57,000
General expenses, 1907-12	42,618
District Board salaries, 1909	39,541
Publicity account, 1908-11	25,081
Graders accounts, 1907-10	24,801
Printing and stationery costs, 1907-11	15,842
Furniture and fixtures, 1908-12	4,993
Rent, 1910-12	2,691
TOTAL	$555,037

SOURCE: "General Ledger, 1907-12," Burley Tobacco Cooperative Records, Special Collections, M.I. King Library, University of Kentucky.

In an age of low prices and tight money, the internal records of the BTS reveal the excessive costs of managing the cooperatives. From 1907 to 1911, $203,605 was spent solely on salaries for officials (see table 10).[5] Since the costs listed in table 10 are incomplete for the six-year period examined, it is very likely that the expenses for the BTS were well in excess of $555,037. While the management of the co-op necessarily required the expenditure of some proceeds from tobacco sales, the fact that over a five-year period farmers, by the terms of the 1908 sale, lost the equivalent of approximately 2.5 million pounds of tobacco, or roughly $15.85 per BTS member, indicates that the BTS leadership could scarcely be considered frugal.

Burley farmers who had gone on strike in 1908 were, of course, fully expected to pool the 1909 crop. As the BTS organizers distributed new pooling contracts, farmers discovered that a new provision had been quietly inserted. In joining the new pool, members were contractually bound to buy stock in a new organization called the Burley Tobacco Company. The company's ambitious intentions were to buy warehouses and build its own manufactories so farmers could compete with the tobacco trust at all levels of the industry. Farmers would buy stock in the company by paying a fee equal to 10 percent of their crops' gross sales. In effect, the new contracts extracted 10 percent of all earnings to be used in a plan in which the farmers had no input.[6]

The "10 percent clause" was too much for many farmers to bear. In the wake of the salary controversy, farmers thought that the BTS was extracting too high a price from their pocketbooks. At BTS meetings in Winchester, a growing clamor was soon directed toward the organization's hierarchy. "The Burley Tobacco Society is no longer the people's organization; it is the personal organization of Clarence Lebus," proclaimed a Cynthiana lawyer, J.J. Osbourne. He added, indignantly: "Threefourths of all the tobacco grown in the Burley Tobacco Belt is grown by tenant farmers. Of the many thousands of them, not a man among them owns a dollar's worth of stock in any corporation. They do not grow tobacco to buy stock. . . . they grow tobacco to buy for themselves and their families the bare necessities of life."[7]

The anger was not only felt in Winchester at BTS meetings. Farmers meeting in Boone County in August 1909 agreed not to sign BTS contracts unless the 10 percent clause was dropped. The same farmers stressed that they also refused to sign unless the proceeds of the crop went directly to the counties and not through BTS headquarters. Similar conclusions were reached in Pendleton County, where burley growers met and refused to support the BTS unless the 10 percent clause was withdrawn and strict limits were placed on salaries.[8] Jessamine County growers did not participate in the 1909 pool, and reports in Scott County indicated that tenant farmers were especially displeased with the new pledge. They said that they would rather have more money than stock.[9]

Behind the resistance to the 10 percent clause was a growing awareness on behalf of tenants and sharecroppers that the BTS was structured to benefit large growers. While large growers were better prepared to wait for satisfactory prices than small farmers, these same wealthier growers often bought poorer growers' crops at low prices and then resold the same crops later for a substantial profit. The small farmer thus remained loyal to cooperation while being exploited by wealthier farmers. Large growers, noted a report to attorney general George W. Wickersham, "are making a fortune by preying upon the necessities of the weak growers of the community." When 1909 pooling contracts were circulated, a contemporary observer wrote, "It need not be a matter for surprise that some of the small farmers should now evince a very lukewarm interest in cooperative selling."[10]

An extraordinary confidential memorandum sent to Kentucky governor Augustus Willson by Lucien Beckner, the first secretary of the BTS, highlighted the growing internal dissatisfaction among BTS members: "There has been a feeling of discontent for some time, but the recent meeting of the Executive Board gave this a tremendous impetus by the allowances it made to Lebus." Beckner charged that "Lebus is imperious and over-bearing." Especially dangerous was the 10 percent clause. "You can easily see," Beckner continued, "how the men with money, who belong to the pool, or outside of it can buy up this ten percent from the poorer individuals and thus become owners of the manufactories."[11] Beckner's memo to Governor Willson emphasized the structural imbalance that favored wealthy growers over small farmers and sharecroppers.

Added to these internal troubles was a rift between the BTS and the American Society of Equity. Led by its Kentucky chairman J. Campbell Cantrill, the Equity had asked for twenty thousand dollars from the BTS following the 1908 sale. The Equity claimed that the money was to be used for operating expenses. After the BTS refused the request, Equity officials lowered the sum to ten thousand dollars. This too was denied. Finally, the Equity asked for a loan from the BTS. Again it was denied. The problem between the two organizations ran even deeper than this dispute suggested. Cantrill felt that the BTS was trying to centralize power, whereas he said that the Equity wished to locate more authority within county unions. Cantrill also strongly opposed the new contracts, feeling that there was no need to change the original cooperative plan, "under which the greatest victory ever won by organized farmers was consummated."[12]

The Winchester *Democrat* quickly defended the local organization, asking: "What right has the State organization of the Society of Equity to any part of the proceeds of the 1906 and 1907 pool?"

Only nominal fees, according to the *Democrat*, were owed the Equity. Yet the Lexington *Herald* saw the brewing conflict differently. The *Herald* claimed that the struggle between the BTS and the Equity was "between conservatives and the extremists, with the BTS representing the more conservative elements of the tobacco growers and the Equity appealing to a more radical faction."[13]

The heart of the matter, as the *Herald* understood, was the desire of the Equity to reform the Burley Tobacco Society. Cantrill and other Equity leaders perceived the high salaries and the 10 percent clause as potential killers of cooperation. Cantrill proposed a list of demands to the BTS that included reduced salaries and prohibiting the 10 percent clause, as well as recognition from the BTS that the Equity was the parent body of the tobacco insurgency. Cantrill's proposals were flatly rejected by Lebus and the BTS.[14]

By August 1909 the split between the two organizations appeared at an end. Lebus and the hierarchy of the BTS, while refusing to acknowledge the Equity as the parent body, agreed to pay ten thousand dollars to the Equity for operating expenses. For its part, the Equity dropped its demands of abolishing the 10 percent clause and instituting lower salaries. Finding no more obstacles to pooling, Clarence Lebus said after the agreement: "If this pool is not a success, you can take my head for a football." Cantrill, on the other hand, reluctantly supported the agreement. Rumors fom the Equity noted, however, that Cantrill privately supported those farmers who refused to sign BTS contracts because of the 10 percent clause.[15]

The uneasy alliance between the BTS and the Equity was soon broken. In late August 1909 growers from numerous burley counties met at the Grand Hotel in Cincinnati and discussed issuing a new cooperative contract independent of the BTS. The meeting was led by national Equity chairman C.O. Drayton, who expressed the dissatisfaction felt by burley growers concerning the 10 percent clause. The meeting produced the formation of the Burley Growers District Union, which began distributing pooling contracts in competition with the BTS. Within weeks, contracts without a 10 percent clause and with strict salary limits were signed in Boone, Bracken, Campbell, Grant, Green, Hardin,

Harrison, Owen, and Pendleton counties in Kentucky and in
Brown and Hamilton counties in Ohio. Lebus thus decided to
relinquish a bonus of ten thousand dollars that the District Board
voted him in June. As the *Western Tobacco Journal* noted, "The
leaders realize that something must be done quickly to change
the sentiment of a certain class of growers, by no means a minority, who are ranked against the BTS."[16]

In late September, the District Union's plan to counter the BTS
was cancelled. Because the effort had started very late in the
growing season, the union had little time to organize. But word
was given that the District Union would continue its effort early
in 1910.[17] To the officials of the BTS, the disappearance of the
bolting farmer's union was welcome, but the threat underlying it
loomed.

Adding to the problems encountered by the BTS was the
natural reluctance of smaller growers to join the 1909 pool. The
burdensome costs involved in withholding two crops and not
raising a third inflicted financial hardship that the salary disputes
and the 10 percent clause only increased. Those burley growers
who had suffered such deprivation were bitter because of the
high prices nonpoolers had received and were continuing to
receive from the trust buyers. Adding to their ills was a growing
reluctance on the part of the BTS leadership to respond to honest
concerns from its constituency. Inevitably, organizers found
their tasks more difficult. The amount of the burley crop that was
pooled by September 1909 was just over one-third of the area's
entire crop, a considerable decline from the 70-80 percent pooled
in 1906-7 (see table 11).

Letters mailed to burley growers by the BTS stipulated that the
1909 crop pooling would not be continued unless at least 80
percent of the crop was pledged. In June 1909 the BTS claimed
that 60 percent had already been signed. This was a gross exag-
geration made in order for the co-op to appear stronger than it
actually was.[18] The critical fact was inescapable: nearly two-
thirds of the 1909 burley crop was not pooled by the end of the
growing season. By October 1 county chairmen were uneasy
about continuing with the pool. Nonetheless, they decided to
keep up the effort by a vote of twenty-nine to eight.[19]

The rapid loss of support for the BTS was further demon-

Table 11. Available Acreage for Crops and Acreage Pooled,
Kentucky Burley Counties, September 1909

County	Total acreage	Pooled acreage	County	Total acreage	Pooled
Barren	3,000	200	Lewis	3,400	700
Boone	2,500	1,198	Jessamine	2,500	50
Bourbon	6,500	600	Madison	4,000	43
Bracken	6,185	4,007	Mason	8,000	3,860
Campbell	1,000	185	Montgomery	3,500	200
Carroll	3,200	1,150	Nicholas	4,000	2,200
Clark	4,200	1,069	Owen	7,000	4,000
Fayette	6,000	550	Pendleton	4,250	485
Fleming	6,100	3,660	Robertson	3,000	2,231
Franklin	4,000	2,780	Scott	7,000	4,168
Gallatin	1,900	1,450	Spencer	2,000	400
Grant	4,250	2,420	Shelby	6,500	500
Harrison	6,500	4,070	Trimble	2,000	850
Hart	3,000	300	Washington	4,000	20
Henry	6,000	1,000	Woodford	4,200	1,212
Kenton	1,500	955			
			Total	131,185	46,513

SOURCE: "Minutebook of the Burley Tobacco Society," Box 2, pp. 372-76,
Burley Tobacco Cooperative Records, Special Collections, M.I. King
Library, University of Kentucky.

strated on November 3, when a suit was filed against the BTS by
former Executive Board member G.W. McMillen. The suit requested that a receiver be appointed to account for the internal
finances of the BTS. Charges against the society concerned the
money distributed from the 1908 sale. Though the overall sale
brought an average price of roughly seventeen cents per pound,
the amount actually distributed to farmers was based on each
county's individual grading system. Each county had an inspector judge the crop and estimate the crop's value, or grade. Few
counties ever graded the leaf at seventeen cents per pound, so
the question arose: Where was the excess money? Though the

suit was judged against the BTS, the Kentucky Court of Appeals later overruled the decision. Nonetheless, the fact that a prominent organizer like McMillen brought the suit reveals the growing internal dissatisfaction that existed within the burley co-op.[20]

During the winter of 1909, just one year after the sale to the American Tobacco Company, the BTS was in deep trouble. With a relatively small amount pooled for 1909, prospects for pooling the 1910 crop seemed remote. Tension against BTS leadership reached its height on January 30, 1910, when a band of twenty night riders raided BTS headquarters in Lexington. The intent of the raid was to "get" Clarence Lebus. Finding only a night watchman, the raiders vowed to return.[21]

Meanwhile, the growers who had signed the 1909 pledge were angered over statements made by the BTS in order to encourage farmers to sign. One Shelby County farmer who had pooled his crop felt he had been misled by the BTS: "I was told that there would be no pool unless at least 75 percent of the entire crop was pledged. Less than 40 percent is pledged, and we poolers are left 'holding the bag.'" Another Shelby County farmer said: "I am a pooler, and, like others, I am a fool. We followed the Burley Society officers like a flock of sheep, and what is the consequence? Our stuff is all tied up, not ready for market." In the future, the farmer added, "I don't propose to be a driveling idiot. Will I pool this year? Not on your life." Such sentiments made the 1910 pool seem even more remote. In Bourbon County, since less than one-fourth of the crop was signed for 1910, the county Board of Control abandoned the 1910 pool. A similar response soon came from Mercer County.[22]

The BTS responded by making the 10 percent clause optional in 1910 contracts.[23] The revision of the contract demonstrated the enormous mistake the BTS had made in changing course without any democratic input from the rank and file. The charge was perceived as excessive by smallholders, who simply could not afford the ten-percent fee.

The dispute between the BTS and the Equity erupted again in 1910. The avowed policy of the BTS was not to endorse candidates for political office. In early 1910, however, the BTS came out in public opposition to a candidate for Congress—none other than J. Campbell Cantrill of the state Equity. Lebus charged that

Cantrill was opposed to the BTS and was undermining the tobacco movement. Cantrill counterattacked by saying that the BTS
was "a miserable failure so far" and that tobacco growers had
"lost confidence in the leaders of the BTS." The farmers would,
he predicted, "no longer follow the arbitrary dictations of Mr.
Lebus."[24]

The *Western Tobacco Journal*, never an organ of the insurgents,
welcomed the political cleavage: "The petty differences of the
leaders thus brought to the light of the public gaze may at least
have the moral effect of discouraging the growers to again place
so much power in the hands of a few men." The outcome, the
Journal hoped, "will likely do much to restore the tobacco industry of the State to a more satisfactory condition." The results of
the election testified to the waning power of Lebus and the BTS:
Cantrill won easily.[25]

With few growers willing to sign the new pledge and with a
pooled crop in storage that was not bought, the BTS saw the
futility of its cause. On August 5, 1910, the BTS elected to dump its
holdings of the 1909 crop on the open market, getting whatever
price it would bring.[26] The open auction of the crop in October
was not, however, attended by buyers for the American Tobacco
Company. At first, independent buyers bid twelve to thirteen
cents per pound for the leaf, but the price soon reached as low as
seven cents. Incredibly, buyers for the American Tobacco Company continued to offer those who had not joined the pool twelve
cents and upward. If any doubt of the trust's adamancy in destroying the burley co-op still existed, it disappeared along with
the Burley Tobacco Society in the fall of 1910.[27]

Though it was not necessary to do so, Lebus announced in
October that the 1910 crop would not be pooled. Lebus remarked,
in words implying defeat, "We are forced to back track, but only
to get a stronger foothold." In a prepared statement, Lebus stated
that the attempted pool would "be unjust to those who have been
so loyal for the past four years." News of the death of the co-op
was welcomed by relieved allies of the BTS—local bankers. Kentucky bank supervisor J.F. Ramey acknowledged that since the
pools "tied up money," the open sale of the 1909 and 1910 crops
"put money into circulation at once, and the banks for the first
time in three years will have money to lend to legitimate business

enterprise." This remarkable alliance of bankers and farmers came to an end, as financiers no longer perceived the tobacco co-op as "legitimate" and worthy of future loans.[28]

Though the BTS was effectively dead after 1910, some erstwhile members continued to hold fast to the hope of cooperation. Future pools and cutouts were often discussed among cooperative leaders from 1911 to 1914, but their efforts were futile.[29] In March 1914 the final disbursement from the 1909 crop was paid by the BTS.[30] This final payment marked the official collapse of the BTS, but the actual end came the day when the 1909 crop was dumped on the open market. Even the shining memory of the 1908 strike soon faded from view.

While the Burley Tobacco Society struggled for survival, the Planters' Protective Association in the Black Patch also underwent serious trials. While the BTS could at least point to the resolution of the 1908 strike as a tangible victory for growers, the PPA found itself bringing prices barely above the cost of production. The Black Patch agrarian movement fought off defeat at every turn. Eventually, however, defeat arrived.

The 1907 financial panic and the devastation left in its wake weakened the ability of the PPA to finance its members. One association farmer, Dan Murphy of Montgomery County, Tennessee, revealed the stress that a withholding campaign created for the local economy: "The merchants say they cannot carry our accounts any longer, as the wholesale houses have shut down on them and will not sell to them unless for cash, and they can't sell to us and wait two or three years for their money." "The farmers," Murphy concluded, "are in a bad hole."[31] Banks in Ashland City, Tennessee, disallowed any further loans to the PPA in 1909 because of stringent monetary markets. The bleak economic picture for association members was not enhanced by the fees that warehouse companies charged farmers during the withholding effort. Jim Hughes of Montgomery County said, "The present methods of handling are too expensive for the average farmer." The entire withholding plan, according to Hughes, was not structured to relieve small farmers and sharecroppers: "It was all right for the man who had a bank account and could wait for the money."[32]

Those farmers who continued to receive advances on half their crop were confronted with bleaker economic circumstances. While warehousemen usually received loans from local banks at interest rates of 6 percent, some warehousemen lent the same money to the farmers at 8 percent. Warehousemen not only earned fees on tobacco stored during the withholding campaign, but they also earned a profit on advances to farmers. It was later rumored that night riders would visit those banks that gave loans to association members at rates higher than 6 percent.[33]

Adding to the costs associated with a withholding campaign was a serious error committed by the PPA. In grading, or placing an estimated value, on the 1907 crop, PPA graders had placed a grade of seven cents per pound on the leaf. In 1909, with the tobacco unsold, the PPA regraded the tobacco at five and a half cents. An estimated $500,000 was lost in the shuffle for Black Patch farmers. A hogshead of 1,600 pounds brought, at seven cents, a price of $112. When the leaf was regraded, the same hogshead brought $88. From this amount, $12.00 was deducted for prizing, $1.75 for warehouse charges, $3.20 for insurance, and $0.82 for commission, a total of $17.77 in expenses. When the farmer finally received his net receipt, he realized $70.23, or just 4.39 cents per pound. After waiting over a year for his money, the association grower received prices on the 1907 crop below the cost of production. Dan Murphy, a tobacco grower, revealed the spirit emanating from the tobacco fields: "Mr. Ewing had our tobacco graded too high," said Murphy. "We don't want a fortune out of a few pounds . . . . but we want a living price."[34]

In fact, it was apparent by 1908 that some Black Patch farmers simply could not afford to join the co-op. In Hopkinsville, Kentucky, the PPA sued an association grower, J.R. Berry, for violating his contract and selling outside the association. The case, however, was dismissed by the county attorney because Berry was "too poor" to join the association and wait for his money.[35]

One of the first overt signs of serious trouble within the ranks of the PPA came from Lyon County, Kentucky, on November 12, 1908. Five hundred county farmers met and passed resolutions calling for immediate sales of the overgraded 1907 crop. Unless the Lyon County growers were allowed to put their crop on the market, they would sever their ties with the PPA. Not long after this meeting, several hundred farmers in Christian County, Kentucky, also adopted resolutions similar to those in Lyon County.[36]

On August 2, 1909, several hundred farmers attended a PPA meeting in Springfield, Tennessee, presided over by PPA chairman Felix Ewing. Charges were heard from the crowd that warehousemen were delaying advances to association members. These charges were strengthened by several district chairmen, who accused members of the Executive Committee of open corruption. The farmers approved of these accusations and reportedly "cheered lustily."[37]

Like BTS leader Clarence Lebus, Felix Ewing was suspected of graft by some association members, who also repudiated his autocratic rule of the PPA. In September 1908 former PPA official C.P. Warfield testified in a night-rider trial that while the farmers' organization had been incorporated with only two hundred dollars, annual profits exceeded one hundred thousand. Since Ewing had orchestrated a new charter in 1906 that gave him control of the largest share of stock in the PPA, charges of flagrant corruption were heard with alarming frequency.[38]

After lengthy public disputes with Ewing, Joel Fort left the PPA in 1909 and later revealed that Ewing had demanded a salary of ten thousand dollars from the Executive Committee, which Ewing later decided to refuse until "a more opportune time." The "opportune time," at least in Fort's estimation, meant one when less public controversy surrounded the issue of salaries. Fort estimated that Ewing's personal budget exceeded twenty thousand dollars and added, "It will cost us $5,000 more at the 'opportune time.'" Fort spoke openly for restoring democratic methods to the PPA. "I advocate the policy we organized by," said Fort, "and that is the affairs of the Association should be ruled and managed by the members."[39]

For the largest tobacco grower in Tennessee to receive a salary of ten thousand dollars, considering that the PPA's constitution forbade an official to receive a salary, was incomprehensible to many sharecroppers and small farmers.[40] The official organ of the PPA, the *Black Patch Tobacco Journal*, moved quickly to defend its chairman, saying that "the people will always be for Ewing. To be different would be base ingratitude." In Fort's view, however, too much emphasis was placed on Ewing's work and not enough on the efforts of more deserving cooperators: "No officer deserves the credit, but I tell you who did the hard work, the disagreeable work. It was the district chairmen, who went from house to house, over plowed fields and met the gibes and jeers of the opposition and all too often without hope of reward."[41]

Central to Ewing's and the PPA's problems was a growing clamor for open sales. Instead of having their tobacco packed by a prizer who charged fees and stored the leaf in a warehouse that also charged rent for the crop, growers increasingly wanted to sell their tobacco loose. Another problem with prizing tobacco was that when the leaf was packed into the hogshead, the tobacco generally lost about 10 percent of its weight in shrinkage. At, say, ten cents per pound, this amounted to a loss of twelve to sixteen dollars per hogshead to the farmer. As the Clarksville *Leaf-Chronicle* noted: "The farmer is demanding quick sales, quick settlement, and at the lowest possible expense. He can have it if he is allowed to market his tobacco through a loose sales house."[42]

When Lyon County farmers demanded the right to sell their crops individually without regard to other counties, Ewing strongly disagreed. After all, Ewing reasoned, such actions defeated the purpose of a cooperative.[43] Ewing's adamancy in disallowing loose sales may also have stemmed from the fact that many banks refused to loan money without a warehouse receipt. It should also be understood that Ewing was in an unenviable situation. Battling tight money and the American Tobacco Company was a task in itself. While hoping to expand his constituency, Ewing had to stave off internal attempts to undermine what he perceived as the core of cooperation. But often Ewing crossed the line between honest democratic leadership and autocratic rule. Charles Fort, president of the PPA, had long hoped that "the people" could have a role in managing their co-op. In Fort's words, "This organization is a movement of the people." Yet he saw Ewing attempt to pass a resolution forbidding PPA board members from criticizing the management of the association in order that the members would "appear before the world as a solid phalanx." Fort saw the movement becoming increasingly ruled by Ewing, and he resigned his post in September 1909.[44]

Loose sales constituted one aspect of the struggle in which Ewing found himself in the minority. By avoiding the expense of warehouse prizing and storage charges, growers hoped to sell earlier and receive better prices. Buyers felt more confident buying tobacco in a loose state, since hogsheads could be packed with stones or inferior tobacco that misrepresented the true weight and quality of the entire hogshead. Ewing, however, felt that when tobacco was prized in hogsheads it was then in a condition to be held indefinitely. Ewing acknowledged that open sales were "the most economical to the member," but a cooperative that allowed each member to sell his crop loose was, in Ewing's opinion, "an Association in name, not in fact." [45]

Charles Barker, chairman of the Christian County PPA, was outspoken in his criticisms of Ewing's steadfast refusal to permit loose sales. In Barker's estimation, such a system unfairly disadvantaged small farmers and sharecroppers. Barker stated that loose sales would be a great benefit to smaller growers: "In this way the man who must sell to pay debts and supply family needs can do so, and is not forced to wait to make a market for his neighbor who has enough of this world's goods to be able to hold for a better price." Barker's Christian County PPA threatened to leave the larger organization unless loose sales were adopted. In desperation Ewing decided to relent and allow the Christian County crop alone to be sold in a loose state. Yet within days, Ewing reversed himself and again denied loose sales. Angry farmers in Christian County went ahead and sold thirty million pounds of dark tobacco loose in 1910. [46]

The dilemma seemed intractable. The Clarksville *Leaf-Chronicle* stated that "unless some solution to the muddle is rapidly found, it is probable that the pool will be broken." Ewing's stance generated hostile reactions. In Graves County, Kentucky, farmers met at the county courthouse in May 1909 and adopted resolutions calling for the dissolution of the PPA unless Ewing was removed as chairman. The tension between growers and PPA leadership was brought to light in a letter to the *Leaf-Chronicle* by W.E. Wall: "When, and for what purpose did such men as Joseph Washington, F.G. Ewing and others, who formerly sat back in their mansions and clipped coupons from their bonds, conceive of such love for the 'dear farmer?'" As the editors of the Clarksville

Table 12. Tobacco Pooled by the Planters' Protective
Association, 1904-1910

Year	Pounds	Average price per pound (cents)
1904	39,531,200	6.67
1905	55,392,140	7.12
1906	61,615,850	8.84
1907	95,316,905	8.54
1908	81,637,144	7.04
1909	36,478,500	9.02
1910	55,000,000	9.00

SOURCE: Clarksville *Leaf-Chronicle*, June 6, 1911.

newspaper reiterated, "This is a movement of the people and they can and should control the business."[47]

The volume of business conducted by the PPA between 1904 and 1910 is illustrated in table 12. The height of the PPA's efforts came in 1907, when over ninety-five million pounds were pledged to the tobacco pool. Despite this apparent success, the average prices the PPA received could never match the offers by trust buyers to nonpoolers. Considering that the American Tobacco Company buyers offered an average of twelve cents per pound, it is obvious that many growers began to question the credibility of a withholding effort. In May 1909 reports from the Clarksville Tobacco Market noted, "Association tobacco is moving very slowly. . . . Independents report good receipts."[48]

Like the BTS, the PPA was sued by former members who charged corruption and demanded that a receiver investigate the financial records of the association.[49] Simply put, by 1910 longtime association members were no longer willing to see nonpoolers receive good prices while cooperators waited. This was expressed in an anonymous letter sent to the *Leaf-Chronicle* in 1909: "Why is it that others can sell loose an inferior grade of tobacco, while we are forced to tie in small hands, prize and hold for twelve months and take less?" The PPA and the night riders could not compete against the capital of the American Tobacco

Company. By 1912 Ewing knew the co-op was dying. At this point he said in a democratic tone that came too late: "I leave the question of the pool with the great majority. The Association is theirs." Even at the height of cooperation, the PPA had only pooled roughly one-third of the dark tobacco crop. When this proportion decreased, the chances of successful cooperation were lost.[50]

In 1914 what vestiges of the PPA that remained were quickly destroyed. A severe drought devastated the region's agricultural economy. A man-made disaster further contributed to the end of the cooperative effort. The outbreak of World War I closed major European shipping lanes, and since dark tobacco was primarily an export crop, this effectively left Black Patch farmers without a market. The official end came in September 1914, when the PPA released all members from their pooling contracts.[51]

Black Patch organizers continued attempts to revive the PPA. The prices for tobacco offered during the early stages of the war reminded many of the conditions that existed in 1904. Average prices of all Tennessee tobacco fell from 8.4 cents per pound in 1913 to 6.3 cents in 1915. Such leaders as Ewing, C.P. Warfield, and even Joel Fort managed to bury their past differences and seek reorganization. Warfield told tobacco growers in 1916 that "our farmers will meet again. . . . they are going to organize." Ewing was even more confident: "The Association has come this time to stay!" Their futile cries were similar to those made by burley organizers after their movement was effectively defunct. The central problem was that the PPA hierarchy had efficiently eradicated any nascent democratic forms within the co-op. Chances of a renewed attempt at cooperation by the same men were nonexistent.[52]

Ironically, the destruction of the tobacco cooperatives corresponded temporally to the nominal dissolution of the American Tobacco Company in the famous Supreme Court antitrust case of 1911. The Court found that Duke's ATC had clearly violated the Sherman Antitrust Act. In the opinion of Chief Justice Edward White, "The combination as a whole, involving all its cooperating parts, constitutes a restraint of trade." Upon the Court's ruling, the case was returned to the circuit court for a decision on the exact nature of the dissolution.[53]

Since this ruling came during the same week in which John D. Rockefeller's Standard Oil trust had also been found in violation of the Sherman Act by the Court, it seemed as though the tactics of James B. Duke and the ATC would finally be put to rest and free competition—the theoretical essence of the American economy—would be restored. A prescient editorialist in the New York *Times* knew otherwise. The decision had dual implications: "Both the government and the Trust win," claimed the *Times*. While the federal government received the plaudits for saving democracy by forcing illegal combinations to dissolve, in reality "the tobacco trust and all the other big corporations get the very thing they have prayed for so long—they got merely a direction by the Supreme Court as to how they may proceed within the law but also a command to the circuit court actually to show them how to reorganize so as to be in harmony with the law."[54]

The details of dissolution were not orchestrated by antitrust experts or court officials. Instead, the essence of the plan was drawn up by James B. Duke and his lawyers and modified somewhat by attorney general George W. Wickersham. At first, James C. McReynolds, who had prosecuted the trust for the government, refused to accept Duke's plan. In McReynolds's opinion, the decree would not secure competition and would continue to leave farmers unprotected from the oligopolistic power of the tobacco buyers. McReynolds proposed instead that the ATC be placed in receivership. This plan drew the anger of President William Howard Taft, who informed Wickersham, "I would not hesitate to run right over [McReynolds]." McReynolds then offered his resignation. Wickersham approved the revised document, based on the framework constructed by Duke's lawyers, which was approved by the Supreme Court in November 1911. The final dissolution decree divided the American Tobacco Company into smaller subsidiaries such as Liggett and Myers, R.J. Reynolds, and P. Lorillard. These new companies, along with the diminished ATC, were essentially controlled by the same stockholders as the original company.[55]

Speaking before Congress, President Taft proclaimed that the "dissolution" of the American Tobacco Company was a landmark antitrust case. "Not in the history of American law," Taft said, "has a decree more effective for such a purpose [dissolving a monopoly] been entered by a court than against the tobacco trust."

A thoroughly disillusioned Louis Brandeis offered a more somber general appraisal of the final result: "The main feature of the plan," Brandeis noted, "is to divide the corporation into three parts; these three parts to be owned by the same persons, in the same proportions, and to be controlled by the same individuals who the Supreme Court considered in a violation of the law."[56]

After 1911, despite presidential claims, the essence of the tobacco monopoly was still intact. In careful maneuvers, the new companies bought only specific types of tobacco for specific uses. For example, Liggett and Myers used particular types for its tobacco products that did not interfere with the programs of other major companies. Either three or four ATC successor companies controlled between 78 and 92 percent of the entire market in cigarettes, smoking tobacco, plug, and fine-cut tobacco. For over thirty years following the original Supreme Court decision, the tobacco industry continued to be an effective oligopoly that produced essentially the same market conditions for farmers that had existed since 1900. In 1946 a jury in Lexington, Kentucky, found the remnants of the American Tobacco Company to have, again, acted in "restraint of trade." Though no direct evidence was brought to prove collusion absolutely, a massive amount of evidence that suggested common action by the major companies successfully persuaded the jury of collusion.[57] In the aftermath of the cooperative movement, liberal reforms by legal and political bodies against the tobacco industry proved futile in dismantling industrial monopolies or improving the economic lot of farmers.

Clearly neither the tobacco cooperatives nor the Supreme Court action ushered in a new day for farmers. A generation after the origins of the first tobacco cooperatives in Kentucky and Tennessee, similar economic conditions testified to the desperate plight of farmers. After wartime inflation increased most agriculture prices, the bottom fell out in 1920. On December 20, 1920, burley markets in Kentucky opened with bids that were less than half those offered in 1919. While tobacco prices had at times reached as high as thirty-five cents per pound in 1918-19, some reports had prices as low as three cents in 1920. The burley market in Lexington witnessed the drawn knives and angry tempers of tobacco farmers, and the market was closed for a short time to calm tensions. While some commentators unhelpfully stressed that low prices were caused by overproduction, the 1920 Kentucky tobacco crop was actually eighty million pounds less than the 1919 crop.[58]

In late 1920, in fact, all farm prices fell drastically. Prices for corn fell from $1.97 per bushel in early 1920 to $0.46 by 1921; cotton fell from 41.0 cents per pound in April 1920 to 10.3 cents fourteen months later.[59] What had caused such a depression in farm prices? By 1919 wartime inflation had sent general prices rising at a rate of 15 percent per year. To correct this course, the newly created Federal Reserve Board raised the discount rate from 4 to 7 percent. This near doubling of the price of credit braked the American economy to such an extent that general prices fell over 50 percent from 1920 to 1922. The Federal Reserve's actions did indeed end inflation, but the severe tightening overwhelmed the nation's farmers. The Board's goals, in fact, were never meant to aid creditors such as agriculturalists. Instead, the "Fed" worked to support the group from which it was created and whose members occupied the chairs of the Federal Reserve Board of Governors—commercial bankers. As William Greider stated, the Federal Reserve Board was intent in 1920 "on eliminating the inflationary fears of financial investors, not on lowering the unemployment rate or restoring farm prices."[60]

The desperate financial conditions farmers experienced in 1920 were not matched, incidentally, by the major tobacco companies. The income of the four major successor companies to the ATC increased from $38.2 million in 1919 to $50.6 million in 1921.[61] Obviously, the Fed's contraction did not have such severe effects throughout the entire economy. It was in this environment in 1921 that tobacco farmers made another attempt at cooperation.

The new attempt was led by Robert W. Bingham, former mayor of Louisville and owner of the *Courier-Journal*. Bingham enlisted the aid of Aaron Sapiro, a California attorney considered an authority on cooperative marketing.[62] Bingham and Sapiro, along with organizer Joseph Passoneau, formed the Burley Tobacco Growers' Cooperative Association. The Association sought to sign burley growers in Kentucky to five-year contracts. In order to finance the movement, Bingham secured the aid of the War Finance Corporation, which agreed to lend farmers money after the burley crop had been redried or after it had been placed on the market and re-stored in warehouses. This money was not, however, available for advances to growers. Bingham secured the support of some local bankers, who agreed to loan $4.6 million, but at the staggering interest rate of 20 percent. Bingham kept the cooperative alive with a personal loan of $1 million.[63]

The Bingham cooperative also extended to the Black Patch. Tobacco farmers were ready to join the cooperative backed by Bingham and the War Finance Corporation. At one point in 1922 the cooperative claimed seventy-seven thousand members. Yet the new cooperators found that the major tobacco companies refused to do business with them. The withholding campaigns of the 1920s produced the same costs that were exacted by the BTS and the PPA. As the waits continued, farmers desperate for a sale saw nonpoolers receive good prices by selling outside the cooperatives, and many farmers sought release from their contracts. The implacable hostility of the tobacco companies caused the burley association to release its growers from their contracts in 1925. Yet when the farmers went to the open market, they found themselves blacklisted by the tobacco companies. Prices fell, and while most of America was enjoying the relative prosperity of the mid-1920s, tobacco farmers groped for ways out of their chronic poverty.[64]

By 1931, as the Great Depression tightened its grip on rural America, the average price received by tobacco farmers fell to 1905 levels.[65] Political leaders ritualistically blamed America's farming ills on inefficient farming methods and overproduction, leaving tobacco growers to anguish about what to do next. Unfortunately, experiments in cooperation over the past twenty-five years provided no clear-cut alternatives.

9

The Decline of the Countryside

The Tobacco Wars occurred at a prominent interval. The U.S. economy was being tranformed from one based on agriculture to one grounded in industrialism. The full effects of this transformation are still being felt. This study has demonstrated that the corporate takeover of the countryside was not accomplished without a frantic defensive struggle by the farmers of Kentucky and Tennessee. Indeed, in the Tobacco Wars, this fight reached stages of unprecedented intensity. It is important to sort out the historical legacy of this passionate struggle at the turn of the century.

Quite simply, the farmers within the tobacco cooperatives were crushed in their attempt to attain a higher standard of living. While buyers offered somewhat higher prices during the peak of cooperation, the only tangible victory came in 1908 with the burley strike and the American Tobacco Company's massive purchase of eighty million pounds of pooled tobacco. After this moment, the co-ops soon withered, and the movement for agrarian self-help collapsed. Throughout the 1910s and 1920s tobacco farmers unsuccessfully fought against agonizingly low prices, regardless of actions taken by the Supreme Court or Congress to alleviate the problems confronting them.

Other writers have reached different conclusions concerning the success of the tobacco co-ops. Historian Dewey Grantham Jr., asserted that the PPA "did help raise prices, the American Tobacco Company was dissolved, as a monopoly, by the federal courts, and some marketing reforms were made." Grantham concluded that the PPA was "partially successful" in changing the rules under which farmers labored. Theodore Saloutos found even less favorable results of the Tobacco Wars, yet he managed to conclude that the farmers "convinced the tobacco industry they were a problem to contend with." Another writer stated that the PPA clearly "was a success" and went so far as to suggest that concurrent with the policies of the PPA "prosperity returned, mortgages were paid, houses and fences painted, and children fed."[1]

Such progressive interpretations have produced a profound misreading of the legacy of the Tobacco Wars. In no uncertain terms, the farmers of Kentucky and Tennessee were unsuccessful in their attempt to change the economic conditions under which they worked. In no social, economic, or political manner did the insurgents win any long-term advantages. To suggest otherwise only adds to the general mystification that surrounds American agriculture.

For farmers in the tobacco belt, the Tobacco Wars verified that their accustomed world had been turned upside down. Tobacco growers in Kentucky and Tennessee did not confront the imposing new social and economic order of industrialism in an abstract or theoretical manner. Their loss involved more than just their livelihoods. The monopolistic power of the tobacco trust to control prices represented to farmers the ominous new order that relegated rural people to the control of centralized urban interests. As industrialism swept millions off the land, some deeply rooted values were swept away with them.

The ideological foundation of the Tobacco Wars was firmly grounded in agrarian republicanism. Cooperative organizers and members lamented time and again the encroaching corporate culture. The farmers involved in the tobacco co-ops rejected a corporate-controlled society that ultimately threatened their independence. Throughout the Tobacco Wars, flash points of agrarian resistance to the new order were revealed: David Amoss anguished over how to achieve "industrial emancipation" for all agricultural toilers; a resolution by five hundred growers in Montgomery County, Tennessee, called the American Tobacco Company "the enemy of the farmer," a force that "places money above man, and dollars above the common good of the people." W.J. Stone characterized the trust as placing the "manacles of slavery upon the tobacco growers"; Joel Fort stressed that "labor must be protected from the oppression of combination and capital and the mad rush to pile wealth into colossal fortunes." Fort added that "the doctrine of the survival of the fittest must give way to fitting a plan that all may survive." James Flowers implored his fellow farmers in Kentucky to "learn from a hive of bees or a nest of ants which work in harmony for the good of all. Let all the farmers do that allotted to each and equity will cover the earth as the waters cover the sea." Noel Gaines defined the work of the Burley Tobacco Society succinctly: "My single idea is—Equality of treatment to all classes. By that I mean that the government should guarantee equal protection to the lives, liberties, and property rights of all classes, and allow destructive privileges to none." While wealthy cooperative leaders like Felix Ewing and Clarence Lebus proudly proclaimed the conservative and unthreatening nature of the tobacco movement, their thoughts clearly did not represent all farmers involved in building the tobacco co-ops.[2]

Often-used terms such as *common good, the good of all, equity,* and *equality of treatment* demonstrated the sense of community that was integral to the cooperative movement. Encroachment on these values by industrial monopoly, or, more specifically, the American Tobacco Company, was the "legitimizing notion" that fueled the Tobacco Wars. Enormous corporate profits combined with rural poverty and the lack of "just" prices for a hard day's work reflected, in E.P. Thompson's phrase, the "moral economy" of the tobacco movement. Undergirding the farmer effort was the inherent understanding that the financial rewards of farming were not commensurate with the work put forth to raise the crop. While academics and other theorists described such notions as the "labor theory of value," for the farmers in Kentucky and Tennessee this line of thinking simply reflected a common value implicit in the republican heritage.[3]

A sense of unity was intensified in the biweekly meetings, the festive barbecues, and small personal acts such as cooperators contributing to a fellow member's fund to rebuild his house. The Clarksville *Leaf-Chronicle* noted, in the waning days of the PPA, that perhaps the foremost benefit of the tobacco movement was "the social life that has been created among the farmers. Farmers, whose lives were confined to a narrow scope, and who knew but few of the citizens of the county, have made fast friends with men in every district, men whom they have learned to love."[4] The idea of a voluntary association of cooperators was subsequently trampled upon, in the eyes of anguished farmers, by greedy "hill-billies" who profited at their neighbor's expense. As the crisis deepened, some desperate and frustrated growers became night riders, lashing out at non-poolers, trust buyers, and African-Americans. Vigilantes perceived these groups as destructive to deeply held notions of justice, equity, and white supremacy.

The bedrock values thus being defended by the farmers in the Tobacco Wars were grounded in the very idea of a just republic. Agrarian republicanism, as Eric Foner has pointed out, was a "belief that independence—the ability to resist personal or eco-nomic coercion—was an essential attribute of the republican citizenry." This notion was rooted in a tradition, as Bruce Laurie notes, that "posed an enduring tension between virtue and com-merce, the self and the market." PPA organizer Joel Fort stated that the tobacco movement "appealed to that power that is higher and more potent than the law . . . that power that nerved the arm of a Robespierre to liberate the enslaved peasantry of France. That power that nerved a Patrick Henry to proclaim freedom and flaunt the American flag in the face of the British Lion." Historian Steven Hahn added that this republicanism was still vital by the 1900s, and linked "freedom and independence with control over productive resources."[5] The tobacco movement therefore did not begin with an ideological *tabula rasa* upon which subsequent events could write. Inherent ideologies that resulted from the activities and beliefs of five generations of agriculturalists since the Revolution remained in the minds of tobacco farmers in 1900.[6]

Had the ideas that generated the Tobacco Wars been successfully translated into mass action, America would be very different today. The notion of the commonweal, or, as the organ of the insurgents termed it, the "brotherhood," was overwhelmed by the emerging corporate culture, represented clearly by the ATC. One cooperator summarized the conflict as "a battle of justice against greed." Accompanying the defeat of the farmers' co-ops was an ethos quite different from that to which many farmers had grown accustomed. The emergence of this new culture was viewed with disdain by the Black Patch farmers, one of whom said, "No man can afford to live for self alone." The one who values self over community "must expect to become an outcast from society and scorned by the community for the lack of that principle which entitles him to the confidence and brotherly help of his neighbors."[7] As evidenced by the Tobacco Wars, these ideas never blossomed into sustained collective action. The leaders of the cooperatives resigned themselves to discussing higher prices in the short term, not structural approaches to battling the industrial shadow expanding over the continent.

In fact, the tobacco movement never evolved into a truly substantial competitor to the new order. Underlying this was the fact that the movement never made the crucial connections between economics and politics. In trying to achieve greater economic equity, some people may become sufficiently knowledgeable that they can further educate themselves about the institutional political constraints under which they operate. With this new ability, these people may proceed to address the underlying structural foundations of their inequity.

In order to learn why the tobacco movement never reached a level of analysis that sought structural solutions, we should direct our focus toward the interior structure of the movement. At the biweekly county meetings of the PPA and the BTS, local cooperators could candidly discuss their concerns about their own movement. These local meetings should not be overlooked: they were, in fact, the lifeblood of the tobacco movement. The Clarksville *Leaf-Chronicle* later noted that the local meetings had "been a source of power for good, as the farmers have stood together shoulder to shoulder as brothers."[8] In schoolrooms, churches, and courthouses, tobacco growers formed, in Sara M. Evans and Harry C. Boyte's phrase, "free spaces," or self-created institutions where they could shape and reshape their own movement.[9] In such "spaces" culturally intimidated people can gather and begin to challenge power. Yet within the tobacco cooperatives of Kentucky and Tennessee, these meetings evolved into scenes of autocratic reaction by cooperative leaders. When farmers openly expressed dissatisfaction in their county meetings—their disapproval of large salaries and expenses, the 10 percent clause, unfair prizing and storage policies, and finally the dictatorial methods of leaders such as Ewing and Lebus—they were often dismissed by county leaders and the officials of the cooperatives. In fact, disagreement with avowed policy often incited a questioning of a member's loyalty to the movement. The *Appeal to Reason* noted that within the PPA, "democratic discussion of association policies in which all members participate is unknown."[10] Rather than discussing potential strategies for addressing their sundry problems, the farmers in the meetings became preoccupied with achieving democratic control of the movement itself. The "free spaces" in the tobacco movement proved to be hardly free at all.

In Kentucky and Tennessee, the tobacco movement was so occupied with economic demystification (a task that it never succeeded in accomplishing) that it could not conceive of political realities. The tobacco cooperatives were steadfast in their determination not to become involved in politics. In the wake of the failure of the People's Party in the 1890s, cooperative leaders (including those in the newly formed Farmers' Union) perceived that the central lesson of the Alliance movement was the unsuccessful elevation of the movement to the political stage. The tobacco movement never achieved the level of self-education reached by the Farmers' Alliance in the 1880s and 1890s. Occasional appearances before congressional committees to testify about the tobacco tax were the extent of organized political participation. In other words, the hierarchies of the tobacco insurgencies never understood that "politics" involved far more than simply the ballot box.

Instead of expressing the concerns of all tobacco farmers, from large landowners to tenants, the cooperatives were structured to disregard the needs of small growers. Inherent in withholding crops are long waits, and small growers desperately needed alternative incomes during the campaign. Because of the central place that tobacco occupied in local economies, small bankers were willing to advance loans in order to aid in financing the movement. But the loans themselves soon became burdensome, and they were issued for only half the estimated value of the crop. This method of financing, simply put, did not adequately address the nagging problem of credit, nor was it a match for the capital reserves of the American Tobacco Company. Adding to

the farmers' costs were warehouse and insurance fees and com-
missions, which continued to eat into smallholders' and tenants'
slim pocketbooks. Large landowners with ample finances did not
suffer as smaller growers did. Consequently, the tobacco movement never became a "popular" expression of common concerns.

What is clear about the attempts by tobacco farmers to organize during the Tobacco Wars is that besides tight money,
night riding, or even the ATC, the central reason why the co-ops
were crushed lies within the co-ops themselves. The PPA and the
BTS experienced early organizing successes because of the democratic forms the movements created at the local level. Here, for a
brief time, the tobacco movement stood poised to challenge
power. The tactics chosen by the farmers were not perfect: some
suggestions were rather naive, others too amorphous. Yet that is
precisely the nature of insurgent movements. Almost necessarily, mistakes are made at every turn. Participants need these
mistakes in order to learn what pitfalls to avoid. As long as local
members of the tobacco co-ops could actively participate and
shape their own movement—mistakes and all—the tobacco insurgency gave itself the opportunity to arrive at a workable
strategy for self-help. Yet when the co-ops ceased operating as
democratic agencies (an event that occurred within the PPA by
1906 and within the BTS by 1909) and, instead, turned into vanguard organizations led by autocratic landowners, they simply
did not have a chance.

As the Tobacco Wars demonstrate, the final result of meshing the
free market with family-farm agriculture is a special kind of
American tragedy. In the twentieth century, financial depressions beginning in 1907, 1920, 1929, and 1937 and the credit crunch
of the 1980s have devastated the ranks of the country's small
farmers, tenants, and sharecroppers. With little choice, farmers
of all types have left the land to seek work in urban mills and
factories. Yet even in periods not regarded as depressions, times
seen by many as "prosperous," farmers have continued to disappear from the American countryside.

From 1920 to 1987 more than twenty-nine million farmers left
the land. Writer Wendell Berry has referred to this mass exodus
as the "forced migration of people greater than any in history."

From 1960 to 1980 alone, the American farm population dropped from 15.6 million to 7.2 million. The number of farming families has declined from 2.45 million in 1970 to 1.44 million in 1987. With this staggering loss of farm labor, it would seem that American agriculture would have reached a crisis in output, yet that is hardly the case. Between 1910 and 1960 total farm output increased over twenty-fold. The acreage of farms has also increased: today average farms exceed 460 acres, more than three times the average size of 1920. The complex dilemma of modern agriculture, in fact, seems to present one of the crucial problems with the concept of progress. Despite massive evidence to the contrary, our collective picture of twentieth-century agriculture in America is clearly progressive. After all, America's farms produce staggering amounts of crops. At the same time, however, farmers have been driven off the land and into increasing poverty. While we collectively celebrate the image of the family farm, America's family farms are on the verge of extinction.[11] Today's farms are no longer operated by an independent yeomanry or even by a flood of sharecroppers and tenants working on small plots. Instead, modern farming is dominated by "agribusiness"—large corporate enterprises designed as models of scientific and efficient agriculture.[12]

One does not lament here the imagined loss of a pastoral Eden presided over by some fancied blissful yeomanry. The truth is that life on the land in America has always been full of endless work and anxiety. The tragedy of the corporate invasion of the countryside is the irreparable damage it inflicted upon millions of farmers and their families and the consequent damage done to the American social fabric. This transformation of the American countryside is an extremely awkward subject. Not surprisingly, it is a topic that has proven difficult for historians to engage. Its implications seem to undercut long-standing popular presumptions concerning America's economic prosperity, which is thought to be partially founded upon the nation's agricultural abundance. The stark reality of the modern farm economy is that enormous profits are generated for banks, life insurance companies, farming supply firms, marketing and manufacturing companies, and retail grocery stores, all at the expense of consumers and the tiny group of remaining smallholders.[13] The time to alter this tragic course of events has passed: the countryside has been irrevocably transformed. The family farm will never return. The time to have acted to redress the "farm problem" was at the turn of the century—around the time of the Tobacco Wars—when America was in the midst of this transforming process.

The methods employed by the American Tobacco Company to dominate the tobacco industry were not restricted to the Gilded Age. Such methods control the modern functioning dynamics of American agribusiness. Today the tobacco industry itself continues to operate as an oligopoly, since only a few corporate giants, such as Philip Morris and R.J. Reynolds-Nabisco, dominate the industry. With their enormous profits, today's tobacco conglomerates have bought out other major corporations in the food and liquor industries to a degree that would humble even James B. Duke.[14]

The American Tobacco Company gained its leverage in the industry in the early 1900s by buying out smaller manufacturers or driving them out of the market through price wars. Modern agribusiness conglomerates follow this same pattern. The coffee industry provides a useful example. In the early 1970s Procter and Gamble decided to enter the lucrative coffee market. Though the company did not own as much as one coffee bean, it solved this problem by employing its massive capital reserves to purchase a coffee manufacturing company, J.A. Folger. To expand its share of the market, Proctor and Gamble followed a simple strategy: drive the price of Folger's coffee low enough in selected regions so that smaller companies could not compete. Targeted areas soon received discounts, free samples, and cost-cutting coupons, publicized through an extensive advertising campaign. The efforts of Procter and Gamble executives were soon successful. In Pittsburgh, the local Breakfast Cheer Coffee Company sold out. A company official lamented, "We were raped." In Syracuse, New York, the profits of the regional Paul de Lima Coffee Company declined 80 percent in three years, and the small enterprise went out of business. In the short term, Procter and Gamble lost approximately sixty million dollars promoting Folger's. In the long run, the company joined General Mills in controlling over 60 percent of the U.S. coffee market by 1980.[15]

Such market control exists today in virtually every aspect of American agriculture. By the 1970s the four largest tractor companies controlled 83 percent of the market; two hybrid seed companies controlled over half of all sales; eight nitrogen fertilizer manufacturers produced almost half of all farm fertilizers; the four leading farming supply firms controlled 67 percent of petroleum products, 71 percent of tires, and 74 percent of chemicals. Through such domination, these companies have enormous leverage over the prices farmers pay for supplies. In 1972 alone, the U.S. Trade Commission estimated that the tractor industry was guilty of overcharging farmers by $251 million and that the feed supply industry had overcharged by over $200 million. During the agriculturally depressed years of the 1980s, as farmers were driven to increasing debt and forfeiture by low prices, R.J. Reynolds averaged a 22.8-percent return on equity.[16]

In Kentucky, more than half of the state's eighty-three thousand tobacco growers received less than fifteen thousand dollars for their crop annually by the mid-1980s. Gross income from tobacco fell almost $450 million from 1984 to 1986. Although the New Deal introduced tobacco price support systems in 1933, the economic position of tobacco growers has subsequently not been enhanced. This system was designed to maintain prices for growers at rates above the cost of production. The benefits of such a program, however, have been received in far greater proportion by absentee owners of large farms than by farmers on small family farms. Many smaller tobacco growers hold second jobs in order to pay their bills. No doubt the increasing awareness of the harmful effects of smoking tobacco has done a great deal to damage local farm communities dedicated to the cultivation of tobacco. Yet during the 1980s, as smoking decreased and farm prices fell, tobacco companies thrived.[17]

American agriculture consequently finds the farmer in a financial squeeze. With competition for farm inputs, such as seed and fertilizer, significantly constrained, farmers pay inflated prices for supplies under an oligopolistic market condition. On the other hand, purchasers of farm outputs, those products produced by the farmers themselves for sale, lack significant competition and effectively determine the prices paid to producers (a condition known as oligopsony). While the total number of current food manufacturing companies exceeds thirty-two thousand, a mere twenty-four food giants account for nearly 57 percent of sales. Consequently, input prices overtake output prices, squeezing the ability of small-scale farmers to survive. While the prices farmers paid for inputs increased 52 percent from 1951 to 1971, the prices they received for their products rose only 8 percent. In 1977 farmers received only eight billion dollars in net income from a total market value of farm products of ninety-six billion.[18] The situation at the turn of the century remains the case today: staggering profits are earned from agriculture, yet the producers of this wealth are left with usually meager returns and mounting debts.

The social consequences of agribusiness are harder to analyze and cannot easily be discerned through numbers or charts. As more and more independent farmers are driven from the land, what is actually lost in social terms? Is the decline of the family farm in America to be pitied only in a nostalgic sense? The only detailed analysis of the impact of corporate agriculture upon social relationships was conducted in the 1940s by anthropologist Walter Goldschmidt. Employed by the Bureau of Agricultural Economics of the U.S. Department of Agriculture, Goldschmidt selected two California towns that were similar in basic economic factors with one exception—farm size. While Arvin had concentrated, large farms using mostly tenants and seasonal labor, Dinuba was selected for its independent small farms. Goldschmidt found that the small farms supported about 20 percent more people at a measurably higher standard of living; the small farm community had improved community facilities, had more schools, parks, and newspapers, and conducted 61 percent more retail business; and "the small farm community had more institutions for democratic decision making and a much broader participation in such activities by its citizenry." Goldschmidt's study was not published by the USDA, and he was ordered to stop further investigations. In 1977 researchers revisited Arvin and Dinuba and found that Goldschmidt's contrasts had appreciably widened. In 1945 the median family income in the small farm community was 12 percent greater than in the area with large farms; by 1975 the difference had increased to 28 percent. It is apparent that with the disappearance of small farm communities throughout America, the chance, in Goldschmidt's words, for a "healthier rural community" is also irretrievably lost.[19]

The reality of modern agriculture consequently does not blend well with a notion widely shared by many Americans: any hard-working entrepreneur with intelligence and tenacity can survive and prosper in the American economy. This belief is rooted in fundamental assumptions about the free market: that markets are ruled by the ironclad law of supply and demand and that those who produce goods held in constant demand by society will therefore profit from these favorable market conditions. In this rather straightforward equation exist America's agricultural producers, who have been historically mired in debt and poverty.

One answer often provided by scholars searching for clues about the nature of agricultural poverty seems to account for most of these conflicting ideas. The root cause of farm poverty, it is reasoned, is a simple reaction of the mechanisms of the free market. Farmers overproduce for a given market, or in other words, supply outruns demand, thus resulting in low prices for agricutural producers. To the farmers involved in the Tobacco Wars, however, the prices offered them had little to do with crop production. Instead, through the ATC's control of the entire industry, the trust simply dictated the prices farmers received. Even in the early 1900s the PPA's Joel Fort knew the power the overproduction thesis held in dismissing the claims of the agrarian poor. Fort said that with the consolidation of the ATC, "the old rule of supply and demand was thrown overboard so that the ship of finance might sail more easily into the port of ill-gotten wealth." He added that the "'song' of overproduction lulled interested observers into 'insensibility'" of the true nature of the tobacco market, while the trust "skillfully plundered the country." Despite Fort's purple prose, it is hard to argue with his conclusion.[20]

Our subsequent "insensibility" to the nature of agricultural poverty has been expanded to include farmers of all types. This tenet has filtered into some of the major works on American farming and farm movements. In the Pulitzer Prize-winning *Age of Reform*, Richard Hofstadter determined that the major flaw of the Farmers' Alliance was its inability to recognize the true problem of agriculture: the market "was oversupplied with agricultural products, that costs, inefficiency, and wastes in distribution and marketing were at the heart of the farm problem." This hoary argument, inappropriate and even innocently romantic, continues to dominate scholarly discourse down to the present day. Writing in 1988, an agricultural historian concluded that all post-Civil War agrarian movements failed to address "the basic problem of surplus reduction" produced by overproduction.[21]

Supporters of this explanation point to controlling production as the best means of raising farm prices over the long term. Gilbert C. Fite stated that the fundamental problem in Gilded Age farming was that "farmers often grew more than the market could absorb at prices profitable to producers. Widely scattered and independent, farmers could not get together to regulate production and avoid price-depressing surpluses."[22] Simply put, if supply is curtailed in some fashion, then prices will automatically rise.

A laboratory for testing this hypothesis was offered in the BTS strike of 1908. The supply of one crop was restricted to an unprecedented degree never since approached. The eventual successful conclusion of the strike lends credence to the overproduction thesis. After all, because of low supplies of burley tobacco, the ATC eventually relented. But the quick demise of the cooperative organization itself revealed the organic weakness in the farmers' attempt to combat low prices merely by restricting supply. More fundamental problems, far transcending production controls, existed for burley growers, as they did for all farmers.

At the root of the failure of the Tobacco Wars is an age-old problem that has dogged agriculturalists in virtually every society—credit. Unlike many other members of the economy, farmers must rely on credit from the time their crops are planted until they are harvested. Because of this controlling economic imperative, agricultural producers have been systematically exploited by creditors. Farmers have always known this, and indeed, this knowledge has been at the heart of every major agrarian insurgency in American history. As evidenced in the 1908 strike and the efforts of the PPA, crop-withholding attempts inflicted greater harm on smallholders and tenants than on large landowners. The smaller growers required much more than production controls to alleviate their seasonal indebtedness. Since the insurgent efforts that characterized the Tobacco Wars involved nothing more than crop-withholding and other "marketing reforms," the structural problem of credit, which produced the economic rules that forced farmers in Kentucky and Tennessee to rely on the cash crop of tobacco in the first place, remained untouched. Quite simply, the casual explanation of overproduction is evidentially thin when considered within the proper context of seasonal indebtedness.

Another time-honored approach in explaining the persistence of agrarian poverty has been to dismiss farmers as lazy and lethargic—in a sense, deserving of their plight because of their own lack of effort.[23] The irony is that this stereotype is often inverted: farmers are also blamed for their own poverty because of their enormous productive capacity, which, parenthetically, results in overproduction.[24] Haunted by a dual personality, "lazy" farmers produce too much for their own good. Similarly, while farmers are perceived as hard-working and embattled, they are also bloodsucking beneficiaries of government subsidies. Lastly, despite the examples afforded by the Farmers' Alliance and other remarkable episodes such as the 1908 strike, academics have conferred on farmers a certain "individualism," which serves to preclude the likelihood of sustained cooperative organization. Thus the lack of meaningful long-term agrarian organizing is explained by yet another organic weakness common only to farmers. Such inconsistent stereotypes serve to deflect critical inquiries into structural economic forces by focusing, instead, on perceived weaknesses with the farmers themselves.[25]

Most people of rural America, we are admonished, have never quite understood the vast and complex market forces under which they have operated. Agricultural experts, often employed by government agencies or agricultural colleges to serve the needs of agribusiness, insist that farmers have simply not been "efficient" producers. Consequently, they assert, the purge of smallholders is nothing more than a market reaction to those who cannot adequately compete.[26] When one thousand Kentucky dairy farms went out of business in 1973, agricultural specialist Dr. John Nicolai of the University of Kentucky remarked that they were simply "inefficient producers" and "needed" to be eliminated. This ethos was once summarized by President Eisenhower's secretary of agriculture Ezra Taft Benson. Benson once placed himself in the position of farmers who were "losing their homes, equipment, and life savings." "If I were in that condition," said Benson, "I would check closely to see if I was operating as efficiently as possible." If this proved no answer, Benson advised: "I would attempt to supplement my income through outside work." Large-scale farms are thus perceived as a product of efficient and scientific management techniques brought to agriculture. It is evident from farm statistics that somebody on the land has indeed gotten more productive: though the farm population decreased by seven million from 1950 to 1971, agricultural output increased by 52 percent. Between 1950 and 1960 cotton production alone increased 60 percent, while corn production rose 58 percent.[27]

Yet greater production in raw numbers and efficiency are not necessarily the same thing. The underlying agricultural reality is far different: when costs are accurately considered, small-scale farms actually produce greater yields per acre. As a leading authority has noted, "the smaller, full-time farmer *must* be efficient or they would not survive, while large farmers can afford to be and indeed often are inefficient." In 1973 the U.S. Department of Agriculture itself concluded that "everyone assumes that large-scale undertakings are inherently more efficient than smaller ones. In fact, the claim of efficiency is commonly used to justify bigness. But when we examine the realities we find that most of the economies associated with size in farming are achieved by the one-man fully mechanized farm."[28]

Studies in other countries have reached the same conclusion: in India, the output per acre is highest on the smallest farms; in Thailand, plots of 2 to 4 acres produce almost 60 percent more rice per acre than farms of 140 acres or more. As Frances Moore Lappé and Joseph Collins noted, smallholders and peasants take care to get the most from their allotted land "precisely because they need to survive on the meager resources allowed to them." Small farms are thus more efficient, yet ultimately less profitable, than large farms, which produce higher volumes and benefit from government subsidies, tax breaks, easier access to credit, and bulk purchasing of supplies. In short, modern American agriculture has substituted mass production for genuine efficiency.[29]

Considering what tobacco farmers confronted in the early 1900s—tight monetary conditions, an unresponsive political structure, and the massive reserves of the tobacco trust—the final outcome is not surprising. Although the odds were remote, farmers in Kentucky and Tennessee resisted nonetheless. Their crushing defeat was repeated, in various ways, all across the American countryside, as millions of rural citizens were driven from the land by agribusiness. The scorched-earth methods of the new industrial order quickly replaced traditional republican concerns about the independence of the smallholder with a disdain for certain values embedded in the agrarian heritage. As such, the events surrounding the Tobacco Wars served as a warning of more ominous things to come.

Appendix

A sequential listing of night-rider activity in Kentucky and Tennessee, along with a few outbreaks in Indiana, Ohio, and West Virginia, from 1905 to 1915 follows. In addition to providing dates, names of victims, and locations, the list categorizes the activities by type: destroying plant beds, burning tobacco barns, whipping or shooting individuals, burning houses, destroying factories or warehouses, and acting in other ways that did not necessarily involve tobacco. In compiling this list of acts of vigilantism, I consulted newspapers such as the Clarksville *Leaf-Chronicle*, the *Western Tobacco Journal*, the Louisville *Courier-Journal*, the Lexington *Herald*, and numerous other smaller papers. A microfilm located at the Kentucky Department for Libraries and Archives, Frankfort, titled "Night Riders" also proved helpful, as did material in the Augustus Everett Willson Papers at the Filson Club, Louisville. To supplement these sources, I also used accounts of night-rider activity by Charles Mayfield Meacham and James O. Nall: Meacham, *A History of Christian County, Kentucky: From Oxcart to Airplane* (Nashville, 1930); and Nall, *The Tobacco Night Riders of Kentucky and Tennessee, 1905-1909* (Louisville, 1939). Though written threats certainly constitute a form of coercion, only overtly violent activities are included in this list. Finally, considering the secretive nature of night riding, it is certain that many acts did not reach available written sources. In this appendix I do not purport to offer a complete list of vigilantism in the Tobacco Wars.

PB	Plant bed destroyed	H	House burned
B	Barn burned	F/W	Factory/warehouse destroyed
W/S	Whippings/shootings	O	Other

1905

12/8	James and B.D. Mason	Daviess Co., Ky.	W/S
12/9	Chestnut, Joseph Russell	Todd Co., Ky.	F/W
12/11	L&N Railroad	Todd Co., Ky.	O
12/12	Mrs. M.B. Penick	Todd Co., Ky.	F/W
12/18	J.W. Scott	Logan Co., Ky.	W/S

PB	Plant bed destroyed	H	House burned
B	Barn burned	F/W	Factory/warehouse destroyed
W/S	Whippings/shootings	O	Other

1906

5/7	J.T. Garnett	Christian Co., Ky.	PB
5/9	A.T. Tilley	Robertson Co., Tenn.	PB
5/12	Owen Davis	Montgomery Co., Tenn.	PB
5/14	J. and T. Ferguson	Montgomery Co., Tenn.	PB
5/14	R.L. Miles	Logan Co., Ky.	PB
5/16	Joe Rosson	Montgomery Co., Tenn.	PB
5/21	W.H. Jeries	Montgomery Co., Tenn.	PB
5/23	L.L. Leavell	Christian Co., Ky.	PB
5/24	Tom Munford	—	PB
6/?	American Snuff Co.	Lyon Co., Ky.	F/W
11/11	Bradshaw Co.	Lyon Co., Ky.	F/W
11/11	Rice Bros.	Caldwell Co., Ky.	F/W
12/1	J.T. Steger	Caldwell Co., Ky.	F/W
12/1	J.G. Orr	Caldwell Co., Ky.	F/W
12/4	James Wilson	Daviess Co., Ky.	B

1907

1/22	W.H. Steger	Caldwell Co., Ky.	B
2/13	H.C. Wallis	Lyon Co., Ky.	B
2/20	—	Caldwell Co., Ky.	B
2/28	H.C. Wallis	Caldwell Co., Ky.	O
3/1	S.M. Holland, W. Wallace	Trigg Co., Ky.	PB
3/4	American Snuff Co.	Caldwell Co., Ky.	O
3/21	John T. Young	Logan Co., Ky.	B
3/22	Tenants of W.P. Cox and W.R. Fourqueen	Christian Co., Ky.	PB
3/26	C. Rogers, J. Woods, and J. McGowan	Caldwell Co., Ky.	PB
3/28	H.C. Wallis	Lyon Co., Ky.	FB
3/30	W. Barefield	Christian Co., Ky.	FB
3/?	—	Trigg Co., Ky.	O
4/9	J. Beshears, M. Thomas	Caldwell Co., Ky.	PB
4/11	Guy S. Dunning	Trigg Co., Ky.	O
4/11	J.C. Thurmond	Christian Co., Ky.	PB
4/17	W.R. Witson	Trigg Co., Ky.	F/W
4/20	H. Hammock, B. Dossett	Christian Co., Ky.	PB

4/23	Wilson Whs.	Trigg Co., Ky.	F/W
4/24	R.W. Bogard	Trigg Co., Ky.	F/W
4/30	Robert Hollowell	Caldwell Co., Ky.	PB, W/S
4/?	B. Foster, G. Dulin, and W. Garnett	Christian Co., Ky.	PB
4/?	S.P. Moseley	Trigg Co., Ky.	PB
5/2	George Swift	Caldwell Co., Ky.	W/S
5/3	Walter Gray	Stewart Co., Tenn.	PB
5/11	W.A. Shirley	Gallatin Co., Ky.	B
5/14	Alex & Lem Thompson	Carroll Co., Ky.	PB
5/15	Arch Ball	Lyon Co., Ky.	W/S
5/17	Edgar Wimpey	Robertson Co., Tenn.	PB
5/18	C. Dowden	Montgomery Co., Tenn.	PB
5/18	Henry Winters	Robertson Co., Tenn.	PB
5/20	Ben Hollins	—	PB
5/20	W.E. Wall, Frank Brown	Caldwell Co., Ky.	PB
5/21	J.D. Taylor	Montgomery Co., Tenn.	PB
5/23	J.B. McCowan	Christian Co., Ky.	PB
5/24	Cullen Atkins	Montgomery Co., Tenn.	PB
5/25	Elias & Ike Shelby	Jordan Springs, Tenn.	PB
5/28	Noble Robinson	Caldwell Co., Ky.	PB
5/29	F.B. McCowan	Christian Co., Ky.	PB
5/?	John M. Rice	—	PB
5/?	Six Sharecroppers of A.M. Henry	Christian Co., Ky.	PB
5/?	—	Christian Co., Ky.	O
6/1	M. Cloyis	Graves Co., Ky.	PB
6/1	M. Dowdy	Graves Co., Ky.	PB
6/1	T.A. Haynes	Montgomery Co., Tenn.	PB
6/1	J.C. Shelton	Graves Co., Ky.	PB
6/5	Mrs. J. Woosley	Christian Co., Ky.	PB
6/6	H.C. Merritt	Todd Co., Ky.	PB
6/12	Gordie Hover	Hopkins Co., Ky.	PB
6/18	Edward Hall	Caldwell Co., Ky.	W/S
6/19	Black tenants of D.W. Wynn	Montgomery Co., Tenn.	W/S
7/1	Harvey Collier	Montgomery Co., Tenn.	PB
7/9	R.D. Fort	Christian Co., Ky.	B
7/9	—	Christian Co., Ky.	O
7/13	Ben Miller	Todd Co., Ky.	B
7/15	J.W. Barefield	Trigg Co., Ky.	W/S
7/15	G.N. Gentry	Montgomery Co., Tenn.	PB
7/17	Thomas Mences	Robertson Co., Tenn.	O
7/18	John Fields	Christian Co., Ky.	O

PB	Plant bed destroyed	H	House burned
B	Barn burned	F/W	Factory/warehouse destroyed
W/S	Whippings/shootings	O	Other

7/18	Royster	Christian Co., Ky.	O
7/23	S.P. Moseley	Trigg Co., Ky.	W/S
7/27	Med Ogburn	Montgomery Co., Tenn.	PB
7/?	Nathan Hester	Trigg Co., Ky.	W/S
8/2	G.B. Pearce	Henry Co., Ky.	B
8/5	John Lockert	—	W/S
8/5	Otis Wilson	Todd Co., Ky.	PB, W/S
8/14	W.E. Wall	Caldwell Co., Ky.	H
8/19	Mrs. E. Nicholson	Montgomery Co., Tenn.	PB
8/23	Johnson-Hendrick Hotel	Trigg Co., Ky.	W/S
9/8	W.J. Ladd, J.M. Crow	Christian Co., Ky.	W/S
10/9	John Harker	Montgomery Co., Tenn.	B
10/9	—	Hopkins Co., Ky.	B
10/26	H.B. Williams	Caldwell Co., Ky.	W/S
10/?	William Green	Daviess Co., Ky.	B
11/5	M. Hendrix	Christian Co., Ky.	H
11/13	—	Graves Co., Ky.	W/S
11/14	John Wicks	Montgomery Co., Tenn.	W/S
11/18	Berry Wallace	Stewart Co., Tenn.	W/S
11/19	W.E. Wall	Caldwell Co., Ky.	H
11/22	Rev. J.A. Lee	McLean Co., Ky.	B
11/22	Frank McGary	Breckinridge Co., Ky.	B
11/22	John Melton	Stewart Co., Tenn.	W/S
11/29	D. Beheimer	Pendleton Co., Ky.	W/S
12/4	W.S. Henderson	Bracken Co., Ky.	W/S
12/6	Clarence Wilson	Trigg Co., Ky.	B
12/7	Hopkinsville citizens	Christian Co., Ky.	W/S, O
12/8	Pearl Wilhoit	Owen Co., Ky.	O
12/15	William Gray	Trigg Co., Ky.	W/S
12/?	Peter Daniels	Campbell Co., Ky.	B
12/?	Mrs. E. Owens	Mason Co., Ky.	O
12/?	—	Bracken Co., Ky.	W/S
12/?	—	Christian Co., Ky.	W/S
12/?	—	Robertson Co., Tenn.	O

1908

| 1/1 | Johnson-Hendrick Store | Trigg Co., Ky. | O |
| 1/3 | Luckett-Wake American Snuff Co. | Logan Co., Ky. | F/W |

1/7	General store	Bath Co., Ky.	O
1/7	Warehouse	Fleming Co., Ky.	F/W
1/13	Enos Dixon	Boone Co., Ky.	H
1/15	William Wright	Butler Co., Ohio	F/W
1/20	Black sharecroppers	Christian Co., Ky.	PB
1/21	J.D. Coleman	Montgomery Co., Tenn.	B
1/25	Arcadia Hotel	Hopkins Co., Ky.	W/S
1/25	—	Caldwell Co., Ky.	W/S
1/27	Press Rodgers	Christian Co., Ky.	W/S
1/29	Jesse Burr	Logan Co., Ky.	B
1/30	J. McDaniel	Montgomery Co., Ky.	B
1/30	W.E. Wall	Montgomery Co., Tenn.	B
1/31	Lige Nichols	Caldwell Co., Ky.	B
1/?	Harp Menser	Hopkins Co., Ky.	W/S
2/1	—	Caldwell Co., Ky.	H
2/3	Pat Chapman	McCracken Co., Ky.	B
2/3	Jack Crawford	Graves Co., Ky.	B
2/4	Henry Bennett	Crittenden Co., Ky.	W/S
2/7	Wash Fletcher	Robertson Co., Tenn.	B
2/7	Neal Lawrence	Robertson Co., Tenn.	B
2/7	Monroe Lowe	Robertson Co., Tenn.	W/S
2/7	—	Caldwell Co., Ky.	H
2/10	A. Cardin Co.	Crittenden Co., Ky.	F/W
2/14	Jake Bagwell	Montgomery Co., Tenn.	B
2/16	Judge Crumbaugh and nine others	Lyon Co., Ky.	W/S
2/16	Twelve farmers	Lyon Co., Ky.	W/S
2/18	V. McKinney	Christian Co., Ky.	PB
2/19	Detective Marshall	Christian Co., Ky.	W/S
2/19	—	Christian Co., Ky.	W/S
2/22	George Butler	Christian Co., Ky.	W/S
2/24	A.W. Merritt	McCracken Co., Ky.	O
2/27	Head & Switzer	Franklin Co., Ky.	F/W
2/27	—	Christian Co., Ky.	B
2/29	Brandon Hurt	Graves Co., Ky.	B
2/?	C. Bravard	Bracken Co., Ky.	PB
2/?	B.A. Gregory	Christian Co., Ky.	H
2/?	D.S. Hendricks	Calloway Co., Ky.	PB
2/?	Lawrence & Vickers	Robertson Co., Tenn.	PB, W/S
2/?	S.W. McKibbon	Bracken Co., Ky.	B
2/?	Lucien Means	Christian Co., Ky.	W/S
3/2	William Rock	McCracken Co., Ky.	W/S
3/4	C.C. Shemwell	Todd Co., Ky.	B
3/4	W. Smithers, W. Wyatt	Robertson Co., Tenn.	PB

PB	Plant bed destroyed	H	House burned
B	Barn burned	F/W	Factory/warehouse destroyed
W/S	Whippings/shootings	O	Other

3/7	John Hull	Bracken Co., Ky.	B
3/7	John Langford	Montgomery Co., Tenn.	O
3/8	John Scruggs	Marshall Co., Ky.	W/S
3/10	James Welch	Montgomery Co., Tenn.	W/S
3/10	TOB Warehouse	Bracken Co., Ky.	F/W
3/11	John Garvey	Owen Co., Ky.	F/W
3/11	Wayne McGahee	Weakley Co., Tenn.	W/S
3/11	Dave Snell	Owen Co., Ky.	F/W
3/11	Robert Stanton	Bracken Co., Ky.	B, W/S
3/13	John Walsh	Montgomery Co., Tenn.	W/S
3/14	G. Graddy, J. Harris	Woodford Co., Ky.	B
3/14	E. Pepper	Scott Co., Ky.	B
3/15	Milton McLain	Mason Co., Ky.	B
3/16	George Strange	Woodford Co., Ky.	B
3/18	Henry Christian	Ballard Co., Ky.	W/S
3/21	Hiram Hedges	Nicholas Co., Ky.	W/S
3/23	Tom Weaver	Trigg Co., Ky.	W/S
3/25	Claude Thomas	Hamilton Co., Ohio	B
3/25	Three Warehouses	Owen Co., Ky.	F/W
3/27	Matson & Prague	Kenton Co., Ky.	F/W
3/27	T.S. Hamilton Co.	Kenton Co., Ky.	F/W
3/30	Steve Whitfield	Marshall Co., Ky.	W/S
3/?	J.B. Carpenter, G.H. Vaughn	Christian Co., Ky.	PB
3/?	Henry Ellis	Shelby Co., Ky.	H
3/?	B.F. Longnecker, B.F. Clift	Mason Co., Ky.	PB
3/?	E.S. Montgomery	Robertson Co., Ky.	W/S
3/?	Thomas Mullins	Carlisle Co., Ky.	O
3/?	J.W. Osborn	Mason Co., Ky.	B,H
3/?	M. Plummer, G. Kelley	Fleming Co., Ky.	PB
3/?	Richard Spann	McCracken Co., Ky.	H
3/?	Eddyville citizens	Lyon Co., Ky.	W/S
3/?	Shepherdsville citizens	Bullitt Co., Ky.	W/S
3/?	Black tenants	Gibson Co., Tenn.	W/S
4/1	R.M. Squires	Fayette Co., Ky.	O
4/6	Henry Forsee	Franklin Co., Ky.	B
4/8	R.E. Statton	Bracken Co., Ky.	B, W/S
4/14	Joe Lilliard	Grant Co., Ky.	O
4/16	Jacob Hardin	Daviess Co., Ky.	PB

4/16	W.E. Whiteley, Thomas French	Daviess Co., Ky.	PB
4/17	George Haley	Harrison Co., Ky.	W/S
4/21	C. Nanney, T. Crews, J. Huddleston	Graves Co., Ky.	PB
4/22	Alvin West	Bracken Co., Ky.	F/W
4/25	R. Watersfield	Brown Co., Ohio	B
4/29	J. Yancey	Mason Co., Ky.	B
5/4	F.M. Crawford	Bracken Co., Ky.	O
5/4	Nelson Cummins	Bracken Co., Ky.	W/S
5/4	H. Gross, G. Gross, L. Kinney	Bracken Co., Ky.	W/S
5/4	John Sanders	Bracken Co., Ky.	W/S
5/4	W.E. Wall	Caldwell Co., Ky.	B
5/5	Ashby Robinson	Mercer Co., Ky.	W/S
5/7	Barney Harburn	Butler Co., Ohio	B
5/7	—	Brown Co., Ohio	PB
5/11	William Shell	Adams Co., Ohio	B
5/12	H. Allen, B. Hunt, C. Jackson	Montgomery Co., Tenn.	PB
5/14	Thomas Cahill	Brown Co., Ohio	PB
5/17	Twenty-eight farmers	Henry Co., Ky.	PB
5/18	J. Bishop	Stewart Co., Tenn.	PB
5/18	H.G. Maddox	Ballard Co., Ky.	B
5/19	R.J. Stone	Cheatham Co., Tenn.	B
5/20	J.R. Stone	Fleming Co., Ky.	B
5/20	James Turner	Montgomery Co., Tenn.	B
5/26	C.F. Egbert	Hopkins Co., Ky.	PB
5/28	R. Smith, O. Adams, E. Sullivan	Boone Co., Ky.	PB
5/29	Irvin Beard	Houston Co., Tenn.	PB
5/30	Thomas Houser	McCracken Co., Ky.	PB
5/31	Palmer & Hazelle	Calloway Co., Ky.	F/W
5/31	J.W. Scott	Logan Co., Ky.	O
6/3	W.W. Baldwin	Mason Co., Ky.	PB
6/3	·Palmer & Bros.	Calloway Co., Ky.	F/W
6/3	John Warner	Henry Co., Ky.	B
6/4	Norval Johns	Brown Co., Ohio	PB
6/5	Edmund Martin	Brown Co., Ohio	O
6/9	Ruef Hunter	Montgomery Co., Ky.	W/S
6/9	J. Phelps, D. Florence	Fayette Co., Ky.	PB
6/10	T. Alexander, I.T. Spilman	Trimble Co., Ky.	PB
6/11	—	Red Oak, Ohio	W/S
6/13	George Strauss	Clark Co., Ky.	PB

PB	Plant bed destroyed	H	House burned
B	Barn burned	F/W	Factory/warehouse destroyed
W/S	Whippings/shootings	O	Other

6/29	Alf Fielder	Montgomery Co., Tenn.	W/S
6/?	Henry Downing	Brown Co., Ohio	PB
7/21	Samuel Ridgon	Mason Co., Ky.	W/S
7/23	Buddy Nickle	—	W/S
7/26	F. Mardis, W. Dyer	Calloway Co., Ky.	W/S
7/26	William Rice	Mason Co., Ky.	O
7/26	G. Turner, J. Riner	Henry Co., Ky.	B
7/28	Walter Goodwin	Trigg Co., Ky.	W/S
7/30	H. Risalger	Brown Co., Ohio	PB
7/30	F. Schatzman	Brown Co., Ohio	B
7/31	J. Browning	Pendleton Co., Ky.	B
7/?	L&N Railroad	Caldwell Co., Ky.	O
7/?	L&N Railroad	Christian Co., Ky.	O
7/?	L&N Railroad	Trigg Co., Ky.	O
8/14	Adam Weickbrock	Pendleton Co., Ky.	O
8/17	D. & S. Hendricks	Calloway Co., Ky.	B
8/17	Tobe Roberts	Calloway Co., Ky.	B
8/20	S. Webber	Harrison Co., Ky.	B
8/21	D. Skinner	McCracken Co., Ky.	B
8/23	Thomas Edwards	Montgomery Co., Tenn.	O
8/24	Walter Galloway	Bracken Co., Ky.	B, W/S
8/31	A.Q. Knight Co.	Calloway Co., Ky.	O
9/15	Pete Knox	Rutherford Co., Tenn.	W/S
9/17	J.W. Shaw	Obion Co., Tenn.	W/S
9/25	Hayes-Sory Whs.	Robertson Co., Tenn.	F/W
10/3	David Walker, Children	Trigg Co., Ky.	W/S
10/23	Edward Loos	Butler Co., Ohio	B
11/23	—	Obion Co., Tenn.	W/S
11/26	R.D. Liddle	Dearborn Co., Ind.	B
11/27	Baker Bros.	Humphreys Co., Tenn.	W/S
11/27	John Walker	Daniels Landing, Tenn.	W/S
12/2	W.H. Gosner	Vanderburgh Co., Ind.	B
12/10	Drew Farrell	Montgomery Co., Tenn.	B
12/23	J. McDonald	Lyon Co., Ky.	B
12/29	M. Owen	Calloway Co., Ky.	B

1909

| 3/17 | Nin Long, J.T. Walker | Christian Co., Ky. | PB |
| 3/26 | J.W. Welbourne | Todd Co., Ky. | F/W |

4/1	C.C. Bell	Robertson Co., Tenn.	F/W
4/6	T.A. Napier	Allen Co., Ky.	PB
4/9	Gentry Miller	Calloway Co., Ky.	B
4/9	Clarence Penny	Calloway Co., Ky.	PB
4/10	O.J. Wood	McCracken Co., Ky.	F/W
4/12	Lewis & Gordon, American Snuff Co.	Graves Co., Ky.	F/W
4/13	J.F. Van Hooser	Christian Co., Ky.	PB
4/16	J.J. Morrow, Alex Week	Blooming Grove, Tenn.	PB
5/14	Seven farmers	Crittenden Co., Ky.	PB
5/18	W.J. Powell	Montgomery Co., Tenn.	PB
5/24	R. Broaddus	Stewart Co., Tenn.	PB
5/26	Sallie Catlett	Lyon Co., Ky.	PB
5/27	L. Phelps, E. Donohew	Bath Co., Ky.	PB
5/27	Denny Washburn	Harrison Co., Ky.	PB
6/3	W.H. Meaks	Fayette Co., Ky.	W/S
6/14	B.C. Wren	Montgomery Co., Tenn.	B
7/23	W.H. Pepper	Bracken Co., Ky.	O
7/24	W. Farris, S. Gross	Edmonson Co., Ky.	W/S
7/29	Obe Clinton	Cheatham Co., Tenn.	O
8/11	Harlan Minton	Edmonson Co., Ky.	W/S
8/23	J. Struve	Bracken Co., Ky.	B
9/30	Tenants of T.J. McDowell	Pendleton Co., Ky.	W/S
10/8	Ed Johnson	Bracken Co., Ky.	B
10/11	J.W. Barnett	Bath Co., Ky.	B
10/11	Theodore Marshall	Scott Co., Ky.	B
10/12	James Deven	Mason Co., Ky.	W/S
10/26	Everett Blake	Cabell Co., W.Va.	B
10/27	Ben Longnecker	Mason Co., Ky.	W/S
10/28	Stephen Eubank	Adams Co., Ohio	B
10/29	George Kreitz	Mason Co., Ky.	W/S
11/2	E.S. Montgomery	Robertson Co., Ky.	W/S
11/6	Thomas Stafford	Jessamine Co., Ky.	B
12/7	Edward Judy	Harrison Co., Ky.	W/S
12/23	Edward Nichols	Spencer Co., Ind.	B

1910

1/30	BTS headquarters	Fayette Co., Ky.	O
3/29	Bonnie Wright	McCracken Co., Ky.	H
4/16	James Woodruff	Clermont Co., Ohio	B
4/23	Danville citizens	Boyle Co., Ky.	O
5/4	George McKibbon	Bracken Co., Ky.	B

PB	Plant bed destroyed	H	House burned
B	Barn burned	F/W	Factory/warehouse destroyed
W/S	Whippings/shootings	O	Other

6/10	Juies Robinson	Caldwell Co., Ky.	W/S
8/1	Axel Cooper	Lyon Co., Ky.	W/S
8/15	M. Buchanan	Barren Co., Ky.	O
9/1	W.D. Elliott	Christian Co., Ky.	B
9/16	W.O. Bradford, G. Kinney	Bracken Co., Ky.	B
10/1	Arris Wiggins	Nicholas Co., Ky.	O

1911

3/13	Robert Haviland	Harrison Co., Ky.	PB
3/17	John Ayler	Calloway Co., Ky.	B
3/18	W.M. Tye	Knox Co., Ky.	B
3/20	J.C. Kellar	Bourbon Co., Ky.	B
4/27	George Meador	Meade Co., Ky.	B
12/11	—	Crittenden Co., Ky.	F/W

1912

1/2	Arthur Jarvis	Crittenden Co., Ky.	F/W
1/28	Gus Evans, W. Davis	Christian Co., Ky.	W/S
5/14	Fifteen farmers	McCracken Co., Ky.	PB
9/23	Bev Reynolds	Christian Co., Ky.	W/S

1913

4/15	George Drury	Union Co., Ky.	PB
4/15	—	Caldwell Co., Ky.	PB
4/18	John Hudson	Henderson Co., Ky.	PB
8/8	L. Hartsfield	Henry Co., Tenn.	PB

1914

| 7/1 | A.W. Sexton | Stewart Co., Tenn. | W/S |
| 11/17 | Henry Allen | Muhlenberg Co., Ky. | W/S |

1915

1/7	James Smithson	Christian Co., Ky.	B
1/14	P. Mohundro	McCracken Co., Ky.	W/S
1/18	William Rose	Christian Co., Ky.	W/S
3/15	—	Ballard Co., Ky.	W/S
3/25	Wash Davis	Stewart Co., Tenn.	B

Notes

Introduction

1. *Appeal to Reason*, Oct. 1, 1910.
2. For example, Theodore Saloutos and John D. Hicks, strongly influenced by the writings of Frederick Jackson Turner, offered the explanation of the "excessive individualism" of the American farmer to account for the apparent decline of sustained organizational forms after the 1890s. In their equation, each farm "was in itself a little frontier," and the "task of organizing the farmers in their own defense was formidable in the extreme." Saloutos and Hicks, *Twentieth-Century Populism: Agricultural Discontent in the Middle West, 1900-1939* (Lincoln: Univ. of Nebraska Press, 1951), 111-12. Gilbert C. Fite explicitly states the farmers' "basic problem": "They simply lacked the organization and bargaining power enjoyed by business and labor." Since farmers are "individualistic by nature, widely scattered physically, busy with their work, and [have] different economic interests," they have been unable to assert the power enjoyed by organized labor. Fite, *American Farmers: The New Minority* (Bloomington: Indiana Univ. Press, 1981), 16, 154.
3. The oft-quoted phrase is taken from Karl Marx, *The Communist Manifesto* (New York: Penguin Books, 1979), 84. Marx enlarged his comments in *The Eighteenth Brumaire of Louis Bonaparte*, where he noted that peasants "live in similar conditions but without entering into manifold relations with one another. Their mode of production isolates them from one another instead of bringing them into mutual intercourse." Because of this isolation, Marx concluded, "the identity of their interests begets no community, no national bond, and no political organization among them. . . . they are consequently incapable of enforcing their class interests in their own name." Marx, *Selected Works* (Moscow: Progress Publishers, 1977), 478-79.

Chapter 1. A Legacy of Peonage

1. Robert P. Sharkey, *Money, Class, and Party: An Economic Study of Civil War and Reconstruction* (Baltimore: Johns Hopkins Univ. Press, 1959), 15-55. For an excellent summary of post-war finances, see Walter T.K. Nugent, *The Money Question during Reconstruction* (New York: Norton, 1967), 65-92.
  In the early 1800s a similar return to the gold standard had sent farmers into poverty in rural England. A financial crisis was set in motion that culminated in the agricultural rebellion of 1830. See Eric Hobsbawm and George Rudé, *Captain Swing: A Social History of the Great English Agricultural Uprising of 1830* (1968; New York: Norton, 1975) 33.
2. A concise study of wartime economic conditions on both sides of the Mason-

Dixon line is James M. McPherson, *Battle Cry of Freedom: The Civil War Era* (New York: Oxford Univ. Press, 1988), 437-50.

3. Sharkey, *Money, Class, and Party*, 50-53, 100. For further discussion of the long-standing tradition of conservatives' relating the gold standard to religious principles, see William Greider, *Secrets of the Temple: How the Federal Reserve Runs the Country* (New York: Simon and Schuster, 1987), 230-31, 234-37, 240, 245, 420-23.

4. Nugent, *Money Question*, 17-20; Walter T.K. Nugent, *Money and American Society, 1865-1880* (New York: Free Press, 1968), 44-55; Irwin Unger, *The Greenback Era: A Social and Political History of American Finance, 1865-1879* (Princeton, N.J.: Princeton Univ. Press, 1964), 73-75; Sharkey, *Money, Class, and Party*, 42, 49, 63, 241; David Montgomery, *Beyond Equality: Labor and the Radical Republicans, 1862-1872* (New York: Alfred A. Knopf, 1967), 345-49; Eric Foner, *Reconstruction: America's Unfinished Revolution, 1863-1877* (New York: Harper and Row, 1988), 22-23; Greider, *Secrets of the Temple*, 245-46.

5. Roger L. Ransom and Richard Sutch, *One Kind of Freedom: The Economic Consequences of Emancipation* (Cambridge: Cambridge Univ. Press, 1977), 106-14. The twelve southern states were South Carolina, Georgia, Mississippi, Alabama, Arkansas, Florida, North Carolina, Tennessee, Texas, Virginia, West Virginia, and Louisiana. See Theodore Saloutos, *Farmer Movements in the South, 1865-1933* (1960; Lincoln: Univ. of Nebraska Press, 1967), 8-10; Lance E. Davis, "The Investment Market, 1870-1914: The Evolution of a National Market," *Journal of Economic History* 25 (Sept. 1965): 388-89; Bruce Palmer, *"Man over Money": The Southern Populist Critique of American Capitalism* (Chapel Hill: Univ. of North Carolina Press, 1980), 81-95; and George L. Anderson, "The South and Problems of Post-Civil War Finance," *Journal of Southern History* 9 (May 1943): 181-95.

6. Ransom and Sutch, *One Kind of Freedom*, 115-16. In their exhaustive study of southern rural banks, Ransom and Sutch conclude, "Our examination of the records on these rural bankers in the Dun and Bradstreet Archives provides no evidence that these individuals provided short-term credit to small farmers unable to offer land or other assets as collateral" (116).

7. Ransom and Sutch, *One Kind of Freedom*, 120-23. For other treatments of the rural furnishing merchant, see Thomas D. Clark, *Pills, Petticoats and Plows: The Southern Country Store* (1944; Norman: Univ. of Oklahoma Press, 1963); idem, "The Furnishing and Supply System in Southern Agriculture since 1865," *Journal of Southern History* 12 (Feb. 1946): 25-43; C. Vann Woodward, *Origins of the New South, 1877-1913* (Baton Rouge: Louisiana State Univ. Press, 1951), 180-84; and Edward L. Ayers, *The Promise of the New South: Life After Reconstruction* (New York: Oxford Univ. Press, 1992), 81-94.

8. Ransom and Sutch, *One Kind of Freedom*, 129-30. A contemporary examination of the southern credit system is D.D. Wallace, "Southern Agriculture: Its Condition and Needs," *Popular Science* (Jan. 1904): 245-48.

9. Ransom and Sutch, *One Kind of Freedom*, 129-37, 148, 237-43; Woodward, *Origins of the New South*, 183-85; Gilbert C. Fite, *Cotton Fields No More: Southern Agriculture, 1865-1980* (Lexington: Univ. Press of Kentucky, 1984), 21-24. Another study by an economist describes the postbellum southern banking system in much the same fashion that credit merchants were described by Ransom and Sutch. High southern interest rates imposed after the Civil War were "responsible for the local monopoly power which enabled southern banks to continue to exact high interest rates." John A. James, "Financial Underdevelopment in the Postbellum South," *Journal of Interdisciplinary History* II (Winter 1981): 445. For more sympathetic treatments of the furnishing mer-

chant, see J. Wayne Flynt, *Dixie's Forgotten People: The South's Poor Whites* (Bloomington: Indiana Univ. Press, 1979), 46; Thomas D. Clark and Albert D. Kirwan, *The South since Appomattox: A Century of Regional Change* (New York: Oxford Univ. Press, 1967), 60-61.

10. Tobacco Ledger, Martin and Johnson Mercantile Records, Special Collections, M.I. King Library, University of Kentucky; *The Mercantile Agency Reference Book, 1885* (New York: R.G. Dun Mercantile Agency, 1885); *The Mercantile Agency Reference Book, 1900* (New York: R.G. Dun Mercantile Agency, 1900). A listing of credit codes given in the reference books and their corresponding meanings is found in Ransom and Sutch, *One Kind of Freedom,* 307-8.

11. Tobacco Ledger, Martin and Johnson Mercantile Records; Woodward, *Origins of the New South,* 180-81; Roger L. Ransom and Richard Sutch, "The 'Lock-In' Mechanism and Overproduction of Cotton in the Postbellum South," *Agricultural History* 49 (April 1975): 405-25. The term *peonage* is applicable to the southern agricultural economy after the Civil War since cotton and tobacco farmers were often compelled to raise the cash crops to suit the economic interests of their creditors. *Debt tenancy* does not adequately relate how many agriculturalists were, in the words of Ransom and Sutch, "locked in" to continual indebtedness and the cultivation of cash crops instead of subsistence edibles. See Ransom and Sutch, *One Kind of Freedom,* 162-70. One of many accounts that take exception to this view is William W. Brown and Morgan O. Reynolds, "Debt Peonage Re-examined," *Journal of Economic History* 33 (Dec. 1973): 862-71. An essential work is Pete Daniel, *The Shadow of Slavery: Peonage in the South, 1901-1969* (Urbana: Univ. of Illinois Press, 1972).

12. Interview with S.P. Boatman, Nov. 2, 1905, File 3084, Tobacco Investigation Records, Bureau of Corporations, Record Group 122, National Archives.

13. Milton Whitney, "Tobacco Soils," *U.S. Department of Agriculture, Farmer's Bulletin,* No. 83 (Washington, 1893), 16-19; W.F. Axton, *Tobacco and Kentucky* (Lexington: Univ. Press of Kentucky, 1975), 69-70; James Harris Clarke, "Geographical Variations in the Prices of Tobacco Grown in Kentucky," M.S. thesis, Univ. of Kentucky, 1937, p. 60.

14. George K. Holmes, "The Peons of the South," *Annals of the American Academy of Political and Social Sciences* (Sept. 1893): 268.

15. Ransom and Sutch, *One Kind of Freedom,* 146-48; Clark, *Pills, Petticoats and Plows,* 274-79.

16. U.S. Bureau of the Census, *Thirteenth Census of the United States, 1910,* vol. 5, *Agriculture* (Washington, D.C., 1913), 104, 130-31. At the turn of the century tenant farms constituted the majority of farms in many southern states. For example, in 1910 the rate of tenancy in Louisiana was 55.3 percent, and in Alabama the rate was 60.2 percent. The highest rate of tenancy in the nation was in Mississippi, where 66.1 percent of farms were operated by tenants. See also Benjamin Horace Hibbard, "Farm Tenancy in the United States," *Annals of the American Academy of Political and Social Sciences* (March 1912): 30.

17. U.S. Bureau of the Census, *Thirteenth Census of the United States, 1910,* vol. 6, *Agriculture,* pp. 609-10; vol. 7, p. 570. A gripping account of the tragic hold that sharecropping had on southern agriculture is Arthur F. Raper and Ira De A. Reid, *Sharecroppers All* (Chapel Hill: Univ. of North Carolina Press, 1941).

18. Interview with Lee Baskett, Nov. 4, 1905, File 3084, Tobacco Investigation Records; interview with Joseph Wilson, Oct. 26, 1905, File 3852, Tobacco Investigation Records.

19. Rent Contracts, Box 13, Folder 2, Washington Family Papers, Tennessee State Library and Archives, Nashville; *Appeal to Reason*, Oct. 1, 1910.

20. Interview with Ben T. Kimsey, Oct. 31, 1905, File 3084, Tobacco Investigation Records. A review of the major economic and social transformations that occurred in southern agriculture after the Civil War is Barbara Jeanne Fields, "The Advent of Capitalist Agriculture: The New South in a Bourgeois World," in *Essays in the Postbellum Southern Economy*, ed. Thavolia Glymph, and John J. Kushma (College Station: Texas A&M Univ. Press, 1985), 73-94.

There is not universal agreement about the debilitating consequences of tenant farming. Robert Higgs, for example, found a progressive aspect of tenantry: "One should not jump to the conclusion that [tenants] were dispossessed former owners or necessarily poor. . . . many tenants were young men accumulating the savings that would ultimately permit them to purchase a farm." This was the "agricultural ladder" that some analysts pictured. Unfortunately, no such ladder existed. The extraordinary rise in tenantry between 1870 and 1930 testifies to the corrosive effect of the lien system. Accounting for farmers' inability to save enough money to own their own land, Higgs suggested that this money was often spent "to pay alimony, erect tombstones, provide daughters with a dowry, and enter horses in races." See Higgs, *The Transformation of the American Economy, 1865-1914* (New York: John Wiley and Sons, 1971), 93-96. The "ladder" continues to find many supporters. See Jeremy Atack, "The Agricultural Ladder Revisited: A New Look at an Old Question with Some Data for 1860," *Agricultural History* 63 (Winter 1989): 1-25.

21. Otto Carl Butterweck, "The Culture of Tobacco," *U.S. Department of Agriculture, Farmers' Bulletin*, no. 82 (Washington, D.C., 1898), 5-22; Rupert B. Vance, *Human Geography of the South: A Study in Regional Resources and Human Adequacy* (Chapel Hill: Univ. of North Carolina Press, 1932), 207-10; Fite, *Cotton Fields No More*, 11.

22. Emma Wilson, *Under One Roof* (New York: Wilfred Funk, 1955), 4. See also Suzanne Marshall Hall, "Breaking Trust: The Black Patch Tobacco Culture of Kentucky and Tennessee, 1900-1940," Ph.D. diss., Emory University, 1989, chap. 2.

23. Pete Daniel, *Standing at the Crossroads: Southern Life in the Twentieth Century* (New York: Hill and Wang, 1986), 6-7.

24. *Appeal to Reason*, Oct. 1, 1910; see also Suzanne M. Hall, "Working the Black Patch: Tobacco Farming Traditions, 1890-1930," *Register of the Kentucky Historical Society* 89 (Summer 1991): 266-86.

25. Harriet A. Byrne, "Child Labor in Representative Tobacco-Growing Areas," U.S. Department of Labor Children's Bureau Publication no. 155 (Washington, D.C.: G.P.O., 1926), 4-16; Vance, *Human Geography*, 212-13. See also Andrew David Holt, *The Struggle for a State System of Public Schools in Tennessee, 1903-1936* (New York: Teacher's College, Columbia University, 1938), 5-10, 109-12.

26. *The Rockefeller Sanitary Commission for the Eradication of Hookworm Disease, Second Annual Report*, (Washington: Offices of the Commission, 1911) 8-62; *Third Annual Report*, (1912) 21-45. John Ettling, *The Germ of Laziness: Rockefeller Philanthropy and Public Health in the New South* (Cambridge, Mass.: Harvard Univ. Press, 1981). While hookworm was more prevalent in the eastern regions of the states, it certainly was not confined to this area. In 1911 ninety-five of ninety-six Tennessee counties reported cases of hookworm. See also Fite, *Cotton Fields No More*, 38-39, 116.

27. C.H. Lavinder, "The Prevalence and Geographic Distribution of Pellagra in the

United States," *Public Health Reports,* Dec. 13, 1912, pp. 2077-85; "Preliminary Vital Statistics," *Bulletin of the State Board of Health of Kentucky, 1912* (Frankfort: Kentucky State Journal Publishing Co., 1912). Deaths from pellagra were discovered in the Kentucky tobacco counties of Crittenden, McCracken, Muhlenberg, and Todd. Cases of pellagra were also discovered in Calloway, Christian, Fayette, and Warren counties. See *Bulletin of the State Board of Health of Kentucky, 1913,* 4-5; I.A. Newby, *Plain Folk in the New South: Social Change and Cultural Persistence, 1880-1915* (Baton Rouge: Louisiana State Univ. Press, 1989), 359-73; Elizabeth W. Etheridge, *The Butterfly Caste: A Social History of Pellagra in the South* (Westport Conn.: Greenwood Publishing Co., 1972), 144.

28. Woodward, *Origins of the New South,* 185. Woodward correctly notes that the prices quoted by the U.S. Department of Agriculture were market prices, or prices received as of December 1. Usually the debt-ridden farmer was forced to sell his crop much earlier, when the markets were glutted and prices were considerably lower.

29. James O. Nall, *The Tobacco Night Riders of Kentucky and Tennessee, 1905-1909* (Louisville: Standard Press, 1939), 8; John L. Matthews, "The Farmer's Union and the Tobacco Pool," *Atlantic Monthly* 102 (Oct. 1908): 484-85. Matthews estimated that even when they earned ten cents per pound for burley, tenant farmers realized only fifty dollars in profit for the entire year. See also *Hearings on the Relief of Tobacco Growers,* 60th Cong., 1st sess., 1903, S. Doc. 390, p. 11.

Ben T. Kimsey, who owned a two-hundred acre farm in Henderson County, Kentucky, related a discussion he once had with Ed Hodge, a representative of the Imperial Tobacco Company, on the cost of producing dark tobacco. Kimsey told Hodge, "The farmer would get nothing out of tobacco at $5 per 100." Hodge replied that "he thought it could be done for $4 per 100 pounds." Interview with Ben T. Kimsey, Oct. 31, 1905, File 3084, Tobacco Investigation Records.

30. U.S. Department of Agriculture, Bureau of Agricultural Economics, *Tobaccos of the United States: Acreage, Yield per Acre, Production, Price, and Value, by States, 1866-1945, and by Types and Classes, 1919-1945* (Washington, D.C., 1948), 6-7, 78-79.

Chapter 2. Monopoly Comes to the Tobacco Belt

1. *Report of the Commissioner of Corporations on the Tobacco Industry,* pt. 1 (Washington, D.C.: G.P.O., 1909), 63-67; Robert F. Durden, *The Dukes of Durham, 1865-1929* (Durham, N.C.: Duke Univ. Press, 1975), 27-48; Patrick G. Porter, "Origins of the American Tobacco Company," *Business History Review* 43 (Spring 1969): 63-76.

2. *United States* v. *American Tobacco Company,* 221 U.S. 106 (1911), p. 189.

3. Durden, *Dukes of Durham,* 48-50; Alfred D. Chandler, Jr., *The Visible Hand: The Managerial Revolution in American Business* (Cambridge, Mass.: Belknap Press, 1977), 290-93, 382-84; Nannie May Tilley, *The Bright-Tobacco Industry, 1860-1929* (Chapel Hill: Univ. of North Carolina Press, 1948), 574-75; Jason Scott, "No Monopoly on Freedom: A Study of the American Tobacco Company from 1890 to 1911," senior thesis, Duke Univ., 1990, pp. 7-12.

4. *Report of the Commissioner of Corporations,* 1-19, 64-66; New York *Times,* May 29, 1906; Emory Martin Matthews, "The Tobacco Industry and the Position of the Tobacco Combination since 1890," M.S. thesis, Cornell Univ., 1932, pp. 4-7. Also helpful is Malcolm R. Burns, "Economies of Scale in Tobacco Manufacture, 1897-1910," *Journal of Economic History* 43 (June 1983): 473-74. An excellent study of the financial organization

of the ATC and its uses of watered stock to obtain greater control of the tobacco industry is Scott, "No Monopoly on Freedom," 15-20, 64-65.

5. Josephus Daniels, *Tar Heel Editor* (Chapel Hill: Univ. of North Carolina Press, 1939), 473.

6. Hans B. Thorelli, *The Federal Antitrust Policy: Origination of an American Tradition* (Stockholm, 1954), 388. As the remarks by Olney and Daniels indicate, Kentucky and Tennessee were not the only states to feel the effects of the monopolization of the tobacco industry. For further antitrust sentiment among farmers in Duke's home state of North Carolina, see Tilley, *Bright-Tobacco Industry*, 267-68, 424-25; idem, *The R.J. Reynolds Tobacco Company* (Chapel Hill: Univ. of North Carolina Press, 1985), 95-127; and Paul D. Escott, *Many Excellent People: Power and Privilege in North Carolina, 1850-1900* (Chapel Hill: Univ. of North Carolina Press, 1985), 242-48.

7. Thorelli, *Federal Antitrust Policy*, 63-82, 214-34, 388, 445-51. Thorelli added that while the Knight case had "a discouraging influence" on enforcement of the Sherman Act, "there is no real indication that enforcement would have been more energetic even if the opinion had been more positive" (598). See also Scott, "No Monopoly on Freedom," 20-23.

8. *Report of the Commissioner of Corporations*, 78-79; *United States* v. *American Tobacco Company*, 11-12.

9. Gabriel Kolko, *The Triumph of Conservatism: A Reinterpretation of American History, 1900-1916* (New York: Free Press, 1963), 125-27.

10. Tobacco Ledger, Martin and Johnson Mercantile Records, Special Collections, M.I. King Library, University of Kentucky; William Hugh McCord, "The Development of the Tobacco Markets in Kentucky with a Preliminary Sketch of the Earliest History of Tobacco," M.A. thesis, Univ. of Kentucky, 1920, pp. 20-21; *United States* v. *American Tobacco Company*, 171.

11. Clarksville *Leaf-Chronicle*, Sept. 6, 1901, and March 21 and Oct. 24, 1902; *Bills for the Relief of Tobacco Growers*, 59th Cong., 2d sess., 1907, S. Doc. 372, p. 116; affidavit of A.O. Dority, A.O. Stanley Papers, Special Collections, M.I. King Library, University of Kentucky.

Washington Anderson, an African-American farmer in Montgomery County, Tennessee, stated, "If the regie buyer buys a crop of snuff tobacco, he turns it over to the buyer for the American Snuff Co."; interview with Washington Anderson, Oct. 23, 1905, File 3085, Tobacco Investigation Records, Bureau of Corporations, Record Group 122, National Archives. Such charges that an "understanding" existed between the Regie and the American Tobacco Company were denied by Joseph Ferigo of the Regie; interview with Joseph Ferigo, Aug. 1, 1905, File 3028, Tobacco Investigation Records. See also "General Information Regarding the Purchase by the Italian Government in the United States of America," File 3028, Tobacco Investigation Records.

12. Affidavit of W.H. Hook, Aug. 1907, A.O. Stanley Papers.

13. J.E. Justice to A.O. Stanley, Aug. 23, 1907, A.O. Stanley Papers.

14. Interview with J.B. Ferguson, Oct. 28, 1905, File 3085, Tobacco Investigation Records; interview with Arthur B. Jarvis, n.d., File 3852, Tobacco Investigation Records.

15. Affidavit of A.O. Dority, A.O. Stanley Papers; *United States* v. *American Tobacco Company*, 143; interview with W.S. Waller, Oct. 16, 1905, Box 3085, Tobacco Investigation Records; interview with Lee Baskett, Nov. 4, 1905, File 3084, Tobacco Investigation Records.

16. Dwight B. Billings, *Planters and the Making of the "New South": Class, Politics, and Development in North Carolina, 1865-1900* (Chapel Hill: Univ. of North Carolina Press, 1979), 113-20; John K. Winkler, *Tobacco Tycoon: The Story of James Buchanan Duke* (New York: Random House, 1942); John Wilbur Jenkins, *Master Builder: The Story of James Buchanan Duke* (New York: George H. Doran and Co., 1927); Matthew Josephson, *The Robber Barons: The Great American Capitalists, 1861-1901* (New York: Harcourt, Brace and Co., 1934). Robert F. Durden's judicious study of the Duke family, *The Dukes of Durham*, primarily discusses the family's philanthropic activities; chapters 3 and 4 describe the rise of the American Tobacco Company. An important recent study is Allen Tullos, *Habits of Industry: White Culture and the Transformation of the Carolina Piedmont* (Chapel Hill: Univ. of North Carolina Press, 1989), 161-66.

Chapter 3. Organizing the Black Patch

1. Clarksville *Leaf-Chronicle*, Sept. 24, 1904; Louisville *Courier-Journal*, Sept. 25, 1904.

2. James O. Nall, *The Tobacco Night Riders of Kentucky and Tennessee, 1905-1909* (Louisville: Standard Press, 1939), 19-23. The crucial decisions regarding the formation of the PPA, according to Nall, were made "by [planter Felix] Ewing and other prominent tobacco growers before the [Guthrie] meeting." After this point, Nall received no connection between insurgent planning and insurgent organizing: "It merely remained necessary for the growers to assemble" (22). Other works that describe the Guthrie meeting as the organizational foundation of the PPA are Dewey W. Grantham, Jr., "Black Patch War: The Story of the Kentucky and Tennessee Night Riders, 1905-1909," *South Atlantic Quarterly* 59 (Spring 1960): 215-25; Bill Cunningham, *On Bended Knees: The Night Rider Story* (Nashville: McClanahan Publishing House, 1983), 41-43; Rick Gregory, "Robertson County and the Black Patch War, 1904-1909," *Tennessee Historical Quarterly* 39 (Fall 1980): 347; Albin Lee Reynolds, "War in the Black Patch," *Register of the Kentucky Historical Society* 56 (Jan. 1958): 2; Christopher Waldrep, "Augustus E. Willson and the Night Riders," *Filson Club History Quarterly* 58 (April 1984): 237; Theodore Saloutos, "The American Society of Equity in Kentucky: A Recent Attempt in Agrarian Reform," *Journal of Southern History* 5 (Aug. 1939): 351-52.

3. This aspect of the insurgent process is addressed in E.J. Hobsbawm and George Rudé, *Captain Swing: A Social History of the Great English Agricultural Uprising of 1830* (1968; New York: Norton, 1975), 56; Sara M. Evans and Harry C. Boyte, *Free Spaces: The Sources of Democratic Change in America* (New York: Harper and Row, 1986); Steven Hahn, *The Roots of Southern Populism: Yeoman Farmers and the Transformation of the Georgia Upcountry, 1850-1890* (New York: Oxford Univ. Press, 1983), 5; and Lawrence Goodwyn, *Breaking the Barrier: The Rise of Solidarity in Poland* (New York: Oxford Univ. Press, 1991), xx-xxi, 263-67. A general summary of the hoary analysis that financial adversity was the "causative agent" that "fomented" agrarian insurgencies throughout America in the late 1880s and 1890s was offered by an economist, Robert A. McGuire, in his article "Economic Causes of Late Nineteenth Century Agrarian Unrest: New Evidence," *Journal of Economic History* 41 (Dec. 1981): 835-52.

4. Edward F. Prichard, Jr., "Popular Political Movements in Kentucky, 1875-1900," senior thesis, Princeton Univ., 1935, pp. 69-70; C. Vann Woodward, *Origins of the New South, 1877-1913* (Baton Rouge: Louisiana State Univ. Press, 1951), 83-84; Michael R. Hyman, *The Anti-Redeemers: Hill Country Political Dissenters in the Lower South from Redemption to Populism* (Baton Rouge: Louisiana State Univ. Press, 1990), 41-42, 194-96.

5. Joseph G. Knapp, *The Rise of American Cooperative Enterprise, 1620-1920* (Danville, Ill.: Interstate Printers and Publishers, 1969), 46-55; Solon Justus Buck, *The Granger Movement: A Study of Agricultural Organization and Its Political, Economic and Social Manifestations, 1870-1880* (Cambridge, Mass.: Harvard Univ. Press, 1913); David Montgomery, *Beyond Equality: Labor and the Radical Republicans, 1862-1872* (New York: Alfred A. Knopf, 1967), 340-56.

6. James D. Bennett, "Some Notes on Christian County, Kentucky, Grange Activities," *Register of the Kentucky Historical Society* 64 (July 1966): 232; Jacqueline Page Bull, "The General Store in the Southern Economy, 1865-1910," Ph.D. diss., Univ. of Kentucky, 1948, pp. 54-55; "Grange Activities, 1875-78," Box 13, Folder 13, Washington Family Papers, Tennessee State Library and Archives, Nashville.

7. The literature of populism is large. The most germane accounts are Woodward, *Origins of the New South;* Lawrence Goodwyn, *Democratic Promise: The Populist Moment in America* (New York: Oxford Univ. Press, 1976); Hahn, *Roots of Southern Populism;* and Bruce Palmer, *"Man over Money": The Southern Populist Critique of American Capitalism* (Chapel Hill: Univ. of North Carolina Press, 1980).

8. N.A. Dunning, ed., *The Farmers' Alliance History and Agricultural Digest* (Washington, D.C.: Farmers' Alliance Publishing Co., 1891), 241-42; Robert C. McMath, Jr., *Populist Vanguard: A History of the Southern Farmers' Alliance* (1975; New York: Norton, 1977), 33; Prichard, "Popular Political Movements," 109; Nashville *Weekly-Toiler*, Sept. 5, 1888; J.A. Sharp, "The Entrance of the Farmers' Alliance into Tennessee Politics," *East Tennessee Historical Society Publications* 9 (1937): 78.

9. Nashville *Weekly-Toiler*, Aug. 1 and Oct. 3, 1888.

10. Ibid., Oct. 24, 1888.

11. *National Economist*, May 18 and Nov. 16, 1889; Nashville *Weekly-Toiler*, Dec. 5, 1888, and Aug. 7, 1889.

12. Nashville *Weekly-Toiler*, June 4, 1890; Gaye K. Bland, "Populism in Kentucky, 1887-1896," Ph.D. diss., Univ. of Kentucky, 1979, p. 55. The impact of the Farmers' Alliance in the tobacco regions of Kentucky and Tennessee remains virtually untreated in national studies. See John D. Hicks, *The Populist Revolt: A History of the Farmers' Alliance and the People's Party* (Minneapolis: Univ. of Minnesota Press, 1931); and Goodwyn, *Democratic Promise.*

13. Corinne Westphal, "The Farmers' Alliance in Tennessee," M.A. thesis, Vanderbilt University, 1929, p. 58. On the national level, the Populist movement was encountering a struggle that was seen in microcosm in Kentucky. "Midroad" Populists, like those in western Kentucky, advocated a flexible currency based on the subtreasury system, which sought public ownership of various industries, and attempted to consolidate a third party from which Populist candidates could obtain political power. The basic statement of "midroad" populism came with the demands expressed in the Ocala convention. Other Alliance members, like those who controlled the Kentucky Alliance, stressed "free silver," or a somewhat less stringent metallic monetary base than gold, and "fusion" with present political parties. Behind this debate of "free silver" and "fusion" was the discussion of what direction populism would take: either a structural reordering of the American economy led by Populist politicians or a simple reform of the gold standard led by contemporary politicians who expressed some Populist sympathies. See C. Vann Woodward, *Tom Watson: Agrarian Rebel* (1938; New York: Oxford

Univ. Press, 1972), 289, 294, 303, 317-23; Woodward, *Origins of the New South*, 235-63; Goodwyn, *Democratic Promise*, 208-11, 213-32, 388-401, 582; Palmer, *"Man over Money,"* 104-10; and Ayers, *Promise of the New South*, 239-43, 250-56.

14. *National Economist*, May 24, 1890; Woodward, *Origins of the New South*, 203, 260; Prichard, "Popular Political Movements," 140-44; Thomas D. Clark, *A History of Kentucky* (Lexington, Ky.: John Bradford Press, 1960), 430-44; Jasper B. Shannon and Ruth McQuown, *Presidential Politics in Kentucky, 1824-1948: A Compilation of Election Statistics and an Analysis of Political Behavior* (Lexington: Bureau of Government Research, College of Arts and Sciences, Univ. of Kentucky, 1950), 64-67; Thomas D. Clark, "The People, William Goebel, and the Kentucky Railroads," *Journal of Southern History* 5 (Feb. 1939): 35; Hambleton Tapp and James C. Klotter, *Kentucky: Decades of Discord, 1865-1890* (Frankfort: Kentucky Historical Society, 1977), 259-60; Gaye K. Bland, "Populism in the First Congressional District of Kentucky, 1892," *Filson Club History Quarterly* 51 (Jan. 1977): 35-36. On populism at the national level, see Peter H. Argersinger, *Populism and Politics: William Alfred Peffer and the People's Party* (Lexington: Univ. Press of Kentucky, 1974).

15. Richard Hofstadter, *The Age of Reform: From Bryan to F.D.R.* (New York: Random House, 1955), 109. Gavin Wright offers a more general conclusion: "It is not surprising that those who stress the exploitative, backward character of the Southern economy tend to write about the 19th century, while those who press the revisionist case for progress tend to write about the first two decades of the 20th century." Wright, *Old South, New South: Revolutions in the Southern Economy since the Civil War* (New York: Basic Books, 1986), 117.

16. U.S. Department of Agriculture, Bureau of Agricultural Economics, *Tobaccos of the United States: Acreage, Yield per Acre, Production, Price, and Value, by States, 1866-1945, and by Types and Classes, 1919-1945* (Washington, D.C., 1948), 78-79; *Western Tobacco Journal*, March 2, 1896.

18. Clarksville *Leaf-Chronicle*, Oct. 21, 1901; Sept. 21 and Oct. 11 and 20, 1901; Nashville *Weekly-Toiler*, Oct. 3, 1888, July 17 and 24, 1889, and Feb. 10, 1892.

19. *Western Tobacco Journal*, Dec. 9, 1901; Clarksville *Leaf-Chronicle*, Sept. 7 and Dec. 10, 1901.

20. *Western Tobacco Journal*, Nov. 3, 1902; Clarksville *Leaf-Chronicle*, Oct. 21, 1902.

21. *Black Patch Tobacco Journal*, Aug. 1907; *Western Tobacco Journal*, June 25, 1900.

22. *Black Patch Tobacco Journal*, Aug. 1907.

23. Ibid.

24. Among those at the meeting were James Foster, James Draughon, Clinton Holman, N.W. Moseley, John W. Starks, George Featherstone, W.W. Payne, G.M. Babb, H.S. Taylor, Frank Rose, Sam Qualls, John Jackson, E.W. Williams, Gideon Morris, A.B. Porter, D.W. Raymer, Frank Durrett, Charley Webster, J.H. Orman, V.A. Bradley, Nick Howard, Boyd Clinard, B.C. Batts, and Robert L. Bell.

25. Clarksville *Leaf-Chronicle*, Dec. 20, 1902; Nall, *Tobacco Night Riders*, 8; W.F. Axton, *Tobacco and Kentucky* (Lexington: Univ. Press of Kentucky, 1975), 87. The tax was removed in 1909.

26. Louisville *Courier-Journal*, Jan. 19, 1903.

27. *Western Tobacco Journal*, Jan. 5, 1903.

28. Clarksville *Leaf-Chronicle*, Jan. 26, 1903.

29. Ibid., Jan. 28 and Feb. 4, 1904; *Hearings on the Relief of Tobacco Growers*, 60th Cong., 1st sess., 1903, S. Doc. 390, p. 7.

30. *Hearings on the Relief of Tobacco Growers*, 20.

31. Ibid., 38-39. Aldrich became one of the major stockholders, along with James B. Duke, of the R.J. Reynolds Tobacco Company following the decree of 1911 dissolving the American Tobacco Company. Historian Allan Nevins concluded that the "extreme laissez-faire" school of the Progressive Era had two chief representatives: Mark Hanna and Senator Nelson W. Aldrich. See Nevins, *John D. Rockefeller: The Heroic Age of American Enterprise* (New York: Charles Scribner's Sons, 1941), 458-59, 555; Nannie May Tilley, *The R.J. Reynolds Tobacco Company* (Chapel Hill: Univ. of North Carolina Press, 1985), 191; Patrick Reynolds and Tom Shachtman, *The Gilded Leaf: Triumph, Tragedy and Tobacco—Three Generations of the R.J. Reynolds Family and Fortune* (Boston: Little, Brown, and Co., 1989), 86-87. It should also be noted that the Independent Tobacco Manufacturers Association of the United States, the lobbying agent for the American Tobacco Company, also exerted considerable effort to block the bill to repeal the tobacco tax. See Nicholas C. Burckel, "A.O. Stanley and Progressive Reform, 1902-1919," *Register of the Kentucky Historical Society* 79 (Spring 1981): 138-39.

32. Clarksville *Leaf-Chronicle*, April 28 and May 4, 1904. In May 1908 the internal organ of the PPA, the *Black Patch Tobacco Journal*, accused Aldrich of owning shares in the American Tobacco Company while the tax repeal bill was before his committee. Additional and more extravagant charges concerning Aldrich's ties to the tobacco trust were levied by Congressman A.O. Stanley of Kentucky. Stanley claimed that James B. Duke operated a ground wire from his office in New York to the committee room in Washington during the hearings on the bill. Stanley charged that Duke had personally wired Aldrich, urging the senator to kill the bill. See A.O. Stanley Speech at Chautauqua, Sept. 4, 1909, A.O. Stanley Papers, Special Collections, M.I. King Library, University of Kentucky.

33. Clarksville *Leaf-Chronicle*, Feb. 3, March 2 and 10, May 20, and June 4, 9, and 15, 1904.

34. *Black Patch Tobacco Journal*, Aug. 1907.

35. Clarksville *Leaf-Chronicle*, July 13, 1904.

36. Ibid., Feb. 2, 1905.

37. Ibid., July 30 and Oct. 22, 1904; *Hearings on the Relief of Tobacco Growers*, 57. Another leader of the PPA, Joel Fort, was also an early opponent of the Farmers' Alliance. In fact, many Alliance men felt that "Joel Fort worked harder to secure our defeat than any other man. . . . he is an eternal hater of the Wheel"; Nashville *Weekly-Toiler*, Jan. 30, 1889.

38. Clarksville *Leaf-Chronicle*, Aug. 13, 1904. Christopher Waldrep details how the PPA hierarchy was composed primarily of large landowners: Waldrep, "Planters and the Planters' Protective Association in Kentucky and Tennessee," *Journal of Southern History* 52 (Nov. 1986): 567-69.

39. *Appeal to Reason*, Oct. 15, 1910; Clarksville *Leaf-Chronicle*, Aug. 13, 1904; *Western Tobacco Journal*, Sept. 12, 1904. The Guthrie fairgrounds was well known to area farmers, since it also hosted the annual Agricultural, Stock and Implement Exhibition. Clarksville *Leaf-Chronicle*, Aug. 20, 1904.

40. Clarksville *Leaf-Chronicle*, Sept. 13, 1904.

41. *Western Tobacco Journal*, Aug. 15, 1904.

42. Clarksville *Leaf-Chronicle,* Sept. 19, 1904.

43. Ibid., Nov. 7, 1905.

44. Since agriculturalists must rely on those who possess access to credit, bankers have historically exploited their organic advantage. The implementation of the modern Federal Reserve System, conceived as a relief to strict monetary policies, has further increased, instead of alleviating, the fundamental antagonism between bankers and farmers. See William Greider, *Secrets of the Temple: How the Federal Reserve Runs the Country* (New York: Simon and Schuster, 1987), 250-54, 295, 451-53, 668-79; Palmer, *"Man over Money,"* 16; Martin Mayer, *The Bankers* (New York: Weybright and Talley, 1974), 240-45; Anna Rochester, *Why Farmers Are Poor: The Agricultural Crisis in the United States* (New York: International Publishers, 1940), 106-12; idem, *Rulers of America: A Study of Finance Capital* (New York: International Publishers, 1936), 232-39.

45. *Black Patch Tobacco Journal,* Aug. 1907; Clarksville *Leaf-Chronicle,* March 15, 1906.

46. Clarksville *Leaf-Chronicle,* Sept. 22, 1904.

47. Ibid., Oct. 17, 1904. Ewing later estimated that 60 percent of the money obtained for the PPA was borrowed from local banks. Marie Taylor, "Night Riders in the Black Patch," M.A. thesis, Univ. of Kentucky, 1934, p. 18.

48. Clarksville *Leaf-Chronicle,* Oct. 17, 1904; Mayfield *Messenger,* Oct. 18, 1904.

49. Clarksville *Leaf-Chronicle,* Sept. 24, 1904; *Western Tobacco Journal,* Oct. 3, 1904; Louisville *Courier-Journal,* Sept. 25, 1904; *Black Patch Tobacco Journal,* August 1908; Nall, *Tobacco Night Riders,* 19-24.

50. *Black Patch Tobacco Journal,* Aug. 1907.

51. Along with the PPA, other lesser tobacco associations emerged in the region during the early 1900s. The Stemming Tobacco Association comprised farmers in the Kentucky counties of Hopkins, Union, Webster, and Henderson. The Stemming group was officially launched on June 16, 1906. At the inaugural meeting, John B. Allen unsuccessfully attempted to persuade the farmers to join the PPA, claiming that it embraced twenty-seven counties. Upon the Stemming group's refusal, Allen grew angry, offending many in attendance who were not as ambitious as Allen in their vision of the organization. The Green River Association, active from 1908 to 1913, comprised farmers in the Kentucky counties of Daviess, Hancock, Breckinridge, Ohio, McLean, and Muhlenberg. The GRA was a very different type of tobacco organization: it was solely a bargaining agency and did not seek to withhold tobacco from the market. James O. Nall estimated that the membership of these groups approached 20,000. This estimation is highly exaggerated. The Stemming Association claimed only 2,200 members in 1909, and it is doubtful that the combined memberships of both groups approached 4,000. See S.E. Wrather, "Tobacco Marketing Organizations in Western Kentucky and Tennessee with Special Emphasis on Early Organizations," M.S. thesis, Univ. of Kentucky, 1933, pp. 55-56. 101-2; Henderson *Daily-Gleaner,* June 17 and 26, 1906; Nall, *Tobacco Night Riders,* 131-35; and Madisonville *Semi-Weekly Hustler,* March 26, 1909.

Chapter 4. Rumors of War

1. *Black Patch Tobacco Journal* Aug. 1907.

2. Ibid.

3. Clarksville *Leaf-Chronicle,* Jan. 12 and Sept. 25, 1905.

4. Clarksville *Leaf-Chronicle*, Nov. 30, 1904, and Jan. 12 and Feb. 1 and 15, 1905; Henderson *Daily-Gleaner*, Jan. 13 and 19, 1905; Mayfield *Messenger*, Jan. 16, 1905. These relatively small local newspapers are critical in uncovering the organizational base of the PPA.

5. Clarksville *Leaf-Chronicle*, April 19, 1905.

6. Henderson *Daily-Gleaner*, Feb. 8, 1905.

7. Organizers were not only interested in recruiting male farmers. A letter from Graves County chairman J.W. Usher showed that organizers also wanted to secure the services of women: "We hope to meet the farmers and explain in detail the plans of our association. . . . A special invitation will be extended the ladies. We are very anxious for them to attend these meetings. We need their influences." Mayfield *Messenger*, May 22, 1907.

8. Clarksville *Leaf-Chronicle*, April 24, 1905.

9. Ibid., March 13, 1905; see also "Minutes of the Dark Tobacco Growers Protective Association of Montgomery County, March 17, 1908, Robertson Yeatman Johnson Papers, Tennessee State Library and Archives, Nashville.

10. Henderson *Daily-Gleaner*, Jan. 7, 1905; Clarksville *Leaf-Chronicle*, March 13, 18, and 21, and April 3, 1905. PPA leaders later charged that the *Western Tobacco Journal* was a "tool" of the ATC.

11. Robertson County *News*, Nov. 12, 1906, in A.O. Stanley Papers, Special Collections, M.I. King Library, University of Kentucky.

12. Mayfield *Messenger*, Dec. 5, 1904. Two months later Ewing estimated that ten thousand farmers had joined the association; see Mayfield *Messenger*, Feb. 1, 1905.

13. Mayfield *Messenger*, Jan. 16, 1905.

14. Ibid., May 2, 1905; Madisonville *Semi-Weekly Hustler*, Jan. 16 and Sept. 11, 1906; Clarksville *Leaf-Chronicle*, Feb. 13, 1905.

15. Unidentified newspaper clipping, ca. 1908, "Night Rider" reel, Kentucky Department for Libraries and Archives, Frankfort; Henderson *Daily-Gleaner*, Feb. 8, 1905. See also S.E. Wrather, "Tobacco Marketing Organizations in Western Kentucky and Tennessee with Special Emphasis on Early Organizations," M.S. thesis, Univ. of Kentucky, 1933, p. 96.

16. *The Tobacco Planters' Yearbook, 1908* (Guthrie, Ky., 1908), 6-7; *Appeal to Reason*, Oct. 15, 1910.

17. *Western Tobacco Journal*, July 3 and 17, Oct. 30, and Nov. 20, 1905. On the sale of three hundred hogsheads, association expenses ran from $1.50 to $1.75 per hundred pounds, leaving $5.50 to $7.75 per hundred pounds remaining for the growers, which was slightly above the cost of production. The *Journal* noted: "We are safe in saying [the prices] were much below the prices quoted by the Association at which they promised the growers."

18. *Tobacco Planters' Yearbook, 1908*, 6; Clarksville *Leaf-Chronicle*, Sept. 25, 1905; Henderson *Daily-Gleaner*, Sept. 24, 1905; James O. Nall, *The Tobacco Night Riders of Kentucky and Tennessee, 1905-1909* (Louisville: Standard Press, 1939), 30.

19. F.G. Ewing to Joseph E. Washington, Oct. 19, 1908, Washington Family Papers, Tennessee State Library and Archives, Nashville; Anna Youngman, "Tobacco Pools of Kentucky and Tennessee," *Journal of Political Economy* 18 (Jan. 1910): pp. 48-49; Forrest Carlisle Pogue, Jr., "The Life and Work of Senator Ollie Murray James," M.A. thesis,

Univ. of Kentucky, 1932, pp. 29-30; memorandum by F.G. Ewing, n.d., A.O. Stanley Papers.

20. Clarksville *Leaf-Chronicle*, July 13, 1906.

21. Both John W. Gaines and Ollie James remained popular officials throughout their careers representing the Black Patch area. Other PPA officials, such as Frank Rives and E.E. Wash, were elected to the Kentucky legislature. Evidently, while they did not officially receive PPA support, their connection with this popular organization proved valuable at the polls.

22. Clarksville *Leaf-Chronicle*, Jan. 1, 1906. At another meeting of the Montgomery County PPA, Garrott Brockman rose to speak about dishonest methods of reporting prices obtained by the PPA. Brockman cited a recent sale by the PPA to the Italian Regie, in which the price quoted by the PPA was $10.85 per hundred pounds. Brockman claimed that the actual price was about two cents per pound less. See the Clarksville *Leaf-Chronicle*, Oct. 29, 1906.

23. Clarksville *Leaf-Chronicle*, Dec. 21, 1905.

24. Ibid., Jan. 2, 1906.

25. Ibid., June 28, 1906.

26. Ibid., March 7 and April 10 and 19, 1906. In 1906 Clarksville warehousemen handled approximately eleven thousand hogsheads of PPA tobacco and about an equal amount of non-PPA tobacco.

27. Ibid., April 7 and 19, 1906.

28. Ibid., April 25, 1906.

29. Ibid., April 24 and 28, 1906. Ewing returned the headquarters to Clarksville in 1910.

30. Ibid., May 3, 1906.

31. Ibid., June 15, 1906.

32. Ibid., Aug. 22, 1906; James Scott Bissett, "Agrarian Socialism in America: Marx and Jesus in the Oklahoma Countryside," Ph.D. diss., Duke University, 1989, pp. 16-20. Early Farmers' Union spokesmen wrote bylaws that allowed the admittance of rural bankers. The rank and file wrote new rules in 1905 that essentially purged all business elements from their organization. Lawrence Goodwyn, "The Cooperative Commonwealth and Other Abstractions: In Search of a Democratic Premise," *Marxist Perspectives* 3 (Summer 1980): 24-25.

33. N.E. Greene to A.O. Stanley, Aug. 17, 1907, A.O. Stanley Papers; Youngman, "Tobacco Pools," 42; Eugene P. Lyle, Jr., "Night Riding—A Reign of Fear," *Hampton's Magazine* (June 1909): 471-72.

34. Clarksville *Leaf-Chronicle*, Sept. 12, 1906.

35. Ibid., Sept. 11 and 12, and Nov. 22, 1906.

36. Ibid., Aug. 1, 6, and 16, 1907. In October 1907 Sheriff Shelton of Todd County served an injunction on the Bank of Guthrie, prohibiting the bank from paying any more money to the PPA because of the rumored high salaries enjoyed by association figures. See the Clarksville *Leaf-Chronicle*, Oct. 8, 1907.

37. Clarksville *Leaf-Chronicle*, Sept. 3 and 13, and Nov. 1, 1907. In a year-long summary of events, Ewing mentioned nothing of association criticisms. See the Clarksville *Leaf-Chronicle*, Nov. 25, 1907.

38. Interview with James B. Walker, Nov. 23, 1907, File 3852, Tobacco Investigation

Records, Bureau of Corporations, Record Group 122, National Archives; *Western Tobacco Journal*, Nov. 12, 1906; Theodore Saloutos, *Farmer Movements in the South, 1865-1933* (1960; Lincoln: Univ. of Nebraska Press, 1967), 171-72.

39. Interview with W.S. Waller, Oct. 16, 1905, File 3085, Tobacco Investigation Records.

40. Eugene P. Lyle, Jr., "Night Riding in the Black Patch," *Hampton's Magazine* (Jan. 1909): 344-45; American Society of Equity *News*, March 17, 1909; *Saturday Evening Post*, Aug. 3, 1907.

41. In the memories of some farmers in the Black Patch, the painful realities of being "hillbillies" were, it appears, forgotten. In 1980 Edna Humphreys recalled that her father, a struggling tenant farmer in western Kentucky, received ten cents per pound for his crop in 1907. Acknowledging that "this was a real good price," Mrs. Humphreys could not remember PPA members or gatherings in her childhood. She did, however, recall seeing "company buyers" with her father. Interview with Edna Humphreys, Oct. 1, 1980, by Nicolette Murray, Forrest C. Pogue Oral History Institute, Murray State University.

42. *Black Patch Tobacco Journal*, Aug. and Nov. 1907; *Western Tobacco Journal*, April 9, 1906.

43. *Appeal to Reason*, Oct. 8, 1910.

44. Federal manuscript census, Montgomery County, Tennessee, 1910; Eugene P. Lyle, Jr., "They That Ride by Night: The Story of Kentucky's Tobacco War," *Hampton's Magazine* (Feb. 1907): 175-87.

45. Federal manuscript census, Montgomery County, Tennessee, 1910; U.S. Bureau of the Census, *Thirteen Census of the United States, 1910*, vol. 3, *Population* (Washington, D.C. 1913), 756.

46. Attending the 1906 meeting was a delegation from Virginia, which officially joined the PPA in February 1906. This alliance, however, was short-lived, and Virginia never sold any tobacco through the PPA. The attempt nonetheless demonstrated the ambitions of PPA leaders to expand the association's membership across the South. See Clarksville *Leaf-Chronicle*, Sept. 24, 1906; and Nall, *Tobacco Night Riders*, 30-36.

47. Milton Friedman and Anna Jacobsen Schwartz, *A Monetary History of the United States, 1867-1960* (Princeton, N.J.: Princeton Univ. Press, 1963), 156-68; Gabriel Kolko, *The Triumph of Conservatism: A Reinterpretation of American History, 1900-1916* (New York: Free Press, 1963), 153-56; Charles A. Conant, *A History of Modern Banks of Issue*, 5th ed. (New York: G.P. Putnam's Sons, 1915), 698-721. Conant traces the cause of the 1907 panic to an organic weakness in an economy ruled by the gold standard. The distinctive feature of this panic was that it was "one of capital and credit rather than of the stock of gold. . . . in spite of the outpour of gold from the mines at a rate never equalled or approached . . . demand outran supply, the new gold did not offset the maladjustments of capital, and the money market found gold an unsatisfactory ailment" (704).

48. Woodford *Sun*, Nov. 28, 1907. Divisions among country bankers and large eastern financiers are discussed in Robert H. Wiebe, *Businessmen and Reform: A Study of the Progressive Movement* (1962; Chicago: Ivan R. Dee, 1989), 24-25, 70-71. The 1907 panic was so severe that many years afterward southern African-Americans incorporated it into a rural folk song. "A nickel worth of meal and a dime of lard / will do while de panic's on. / Save up yo' money / Don' you buy no corn / 'Cause de panic's on. / I wear shoes made of all kinds of leather, / I wear clothes made for all kinds of weather / 'Cause

de panic's on." Lawrence W. Levine, *Black Culture and Black Consciousness: Afro-American Folk Thought from Slavery to Freedom* (New York: Oxford Univ. Press, 1977), 257.

49. Christopher Waldrep, ed., "A 'Trust Lawyer' Tries to Help Kentucky's Farmers: Augustus E. Willson's 1907 Letter to George B. Cortelyou," *Register of the Kentucky Historical Society* 83 (Autumn 1985): 347-49. Bankers in Hopkinsville, Kentucky, were praised by the local press for not making loans to farmers during the panic and for leaving an adequate supply of cash on hand. After a night-rider raid on Hopkinsville in December 1907, bankers there resumed extending loans to PPA members.

50. Madisonville *Semi-Weekly Hustler*, Nov. 12, 1907; Clarksville *Leaf-Chronicle*, Dec. 16, 1907, and Jan. 1 and 15, 1908.

51. Mayfield *Messenger*, Dec. 11, 1907.

52. Madisonville *Semi-Weekly Hustler*, Jan. 7, 1908; Clarksville *Leaf-Chronicle*, Nov. 25, 1907; *Western Tobacco Journal*, Dec. 2, 1907.

53. Winchester *Democrat*, Dec. 27, 1907.

Chapter 5. Night Riders

1. Armed bands of night riders, intent upon destroying tobacco plant beds in order to decrease supply and raise prices, did not first appear in the twentieth century. As early as 1680 night riders emerged in Virginia in reaction to a voluntary agreement to curtail acreage among farmers. When some planters decided to ignore the curtailment, "tobacco cutters" destroyed plant beds and crops. See Matthew Page Andrews, *Virginia: The Old Dominion* (New York: Doubleday, 1937), 166-67.

2. The notion that aggression varies with the degree of frustration is a hypothesis that has found support in sociological and psychological testing. Studies have determined, for example, that more lynchings occurred in states where economic frustration (measured by low farm prices) was at its greatest. See John Dollard et al., "Frustration and Aggression: Definitions," in *When Men Revolt and Why: A Reader in Political Violence and Revolution*, ed. James Chowning Davies (New York: Free Press, 1971), 166-76. For a discussion of vigilantism at the turn of the century as a defensive response to industrialization, see William F. Holmes, "Moonshining and Collective Violence: Georgia, 1889-1895," *Journal of American History* 67 (Dec. 1980): 589-611; and David Thelen, *Paths of Resistance: Tradition and Dignity in Industrializing Missouri* (New York: Oxford Univ. Press, 1986), 86-99.

3. C. Vann Woodward, *Origins of the New South, 1877-1913* (Baton Rouge: Louisiana State Univ. Press, 1951), 158-60. Historian Suzanne Marshall Hall examines the "long heritage" of Black Patch violence in "Breaking Trust: The Black Patch Tobacco Culture of Kentucky and Tennessee, 1900-1940," Ph.D. diss., Emory Univ., 1989, chap. 3.

4. Woodward, *Origins of the New South*, 158-60; Thomas D. Clark, *The Southern Country Editor* (1948; Gloucester, Mass.: Peter Smith, 1964), 216-19, 224. See also Joseph C. Kiger, "Social Thought as Voiced in Rural Middle Tennessee Newspapers, 1878-1898," *Tennessee Historical Quarterly* 9 (June 1950): 134-35. The culture of violence in the antebellum South is treated in Bertram Wyatt-Brown, *Southern Honor: Ethics and Behavior in the Old South* (New York: Oxford Univ. Press, 1982), 366-71.

British historian E.J. Hobsbawm found American vigilantism during this period characteristic of a country that witnessed "the total absence of any kind of control over business dealings." The federal and state governments clung to notions of laissez-faire and remained unconcerned about the internal injustices that various companies were inflicting and about the concurrent employment of private police squads by corporations. Hobsbawm argues, therefore, that Americans had little choice but to resort to such vigilantism. Hobsbawm, *The Age of Capital, 1848-1875* (New York: Charles Scribner's Sons, 1975), 144.

5. In the 1880s and 1890s lynchings were by no means confined exclusively to African-Americans. From 1889 to 1900, 1,843 reported lynchings occurred in America, and roughly one-third of those crimes had white victims. After the 1890s, however, lynchings became even more racially focused. From 1900 to 1910 almost 90 percent of all reported lynchings involved black victims. In some quarters lynchings have been also associated in historical memory as white male reactions to black assaults on white women. Actually only one-sixth of lynch victims between 1889 and 1929 were accused of rape. See the Southern Commission on the Study of Lynching, *Lynchings and What They Mean* (Atlanta, 1931), 18-19, 73; Wyatt-Brown, *Southern Honor*, 436-40, 453-61; Sig Synnestvedt, *The White Response to Black Emancipation* (New York: Macmillan, 1972), 58-59.

6. Clarksville *Leaf-Chronicle*, Jan. 22, 1906, and Aug. 11, 1909; George C. Wright, *Racial Violence in Kentucky, 1865-1940: Lynchings, Mob Rule, and "Legal Lynchings"* (Baton Rouge: Louisiana State Univ. Press, 1990), 61-126; Edward Coffman, *The Story of Logan County* (Nashville: Parthenon Press, 1962), 230. See also Richard P. Gildrie, "Lynch Law and the Great Clarksville Fire of 1878: Social Order in a New South Town," *Tennessee Historical Quarterly* 42 (Spring 1983): 58-75; and Robert Minor, *Lynching and Frame-Up in Tennessee* (New York: New Century Publishers 1946), 12-19.

7. Clarksville *Leaf-Chronicle*, May 8, 1905; Eugene P. Lyle, Jr., "Night Riding in the Black Patch," *Hampton's Magazine* (Jan. 1909): 344.

8. Clarksville *Leaf-Chronicle*, Nov. 22 and Dec. 27, 1905; James O. Nall, *The Tobacco Night Riders of Kentucky and Tennessee, 1905-1909* (Louisville: Standard Press, 1939), 43-46; Eugene P. Lyle, Jr., "Night Riding—A Reign of Fear," *Hampton's Magazine* (June 1909): 466-67.

9. Clarksville *Leaf-Chronicle*, Oct. 3 and Dec. 9, 1905. In *The Tobacco Night Riders of Kentucky and Tennessee*, Nall incorrectly says that the fire was extinguished before damage was done (46).

10. Clarksville *Leaf-Chronicle*, Jan. 31 and Sept. 15, 1905.

11. Clarksville *Leaf-Chronicle*, Dec. 1, 1906; Nall, *Tobacco Night Riders*, 50, 67-72; Charles Mayfield Meacham, *A History of Christian County, Kentucky: From Oxcart to Airplane* (Nashville: Marshall and Bruce, 1930), 346-47.

12. Mayfield *Messenger*, Dec. 13, 1906.

13. Clarksville *Leaf-Chronicle*, Oct. 3, 1905; Paducah *News-Democrat*, Dec. 12 and 19, 1907. M.V. Ingram wrote a scathing article condemning Ferigo's actions, stating that Ferigo and his fellow buyers were "robbing our people of the fruits of their labor, bringing suffering on the laboring class . . . and reducing the owners of the land to poverty." This article was subsequently not published by the *Leaf-Chronicle*, because of threatened legal action by the Regie against the newspaper. The article is located in File 3028, Tobacco Investigation Records, Bureau of Corporations, Record Group 122, National Archives.

14. Clarksville *Leaf-Chronicle*, December 7 and 10, 1907; New York *Times*, Dec. 8,

1907; *Commonwealth of Kentucky* v. *Dr. David Amoss*, Hopkinsville, Ky., 1911, p. 36; Meacham, *History of Christian County*, 351-55; Nall, *Tobacco Night Riders*, 72-80; Day Allen Willey, "The Night Riders: An Account of the Tobacco War," *Metropolitan Magazine* 28 (July 1908): 355-57, 361-62. The Italian government requested federal protection of its property in a letter to U.S. secretary of state Elihu Root. See *Western Tobacco Journal*, Dec. 30, 1907.

15. New York *Times*, Jan. 29, 1908; *Report of the Commissioner of Corporations on the Tobacco Industry*, pt. 1 (Washington, D.C.: G.P.O., 1909), 9-10, 60-61, 78-79.

16. *Appeal to Reason*, Oct. 15, 1910; Lyle, "Night Riding—A Reign of Fear," 465.

17. Lyle, "Night Riding—A Reign of Fear," 466; *Appeal to Reason*, Oct. 15, 1910. The *Appeal*'s leading reporter, George Shoaf, investigated the Tobacco Wars in 1910 and was unabashed in his approval of Amoss and the night riders: "Without reserve the writer admits his admiration for the Night Riders. . . . in the spirit of resistance and audacity shown by the Night Riders in their fight to preserve their economic freedom he realizes there still burn the unquenchable fires of 1776 and 1861, and in the lurid glare of the blazing tobacco barns and warehouses he sees revealed a resolute determination not to submit to industrial slavery." See *Appeal to Reason*, Sept. 10, 1910. The *Appeal*'s role in the Socialist movement in America is treated in Elliott Shore, *Talkin' Socialism: J.A. Wayland and the Role of the Press in American Radicalism, 1890-1912* (Lawrence: Univ. Press of Kansas, 1988), 3-5, 75-93, 172-77; James R. Green, *Grass-Roots Socialism: Radical Movements in the Southwest, 1895-1943* (Baton Rouge: Louisiana State Univ. Press, 1978), chap. 1, pp. 137-41; and Nick Salvatore, *Eugene V. Debs: Citizen and Socialist* (Urbana: Univ. of Illinois Press, 1982), 191-93, 198, 220. Amoss died in 1915. Nall, *Tobacco Night Riders*, 197.

18. *Commonwealth of Kentucky* v. *Dr. David Amoss*, 225; Lyle, "Night Riding—A Reign of Fear," 466-67; Nall, *Tobacco Night Riders*, 56-60, 78-79; G.N. Albrecht to A.E. Willson, March 29, 1908, and John Stites to Willson, March 18, 1908, Augustus Everett Willson Papers, Manuscript Department, Filson Club, Louisville.

19. *Commonwealth of Kentucky* v. *Dr. David Amoss*; New York *Times*, July 26, 1908; *The Tobacco Planters' Yearbook, 1908* (Guthrie, Ky., 1908), 7; Nall, *Tobacco Night Riders*, 60-61. By all accounts, Amoss and Dunning were community leaders, active in local civic affairs and their churches. Historian Allen W. Trelease found these same qualities in the founders of the Ku Klux Klan. See Trelease, *White Terror: The Ku Klux Klan Conspiracy and Southern Reconstruction* (New York: Harper and Row, 1971), 3.

20. New York *Times*, July 26, 1908; Lyle, "Night Riding in the Black Patch," 345; Nall, *Tobacco Night Riders*, 49.

21. *Kentucky Evening Gazette*, March 14, 1908.

22. Edward A. Jonas, "The Night Riders: A Trust of Farmers," *World's Work* 17 (Feb. 1909): 11216; Nall, *Tobacco Night Riders*, 52-56. See also Cincinnati *Enquirer*, Dec. 6, 1908. The elaborate rituals of swearing oaths in antebellum southern culture are discussed in Wyatt-Brown, *Southern Honor*, 34, 55-59.

23. Lyle, "Night Riding—A Reign of Fear," 466-67. See also Gladys-Marie Fry, *Night Riders in Black Folk History* (Knoxville: Univ. of Tennessee Press, 1975), 3, 110-34.

24. *Tobacco*, Oct. 24 and 31, 1907.

25. In 1897 Willson was appointed to attend a convention in Indianapolis to discuss "currency reform" and to recommend policies designed to maintain the gold standard. Among those selected were bank presidents, advisers to President McKinley, and other representatives of the nation's financial sector. Willson attended the meeting as an

official representative of the Union for Sound Money. A scholar recently remarked that the composition of these groups had one common trait: "their associations with the most advanced forms of business enterprise and technical innovation—the new corporations." The Indianapolis convention subsequently laid the groundwork that led to the Gold Standard Act of 1900, which alleviated financial tensions among the nation's business elite at the expense of agriculturalists. James Livingston, *Origins of the Federal Reserve System: Money, Class, and Corporate Capitalism, 1890-1913* (Ithaca, N.Y.: Cornell Univ. Press, 1986), 21-22, 105-6, 110-25.

26. Robert K. Foster, "Augustus E. Willson and the Republican Party of Kentucky, 1895-1911," M.A. thesis, Univ. of Louisville, 1955, p. 64.

27. Ibid., 63; Louisville *Courier-Journal,* Oct. 31, 1907.

28. Foster, "Augustus E. Willson and the Republican Party," 55-68; Thomas H. Appleton, Jr., "'Like Banqho's Ghost': The Emergence of the Prohibition Issue in Kentucky Politics," Ph.D. diss., Univ. of Kentucky, 1981.

29. Nicholas C. Burckel, "From Beckham to McCreary: The Progressive Record of Kentucky Governors," *Register of the Kentucky Historical Society* 76 (Oct. 1978): 285-306; Louisville *Courier-Journal,* Nov. 1, 2, and 7, 1907.

30. Cortelyou, who chaired the Republican National Committee during the 1904 presidential election, later denied allegations that he had accepted illegal campaign donations from the American Tobacco Company. *Western Tobacco Journal,* Oct. 28, 1912.

31. Christopher Waldrep, ed., "A 'Trust Lawyer' Tries to Help Kentucky Farmers: Augustus E. Willson's 1907 Letter to George B. Cortelyou," *Register of the Kentucky Historical Society* 83 (Autumn 1985): 354-55.

32. Christopher Waldrep, "The Night Riders and the Law in Kentucky and Tennessee, 1870-1911," Ph.D. diss., Ohio State Univ., 1990, pp. 320-21.

33. James B. Duke to Willson, Dec. 17, 1907, and F.G. Ewing to Willson, Dec. 19, 1907, Augustus Everett Willson Papers; *Western Tobacco Journal,* Jan. 6, 1908; Clarksville *Leaf-Chronicle,* Dec. 13 and 20, 1907.

34. In 1910 tenant farmer J.T. Strand said: "I'd see Willson in hell before I'd vote fur him." *Appeal to Reason,* Oct. 1, 1910.

35. *Western Tobacco Journal,* Aug. 28, 1911; State of the Commonwealth message, Jan. 8, 1908, in A.E. Willson's Vertical Files, Kentucky Historical Society, Frankfort; *Black Patch Tobacco Journal,* Dec. 1908; Christopher Waldrep, "Augustus E. Willson and the Night Riders," *Filson Club History Quarterly* 58 (April 1984): 237-42; Foster, "Augustus E. Willson and the Republican Party," 75-79, 91. Willson also pardoned numerous confessed night riders who had provided evidence to the state, as well as many convicted of killing night riders.

36. After Governor Patterson offered rewards for captured night riders, an enraged Polk Prince of the Montgomery County PPA launched a brief campaign for governor against Patterson. See Lyle, "Night Riding in the Black Patch," 347.

37. G.W. Long to Willson, Dec. 12, 1907, Augustus Everett Willson Papers.

38. G.N. Albrecht to Willson, Feb. 23 and 25, 1908, Augustus Everett Willson Papers.

39. G.N. Albrecht to Willson, Feb. 27, 1908, Augustus Everett Willson Papers; Lexington *Herald,* June 24, 1908.

40. Clarksville *Leaf-Chronicle,* March 23, 1908.

41. Theodore Roosevelt to Willson, March 6, 1908, Augustus Everett Willson Papers.

42. A.O. Stanley to George Snadon, Aug. 20, 1907, and A.O. Stanley to the Committee on Mines and Mining, A.O. Stanley Papers, Special Collections, M.I. King Library, University of Kentucky; *Tobacco*, Sept. 19, 1907, and June 4, 1908; Mayfield *Messenger*, Sept. 6, 1907; Nicholas C. Burckel, "A.O. Stanley and Progressive Reform, 1902-1919," *Register of the Kentucky Historical Society* 79 (Spring 1981): 141. Among some agrarian "radicals," the methods used by night riders were commendable. Tom Watson's *Jeffersonian Magazine* in 1908 noted: "Congress could have given these men relief, but Congress is too busy making and upholding the laws that produce the Trusts. Those are best helped who help themselves, and the brave men of Kentucky went to war. . . . Some crimes were committed which must be deplored. But crime is always the incident of war; I glory in their spunk. . . . Let the Farmers Union study the methods of the Night Riders of Kentucky!" Quoted in the *Black Patch Tobacco Journal*, Sept. 1908.

43. Clarksville *Leaf-Chronicle*, Sept. 24, 1906; J. Morgan Kousser, *The Shaping of Southern Politics: Suffrage Restriction and the Establishment of the One-Party South, 1880-1910* (New Haven, Conn.: Yale Univ. Press, 1974), 120, 122, 239; Pete Daniel, *Standing at the Crossroads: Southern Life in the Twentieth Century* (New York: Hill and Wang, 1986), 50-54. See also Joseph H. Cartwright, *The Triumph of Jim Crow: Tennessee Race Relations in the 1880's* (Knoxville: Univ. of Tennessee Press, 1976).

44. Interview with Washington Anderson, Oct. 23, 1905, File 3085, Tobacco Investigation Records.

45. Clarksville *Leaf-Chronicle*, March 10 and Oct. 5, 1908; *Western Tobacco Journal*, May 11, 1908. See also Wright, *Racial Violence in Kentucky*, 123-43; and William F. Holmes, "Whitecapping: Agrarian Violence in Mississippi, 1902-1906," *Journal of Southern History* 35 (May 1969): 165-85. The Hopkins County attack was later strangely connected to a conversation David Amoss had with a representative of the United Mine Workers in the county. In exchange for funds to help pay his lawyer's fees, Amoss told the miners' union that at "anytime it was necessary for anything to be done in Hopkins Co., he would furnish the men to do it." Paul Moore to Willson, July 16, 1910, Augustus Everett Willson Papers.

46. Wright, *Racial Violence in Kentucky*, 123-24.

47. Harrodsburg *Democrat*, May 1, 1908; *Western Tobacco Journal*, March 24, 1908; Clarksville *Leaf-Chronicle*, Dec. 30, 1907, and Sept. 24, 1908; Mayfield *Messenger*, April 30, May 1, and July 10, 1908; Paducah *Evening Sun*, Jan. 25, Feb. 19, and March 10 and 23, 1908; *Appeal to Reason*, Nov. 14, 1908; Woodford *Sun*, May 21, 1908; Wright, *Racial Violence in Kentucky*, 137-39. See also Minor, *Lynching and Frame-Up in Tennessee*, 17-18.

48. *Black Patch Tobacco Journal*, Feb. 1908. The *Journal* also noted that "the negro is by nature fitted for the South. He shivers and freezes in the North. The Southern sun is good for his complexion and feels good to his 'pusson.' The Southern white knows the negro and can get along with him if they are left unmolested."

49. Clarksville *Leaf-Chronicle*, May 3, 1907.

50. Federal manuscript census, Montgomery County, Tennessee, 1910.

51. Clarksville *Leaf-Chronicle*, April 11, 1907; *Tobacco*, Jan. 21, 1909. Not all visitations by night riders, incidentally, were of a violent or coercive nature. In July 1909 night riders visited the home of a non-association farmer, W.H. Pepper of Bracken County, Ken-

tucky. Though a tobacco grower, Pepper was an invalid and had great difficulty tending his crop. Pepper awoke early one morning to find night riders in his field, planting his crop for him. Pepper heard the riders yell, "Sign Up, Cecil. Sign up!" Clarksville *Leaf-Chronicle*, July 23, 1909.

52. C.H. Branch to Willson, Dec. 20, 1907, Augustus Everett Willson Papers; Princeton *Twice-A-Week Leader*, Sept. 1, 1908.

53. Lyle, "Night Riding—A Reign of Fear," 468-69; Jonas, "Night Riders," 11213-18; John G. Miller, *The Black Patch War* (Chapel Hill: Univ. of North Carolina Press, 1936), 21-25; Christopher Waldrep, "'Human Wolves': The Night Riders and the Killing of Axiom Cooper," *Register of the Kentucky Historical Society* 81 (Autumn 1983): 420-24. In popular revolts, those who commit crime on the forces that are perceived as taking traditional rights away from society are often looked upon as folk heroes. See E.J. Hobsbawm, *Primitive Rebels: Studies in Archaic Forms of Social Movements in the 19th and 20th Centuries* (Manchester: Manchester Univ. Press, 1959), 14-16; Richard Maxwell Brown, "Historical Patterns of American Violence," in *Violence in America: Historical and Comparative Perspectives*, ed. Hugh Davis Graham and Ted Robert Gurr (Beverly Hills, Calif.: Sage Publications, 1979), 27; Thelen, *Paths of Resistance*, 59-77.

54. *Appeal to Reason*, Oct. 1, 1910.

55. Miller, *Black Patch War*, 25-36, 62-72; Nall, *Tobacco Night Riders*, 165-68; New York *Times*, May 14, 1908.

56. Wright, *Racial Violence in Kentucky*, 141-42.

57. *Commonwealth of Kentucky* v. *Dr. David Amoss*; Nall, *Tobacco Night Riders*, 192-97.

Chapter 6. Organizing the Bluegrass

1. Brief discussions of the burley movement are contained in Helen Morris Bleidt, "A History of the Development of Growers' Organizations and Tobacco Pools in the Burley District of Kentucky, 1902-1927," M.A. thesis, Univ. of Kentucky, 1932, pp. 22-37; Theodore Saloutos and John D. Hicks, *Twentieth-Century Populism: Agricultural Discontent in the Middle West, 1900-1939* (Lincoln: Univ. of Nebraska Press, 1951), 122-26, an account largely based on Saloutos's earlier article, "The American Society of Equity in Kentucky: A Recent Attempt in Agrarian Reform," *Journal of Southern History* 5 (Aug. 1939): 347-63; and Joseph G. Knapp, *The Rise of American Cooperative Enterprise, 1620-1920* (Danville, Ill.: Interstate Printers and Publishers, 1969), 185-88.

2. *Western Tobacco Journal*, May 9, 1898.

3. *Report of the Commissioner of Corporations on the Tobacco Industry*, pt. 1 (Washington, D.C.: G.P.O., 1909), 53; U.S. Department of Agriculture, Bureau of Agricultural Economics, *Tobaccos of the United States: Acreage, Yield per Acre, Production, Price, and Value, by States, 1866-1945, and by Types and Classes, 1919-1945* (Washington, D.C., 1948), 6-7; U.S. Bureau of the Census, *Statistical Abstract of the United States, 1889* (Washington, D.C., 1890), 269-70; idem, *Statistical Abstract of the United States, 1897* (Washington, D.C., 1898), 313-14.

4. *Western Tobacco Journal*, July 18, 1898. Eleven growers attended this meeting: Hampton; M.W. Neal of Lousville; W.O. Coleman, J.H. Alexander, and J.P. Powell of Trimble County; Luther B. Strader of Barren County; Nathan Sorrell, T.S. Robertson, and J.R. Peters of Bath County; Ambrose Dudley of Henry Co.; and T.M. Dixon.

5. *Western Tobacco Journal*, Nov. 7, 1898.

6. Ibid., Nov. 21 and 28, 1898.

7. Ibid., Nov. 28 and Dec. 12, 1898. The counties represented at the meeting were Barren, Bath, Bourbon, Boyle, Carroll, Clark, Fayette, Franklin, Garrard, Harrison, Hart, Henry, Jessamine, Mason, Nelson, Nicholas, Owen, Pendleton, Scott, Shelby, Spencer, Trimble, Washington, and Woodford.

8. Ibid., Dec. 12, 1898.

9. Louisville *Courier-Journal*, Dec. 6, 1896; *Appeal to Reason*, Nov. 12, 1910; James O. Nall, *The Tobacco Night Riders of Kentucky and Tennessee, 1905-1909* (Louisville: Standard Press, 1939), 149. In January 1907 James A. Scott, a BTS member and prominent local attorney, spoke admiringly of the legacy of the tollgate riders and suggested that the same vigilantism might be inflicted on representatives of the tobacco trust. Winchester *Democrat*, Jan. 4, 1907.

10. *Western Tobacco Journal*, Dec. 12, 1898. The term *lecturer* no doubt was a holdover from the Farmers' Alliance and its network of lecturers.

11. Ibid., Jan. 16, Feb. 27, and April 17, 1899; Lexington *Morning Herald*, Dec. 6, 1898.

12. *Western Tobacco Journal*, March 10 and April 14, 1902; Lexington *Herald*, Oct. 31, 1902; Bleidt, "History of the Development of Growers' Organizations," 11-14.

13. Lexington *Herald*, Nov. 7, 1902.

14. James B. Duke to W.B. Hawkins, Sept. 4, 1903, Letterbrook no. 2, James B. Duke Papers, Manuscript Department, Perkins Library, Duke University; Lexington *Herald*, Sept. 20, 1903. From 1903 to 1908, a period of desperately low prices for farmers, the ATC amassed its greatest profits. After paying 6-percent dividends on preferred stock and 4 to 6 percent on bonds, both totalling over eleven million dollars, the average remaining surplus was sixteen million dollars. Jason Scott, "No Monopoly on Freedom: A Study of the American Tobacco Company from 1890 to 1911," senior thesis, Duke Univ. 1990, pp. 64-65.

15. *Western Tobacco Journal*, Feb. 8, 1904; Lexington *Herald*, Sept. 20, 1903; Clarksville *Leaf-Chronicle*, Dec. 10, 1903; Theodore Saloutos, *Farmer Movements in the South, 1865-1933* (1960; Lincoln: Univ. of Nebraska Press, 1967), 168-69.

16. "Minutebook of the Burley Tobacco Growers Company," Box 2, pp. 1-4, Burley Tobacco Cooperative Records, Special Collections, M.I. King Library, University of Kentucky; Lexington *Herald*, June 10, 1904; Bleidt, "History of the Development of Growers' Organizations," 15-16.

17. Lexington *Herald*, Sept. 18 and Oct. 31, 1904; *Western Tobacco Journal*, June 19, 1905; *Wisconsin Equity News*, June 1, 1908; Cincinnati *Enquirer*, May 11, 1905; Bleidt, "History of the Development of Growers' Organizations," 15-16.

18. Lexington *Herald*, May 24, 1905; Clarksville *Leaf-Chronicle*, Feb. 10, 1905.

19. "Minutebook of the Burley Tobacco Growers Company," Box 2, pp. 46-48, 57-58; Lexington *Leader*, Feb. 8 and 24, 1905; Bleidt, "History of the Development of Growers' Organizations," 18.

20. Paducah *News-Democrat*, Jan. 15, 1905; Clarksville *Leaf-Chronicle*, Feb. 13, 1905. The Tobacco Growers Association was officially dissolved on March 5, 1907. Lexington *Herald*, March 6, 1907.

21. J.A. Everitt, *The Third Power: Farmers to the Front* (Indianapolis: J.A. Everitt, 1907), 18; Robert H. Bahmer, "The American Society of Equity," *Agricultural History* 14 (Jan. 1940): 33-35; Saloutos, "American Society of Equity in Kentucky," 351.

22. Everitt, *Third Power*, 240-41, 63; *Appeal to Reason*, Oct. 15, 1910.

23. Everitt, *Third Power*, 240-41; Saloutos, "American Society of Equity in Kentucky," 352. The Equity also appeared in North Dakota in 1907, promising higher prices for midwestern farmers. Without any adequate marketing programs, however, the Equity was unable to deliver a new day. Concerning the role of Everitt in North Dakota, one scholar has remarked: "The success of the Equity came in spite of, rather than because of, the efforts of its promotion-oriented founder." Scott Ellsworth, "Origins of the Nonpartisan League," Ph.D. diss., Duke Univ., 1982, pp. iii-iv, 105. An earlier student also noted: "Cooperatives can not achieve permanent success by arbitrary price fixing." The Equity plan was not structurally organized to meet the long-term needs of growers, who "were not equipped to store their tobacco nor to finance the holding process." O.B. Jesness, "The Cooperative Marketing of Tobacco," *Kentucky Agricultural Experiment Station Bulletin*, no. 288 (1928): 276-305.

24. In Everitt's estimation, the Grange and the Alliance had been "misdirected" by their leadership. Everitt thus sought the Alliance's constituency while advocating a plan that dealt only with market prices. Everitt, *Third Power*, 60-63, 112, 214. See also Knapp, *Rise of the American Cooperative Enterprise*, 182-83; Bahmer, "American Society of Equity," 37; and Saloutos and Hicks, *Twentieth-Century Populism*, 117.

25. Saloutos, *Farmer Movements*, 170-71; Bahmer, "American Society of Equity," 46; Knapp, *Rise of the American Cooperative Enterprise*, 184-85; Bleidt, "History of the Development of Growers' Organizations," 12.

26. *Western Tobacco Journal*, Feb. 19, 1906.

27. Lexington *Herald*, Aug. 27, 1909; "Minutebook of the Burley Tobacco Society," Box 2, p. 1, Burley Tobacco Cooperative Papers, Special Collections, M.I. King Library, University of Kentucky; Everitt, *Third Power*, 289-90; Saloutos, *Farmer Movements*, 172-73.

28. Winchester *Democrat*, Oct. 23, 1906.

29. "Minutebook of the Burley Tobacco Society," Box 2, pp. 1-3; Saloutos, "American Society of Equity in Kentucky," 352; Lexington *Herald*, Aug. 27, 1909. Rankin was elected Kentucky commissioner of agriculture in 1907.

30. Lexington *Herald*, Aug. 27, 1909.

31. Winchester *Democrat*, Nov. 6, 1906.

32. The pooling agreement called for the 1905 crop to be sold for not less than fifteen cents per pound, almost double the price burley farmers were receiving in 1904. "Minutebook of the Burley Tobacco Society," Box 2, pp. 3-12; *Western Tobacco Journal*, Nov. 19, 1906; *Wisconsin Equity News*, June 1, 1908; Lexington *Herald*, Aug. 27, 1901. Everitt said that local growers portrayed him as "the Moses who pointed the way" and Sherman as Aaron (*Third Power*, 289).

33. *Appeal to Reason*, Jan. 25, 1908; Woodford *Sun*, Dec. 13, 1906.

34. "Minutebook of the Burley Tobacco Society," Box 2, pp. 14-15; Lexington *Herald*, Jan. 2, 1907.

35. "Minutebook of the Burley Tobacco Society," Box 2, pp. 20-21; Clarksville *Leaf-Chronicle*, Jan. 14, 1907; Bleidt, "History of the Development of Growers' Organizations," 28-29.

36. Everitt, *Third Power*, 289; Lexington *Herald*, Aug. 27, 1909; Woodford *Sun*, May 23, 1907.

37. Lexington *Herald*, Jan. 17, 1907; Woodford *Sun*, Feb. 7, 1907; U.S. Bureau of the

Census, *Thirteenth Census of the United States, 1910*, vol. 6, *Agriculture* (Washington, D.C., 1913), 633.

38. Kentucky Board of Fire Underwriters, *Final Report*, Oct. 8, 1907, in Augustus Everett Willson Papers, Manuscript Department, Filson Club, Louisville. Support among businessmen for the BTS was reflected in the actions of two Woodford County bankers. J.N. Camden, president of the Woodford County Bank, and cashier Louis Marshall pledged their crops to the BTS shortly after the American Tobacco Company withdrew its deposits from the bank. Woodford *Sun*, March 14, 1907.

39. *Final Report*, Oct. 8, 1907, Willson Papers; Lexington *Leader*, Dec. 8, 1907; Bleidt, "History of the Development of Growers' Organizations," 29. In January 1908 five wealthy members of the BTS—Wilson Berry, C.C. Patrick, John T. Denton, Charles Lamb, and Charles Prather—announced that they would provide part of their "fortunes" in financing the movement. See Lexington *Herald*, Jan. 26, 1908.

40. Winchester *Democrat*, Jan. 22 and 25, Feb. 8 and 26, and Aug. 20, 1907; *Western Tobacco Journal*, Feb. 11, 1907, and March 23, 1908; *Wisconsin Equity News*, June 1, 1908; Lexington *Herald*, July 8, 1907; *Tobacco*, May 23, 1907.

41. Lexington *Herald*, March 12 and April 26, 1907. National Equity organizers M.F. Sharp and W.B. Sherman attended the barbecue. The Equity, however, had no organizational structure in place to host such a meeting. Instead, the BTS depended on local organization.

42. "Minutebook of the Burley Tobacco Society," Box 2, p. 105.

43. *Western Tobacco Journal*, March 2, 1908.

Chapter 7. Farmers on Strike

1. Lexington *Herald*, Dec. 8, 1907; *Western Tobacco Journal*, Nov. 4, 1907.

2. "Minutebook of the Burley Tobacco Society," Box 2, pp. 126-29, 155-61, Burley Tobacco Cooperative Records, Special Collections, M.I. King Library, University of Kentucky; *Kentucky Evening Gazette*, Oct. 19, 23, 1907.

3. "Minutebook of the Burley Tobacco Society," Box 2, 171-75; *Tobacco*, Nov. 7 and Dec. 26, 1907.

4. Kentucky Board of Fire Underwriters, *Final Report*, Oct. 8, 1907, in Augustus Everett Willson Papers, Manuscript Department, Filson Club, Louisville.

5. The idea of eliminating an entire crop in order to increase market prices has been discussed at various times in twentieth-century American agriculture. The 1908 tobacco strike remains the only such successful effort. An attempt on a far grander scale in 1931 first brought Louisiana governor Huey P. Long to national prominence when he proposed that all southern cotton-growing states forbid the planting of cotton. Only Arkansas and South Carolina passed moratorium laws, and when Texas refused to comply, the matter was soon dropped. Long's plan, however, resonated deeply among thousands of southern cotton farmers, who were driven to the brink of economic disaster by the oncoming rush of the Great Depression. See Robert E. Snyder, *Cotton Crisis* (Chapel Hill: University of North Carolina Press, 1984); Alan Brinkley, *Voices of Protest: Huey Long, Father Coughlin, and the Great Depression* (New York: Vintage Books, 1982), 37-40; and T. Harry Williams, *Huey Long* (New York: Alfred A. Knopf, 1969), 531-33.

Most agricultural strikes in America have involved seasonal or migratory farm workers, and most occurred in the depression years of the 1930s. In general, these migratory strikes were small, lasted only a few weeks, and were often directed toward large landowners. Faced with the prospect of not having their crops harvested, the landowners usually agreed to nominal pay increases, but they returned to low wages the following year when the migrants returned. See U.S. Department of Labor, Bureau of Labor Statistics, *Labor Unionism in American Agriculture*, bulletin 836 (Washington, D.C., 1945); John L. Shover, "The Farmers' Holiday Association Strike, August, 1932," *Agricultural History* 39 (Oct. 1965): 196-203; A. William Hoglund, "Wisconsin Dairy Farmers on Strike," *Agricultural History* 35 (Jan. 1961): 24-34; John T. Schlebecker, "The Great Holding Action: The NFO in September, 1962," *Agricultural History* 39 (Oct. 1965): 204-13; and Frank W. Groves, "Twentieth-Century Farm Strikes: A Comment," *Agricultural History* 39 (Oct. 1965): 217-19. An account of an earlier strike is William F. Holmes, "The Arkansas Cotton Pickers' Strike of 1891 and the Demise of the Colored Farmers' Alliance," *Arkansas Historical Quarterly* 32 (Summer 1973): 107-19. A useful comparative study is Robert Edelman, *Proletarian Peasants: The Revolution of 1905 in Russia's Southwest* (Ithaca, N.Y.: Cornell Univ. Press, 1987), 82-168. Edelman understates the case when he remarks: "Plantation fields are not factory floors. Organizing a rural proletariat, strictly defined, has never been an easy process" (175).

6. Lexington *Herald*, Jan. 6, 1908. The 1908 organizing effort revealed the possibilities and the limits of the BTS recruiting drive. BTS organizers were mostly men, who limited their work to BTS meetings or personal contact. In 1910, after the BTS was essentially dead, the organization enlarged its recruiting staff to include women. The 1910 effort embraced local churches, of all denominations. This ambitious approach, however, was tried too late. *Western Tobacco Journal*, Sept. 12, 1910.

7. Lexington *Herald*, Jan. 20 and 28, and Feb. 4 and 18, 1908.

8. *Kentucky Evening Gazette*, Jan. 2 and 4, 1908; Lexington *Herald*, Jan. 2, 3, and 4, 1908; "Minutebook of the Burley Tobacco Society," Box 2, 184-86, 195.

9. "Minutebook of the Burley Tobacco Society," Box 2, 171-175, 184-86, 195. The Kentucky commissioner of agriculture estimated in April 1908 that approximately 11 percent of tobacco beds in the burley tobacco region had been set out for planting. *Farmers Equity Journal*, April 11, 1908.

10. *Tobacco*, March 12, 1908.

11. Lexington *Herald*, Feb. 10 and 22, 1908.

12. John L. Matthews, "The Farmers' Union and the Tobacco Pool," *Atlantic Monthly* 102 (Oct. 1908): 488.

13. *Kentucky Evening Gazette*, March 16, 1908; New York *Times*, July 26, 1908; Lexington *Herald*, May 31, 1908; Harrodsburg *Democrat*, Nov. 10, 1908.

14. *Kentucky Evening Gazette*, March 26 and 31, 1908.

15. Lexington *Herald*, March 5, 1908.

16. "Minutebook of the Burley Tobacco Society," Box 2, 195, 199-208; *Tobacco*, Aug. 20, 1908; *Western Tobacco Journal*, May 5, 1908.

17. Night riding also occurred within the far western section of Tennessee, in areas near the Black Patch. The causes of violence, however, had nothing to do with tobacco. Entrepreneurs claimed legal title to land surrounding Reelfoot Lake, preventing fishermen from earning a livelihood, and demanded rents from squatters. The conflict saw armed night riders appear in 1908, attempting to retain rights that many generations had

held. Two lawyers were murdered, some piers were damaged, and a black family was murdered outside Hickman, Tennessee. See Paul J. Vanderwood, *Night Riders of Reelfoot Lake* (Memphis, Tenn.: Memphis State Univ. Press, 1969).

18. *Kentucky Evening Gazette*, Feb. 19, 1908.

19. *Kentucky Evening Gazette*, March 14, 1908; *Appeal to Reason*, Oct. 29, 1910; *Western Tobacco Journal*, March 16, 1908; Lexington *Herald*, March 22, 1908.

20. Memorandum from W.B. Hawkins, March 1908, Augustus Everett Willson Papers.

21. U.S. Bureau of the Census, *Thirteenth Census of the United States, 1910*, vol. 6, *Agriculture* (Washington, D.C., 1913), 622-45; vol. 7, *Agriculture*, pp. 573-611. The twenty-four counties are: Anderson, Boone, Bourbon, Bracken, Campbell, Carroll, Clark, Fayette, Franklin, Gallatin, Grant, Harrison, Henry, Jessamine, Kenton, Madison, Mason, Mercer, Owen, Pendleton, Scott, Shelby, Trimble, and Woodford.

22. *Appeal to Reason*, Oct. 29, 1910.

23. Winchester *Democrat*, Dec. 17, 1907; F.G. Snyder to Willson, Dec. 13, 1907, Augustus Everett Willson Papers.

24. Lexington *Herald*, March 22, 1908; Harrodsburg *Democrat*, April 24, 1908; *Kentucky Evening Gazette*, March 24, 1908; Jessie Taylor to Willson, March 27, 1908, Augustus Everett Willson Papers.

25. *Kentucky Evening Gazette*, June 5, 1908. Dr. Samuel Halley of Fayette County was one of the few Bluegrass farmers who successfully raised a tobacco crop in 1908. To do so, however, he had to hire full-time armed guards to protect his plants. *Western Tobacco Journal*, July 20, 1908.

26. U.S. Department of Agriculture, *Annual Summary, 1908: Kentucky Section of the Climatological Section of the Weather Bureau* (Louisville, 1909), 99; idem, *Report for October, 1908: Kentucky Section of the Climatological Service of the Weather Bureau* (Louisville, 1908), 76; idem, *Crop Reporter* 9 (Dec. 1907): 100; idem, *Crop Reporter* 10 (Dec. 1908): 98; Lexington *Herald*, Feb. 17, May 8, July 15 and 27, and Aug. 31, 1908; *Kentucky Evening Gazette*, Feb. 14 and 29, 1908.

27. Lexington *Leader*, Dec. 8, 1907; Kentucky Board of Fire Underwriters, *Final Report*, 4.

28. *Report of the Commissioner of Corporations on the Tobacco Industry*, pt. 1 (Washington, D.C.: G.P.O., 1909), 43-48, 254; Patrick Reynolds and Tom Shachtman, *The Gilded Leaf: Triumph, Tragedy, and Tobacco—Three Generations of the R.J. Reynolds Family and Fortune* (New York: Little, Brown, and Co., 1989), 80; *Burley Tobacco Grower*, June 1924; *Commercial and Financial Chronicle*, Nov. 7 and 20, 1908. The *Chronicle* reported to its readers that tobacco prices would rise in 1908 because of low supplies on hand in manufactories.

29. Cincinnati *Enquirer*, Nov. 21, 1908.

30. "Minutebook of the Burley Tobacco Society," Box 2, 276-79; *Tobacco*, Nov. 26, 1908; *Wisconsin Equity News*, Dec. 15, 1908; Lexington *Herald*, Nov. 20 and 25, 1908; *Western Tobacco Journal*, Nov. 23, 1908; Cincinnati *Enquirer*, Nov. 20, 1908; New York *Times*, Nov. 20, 1908.

31. Cincinnati *Enquirer*, Nov. 21, 1908.

32. Louisville *Courier-Journal*, Nov. 20 and 21, 1908; Cincinnati *Enquirer*, Nov. 20 and 21, 1908; Theodore Saloutos and John D. Hicks, *Twentieth-Century Populism: Agricultural Discontent in the Middle West, 1900-1939* (Lincoln: Univ. of Nebraska Press, 1951), 125.

33. *Wisconsin Equity News*, Dec. 15, 1908; *Tobacco*, Nov. 26, 1908; Cincinnati *Enquirer*, Nov. 21, 1908; *Appeal to Reason*, Oct. 29, 1910.

34. Lexington *Herald*, Nov. 20, 1908.

35. Louisville *Courier-Journal*, Nov. 20, 1908.

36. *Western Tobacco Journal*, Nov. 30, 1908.

37. Lexington *Herald*, Dec. 9, 1908; Cincinnati *Enquirer*, Nov. 20, 1908; *Wisconsin Equity News*, Dec. 15, 1908.

38. The language used by auto organizers in 1937 to describe the settlement reached with General Motors sounds remarkably similar to that used by tobacco organizers in 1908. For example, one member of the UAW claimed that the workers' strike was "the greatest advance of any single event in the history of the labor movement." See Sidney Fine, *Sit-Down: The General Motors Strike of 1936-1937* (Ann Arbor: Univ. of Michigan Press, 1969), 306-7.

39. Cincinnati *Enquirer*, Nov. 22, 1908.

Chapter 8. The Demise of Agrarian Cooperation

1. Lexington *Leader*, Dec. 8, 1907.

2. *Appeal to Reason*, Oct. 22, 1910; Anna Youngman, "Tobacco Pools of Kentucky and Tennessee," *Journal of Political Economy* 18 (Jan. 1910): 45.

3. "Minutebook of the Burley Tobacco Society," Box 2, pp. 290-94, 319-27, Burley Tobacco Cooperative Records, Special Collections, M.I. King Library, University of Kentucky; *Tobacco*, June 17, 1909. In January 1909 Lebus suddenly resigned his presidency, only to reconsider and return. See "Minutebook of the Burley Tobacco Society," 306-10; Lexington *Herald*, Jan. 29, 1909.

4. *Kentucky Evening Gazette*, April 2, 1908.

5. "General Ledger, 1907-1912," Burley Tobacco Cooperative Records. In addition to negotiating his salary, the BTS also cleared Lebus of any guilt in allegedly selling large holdings of his crop outside the pool for a hefty price. Lexington *Herald*, Aug. 23, 1908.

6. "Minutebook of the Burley Tobacco Society," Box 2, pp. 181-82, 331; Helen Morris Bleidt, "A History of the Development of Growers' Organizations and Tobacco Pools in the Burley District of Kentucky, 1902-1927," M.A. thesis, Univ. of Kentucky, 1932, p. 36.

7. Clarksville *Leaf-Chronicle*, Aug. 2, 1909.

8. *Western Tobacco Journal*, Aug. 9, 1909. The salary limit proposed by Pendleton County farmers was placed at five thousand dollars for President Lebus.

9. *Western Tobacco Journal*, Aug. 16, 1909.

10. James W. Noel to G.W. Wickersham, Nov. 24, 1909, in Augustus Everett Willson Papers, Manuscript Department, Filson Club, Louisville; Youngman, "Tobacco Pools," 45.

11. Confidential memorandum, Beckner and Beckner Attorneys to Willson, June 24, 1909, Augustus Everett Willson Papers.

12. Winchester *Democrat*, July 20, 1909; Lexington *Herald*, July 14, 1909; New York *Times*, July 24, 1909; *Western Tobacco Journal*, July 19, 1909.

13. Winchester *Democrat*, Aug. 13, 1909; Lexington *Herald*, July 14, 1909.

14. *Western Tobacco Journal*, July 26, 1909.

15. Lexington *Herald*, Aug. 11, 1909; *Western Tobacco Journal*, Aug. 23 and 30, 1909.

16. *Western Tobacco Journal*, Sept. 6, 13, and 20, 1909.

17. Ibid., Sept. 27, 1909.

18. Ibid., Feb. 15 and June 14, 1909.

19. "Minutebook of the Burley Tobacco Society," Box 2, pp. 372-85.

20. *Western Tobacco Journal*, Nov. 8 and 15, 1909, and Jan. 31, 1910.

21. Ibid., Jan. 31, 1910.

22. Ibid., April 18 and May 9 and 23, 1910.

23. Ibid., March 14, 1910.

24. Scrapbook, June 2, 1910, James Campbell Cantrill Papers, Special Collections, M.I. King Library, University of Kentucky.

25. *Western Tobacco Journal*, May 30 and June 6, 1910.

26. The Equity disapproved of the BTS decision to sell the 1909 pool and vowed to canvass the area to find more support for the Equity. Ibid., Aug. 8, 1910.

27. Ibid., Aug. 8 and Oct. 10 and 17, 1910.

28. Lexington *Herald*, Oct. 16, 1910; *Western Tobacco Journal*, Sept. 26 and Oct. 17 and 24, 1910. Bankers in Cincinnati refused to support the BTS in seeking new loans in 1910.

29. *Western Tobacco Journal*, Dec. 26, 1910, Jan. 9, Feb. 13, 20, and 27, March 6, May 22, and Aug. 14, 1911, and April 15, Sept. 2, and Oct. 7 and 21, 1912.

30. Ibid., March 30, 1914. The BTS was replaced by the Burley Tobacco Company, the organization for which the 10 percent clause was aimed. With Clarence Lebus at its head, the BTC bought warehouses and the Schrader Tobacco Company in Louisville for six hundred thousand dollars. By World War I the BTC had sold its holdings to the R.J. Reynolds Company. The Burley Tobacco Company officially dissolved in 1919. See Bleidt, "History of the Development of Growers' Organizations," 38-40.

31. Clarksville *Leaf-Chronicle*, Jan. 18, 1909.

32. Ibid., Feb. 1 and April 8, 1909.

33. Unidentified newspaper clipping, ca. 1908, "Night Rider" reel, Kentucky Department for Libraries and Archives, Frankfort; *Appeal to Reason*, Nov. 14, 1908.

34. Clarksville *Leaf-Chronicle*, Jan. 7 and 18, and April 6, 1909; *Western Tobacco Journal*, Dec. 14, 1908; Mayfield *Messenger*, Oct. 9, 1909.

35. *Western Tobacco Journal*, June 21, 1909.

36. Clarksville *Leaf-Chronicle*, Nov. 12 and Dec. 1 and 2, 1908.

37. Ibid., Aug. 9, 1909.

38. *Western Tobacco Journal*, Sept. 28, 1908.

39. Ibid., Sept. 28, 1908, and May 17, 1909; Clarksville *Leaf-Chronicle*, May 24, 1909.

40. Clarksville *Leaf-Chronicle*, May 24, 1909; *Western Tobacco Journal*, May 17, 1909.

41. Clarksville *Leaf-Chronicle*, May 24, 1909; *Black Patch Tobacco Journal*, Aug. 1908. Not all members of the PPA were critical of Ewing. J.D. McClurdy wrote in 1909: "Jesus Christ died that we might live spiritually. F.G. Ewing came near dying that we might live temporarily. Ingratitude, ingratitude, ingratitude!" Clarksville *Leaf-Chronicle*, Feb. 10, 1909.

42. Clarksville *Leaf-Chronicle*, Oct. 29, 1909; Lexington *Herald*, Aug. 23, 1908.

43. Louisville *Courier-Journal*, Nov. 17, 1908.

44. "Minutes of the Dark Tobacco Growers Protective Association of Montgomery County," Oct. 28, 1907, in Robertson Yeatman Johnson Papers, Tennessee State Library and Archives, Nashville; Clarksville *Leaf-Chronicle*, May 6 and Sept. 27, 1909, and Aug. 29, 1914.

45. Clarksville *Leaf-Chronicle*, Feb. 11 and April 6, 1909.

46. Ibid., Jan. 16 and Feb. 13, 17, and 26, 1909, and July 18, 1910.

47. Ibid., Feb. 27, May 18, and Aug. 18, 1909.

48. Ibid., April 8 and May 12, 1909.

49. Louisville *Courier-Journal*, Dec. 3, 1908.

50. Clarksville *Leaf Chronicle*, Jan. 26, 1909, and June 7, 18, and 20, 1912.

51. Ibid., June 13 and 27, Aug. 6 and 8, Sept. 1 and 5, and Oct. 26, 1914, and Jan. 5, May 6, and July 1, 1915; *Western Tobacco Journal*, Nov. 8, 1915; S.E. Wrather, "Tobacco Marketing Organizations in Western Kentucky and Tennessee with Special Emphasis on Early Organizations," M.S. thesis, Univ. of Kentucky, 1933, pp. 45, 97.

52. U.S. Department of Agriculture, Bureau of Agricultural Economics, *Tobaccos of the United States: Acreage, Yield per Acre, Production, Price, and Value, by States, 1866-1945, and by Types and Classes, 1919-1945* (Washington, D.C., 1948), 80; Clarksville *Leaf-Chronicle*, Feb. 14, 19, and 28, March 1 and 8, and June 15, 1916.

53. *United States* v. *American Tobacco Company*, 221 U.S. 106 (1911), pp. 160-87.

54. New York *Times*, May 29, 1911.

55. Richard B. Tennant, *The American Cigarette Industry: A Study in Economic Analysis and Public Policy* (New Haven, Conn.: Yale Univ. Press, 1950), 59-64; Josephus Daniels, *Tar Heel Editor* (Chapel Hill: Univ. of North Carolina Press, 1939), 475; Gabriel Kolko, *The Triumph of Conservatism: A Reinterpretation of American History, 1900-1916* (New York: Free Press, 1963), 168-70. In his magisterial study of antitrust policy in America, Hans B. Thorelli discarded notions that combinations such as the ATC were necessary to increase "efficiency" in production and output. Thorelli found that combinations during this time were involved with "predacity" rather than obtaining efficiency and were "no sure-fire short-cuts to either greater efficiency or greater profits." Thorelli concludes that "economic power in the Golden Era of industrial expansion too often tended to be used in the interest of the favored few rather than that of the public." The events of the ATC case that transpired between 1907 and 1912 support this claim. Thorelli, *The Federal Antitrust Policy: Origination of an American Tradition* (Stockholm, 1954), 564, 560, 574. See also Ralph L. Nelson, *Merger Movements in American Industry, 1895-1956* (Princeton, N.J.: Princeton Univ. Press, 1959), 100-103.

Wickersham at this time also had fourteen Secret Service agents in Kentucky working to collect evidence that the tobacco cooperatives were "in restraint of trade" and could thus be prosecuted for violating the Sherman Act. See the Lexington *Herald*, Jan. 9, 1910.

56. Taft quoted in Jason Scott, "No Monopoly on Freedom: A Study of the American Tobacco Company from 1890 to 1911," senior thesis, Duke Univ., 1990, p. 89. Tennant, *The American Cigarette Industry*, 59-64. For a more general indictment of industrial monopoly, see Louis D. Brandeis, "Trusts, Efficiency, and the New Party," *Collier's Weekly* 26 (Sept. 1912): 14-15.

57. Tennant, *American Cigarette Industry*, 322-25, 340, 367; Reavis Cox, "Competition in the American Tobacco Industry, 1911-32: A Study of the Effects of the Partition of the American Tobacco Company by the United States Supreme Court," Ph.D. diss., Columbia Univ., 1933; Emory Martin Matthews, "The Tobacco Industry and the Position of the Tobacco Combination since 1890," M.S. thesis, Cornell Univ., 1932; Scott, "No Monopoly on Freedom," p. 88-89; Nannie May Tilley, *The R.J. Reynolds Tobacco Company* (Chapel Hill: Univ. of North Carolina Press, 1985), 415-26;

William H. Nicholls, *Price Policies in the Cigarette Industry: A Study of "Concerted Action" and Its Social Control, 1911-1950* (Nashville: Vanderbilt Univ. Press, 1951), 26-32; T.J. Woofter, Jr., *The Plight of Cigarette Tobacco* (Chapel Hill: Univ. of North Carolina Press, 1931), 32-38.

58. Joseph C. Robert, *The Story of Tobacco in America* (New York: Alfred A. Knopf, 1949), 201-2; James H. Shideler, *Farm Crisis, 1919-1923* (Berkeley: Univ. of California Press, 1957); U.S. Department of Agriculture, *Tobaccos of the United States*, 78.

59. Shideler, *Farm Crisis*, 46-52.

60. William Greider, *Secrets of the Temple: How the Federal Reserve Runs the Country* (New York: Simon and Schuster, 1987), 290-91. For other accounts that exonerate the Fed's actions in the farming crisis of 1920, see Shideler, *Farm Crisis*, 54-56; Arthur S. Link, "The Federal Reserve Policy and the Agricultural Depression of 1920-1921," *Agricultural History* 20 (July 1946): 166-75; George Brown Tindall, *The Emergence of the New South, 1913-1945* (Baton Rouge: Louisiana State Univ. Press, 1967), 111-14. A congressional committee examining the 1920 farm depression concluded that overproduction was not a factor in the crisis. Rather, the overly strict actions of the Federal Reserve Board were blamed. See Report of the Joint Commission of Agricultural Inquiry, *The Agricultural Crisis and Its Causes*, 67th Cong., 1st sess., 1921, H. Rept. 408, pp. 88-147.

61. Nicholls, *Price Policies*, 43. The four companies were the American Tobacco Company, Liggett and Myers, R.J. Reynolds, and P. Lorillard.

62. For a review of Sapiro's early career, see Grace H. Larsen and Henry E. Erdman, "Aaron Sapiro: Genius of Farm Cooperative Promotion," *Mississippi Valley Historical Review* 49 (Sept. 1962): 242-68. A recent sympathetic treatment is Henry N. Wallace, "Aaron Sapiro: The Man, His Philosophy, and the California School of Cooperative Thought," in *American Cooperation, 1988* (Washington, D.C.: American Institute of Cooperation, 1988), 133-43.

63. *Burley Tobacco Grower*, May 1922 and June 1922; William E. Ellis, "Robert Worth Bingham and the Crisis of Cooperative Marketing in the Twenties," *Agricultural History* 56 (Jan. 1982): 100-104.

64. *Burley Tobacco Grower*, July 1922; Ellis, "Robert Worth Bingham," 108; Tindall, *Emergence of the New South*, 119-20: George O. Gatlin, "Cooperative Marketing in the Black Patch," *Cooperative Marketing Journal* 1 (Feb. 1927): 69-71. See also Julian LaFar Smith, "Farmers' Cooperatives in Kentucky," M.A. thesis, Univ. of Kentucky, 1942, pp. 76-83; Harold Brown Clark, "The Role of Farmers' Cooperative Associations in the Marketing of Dark Tobacco in Kentucky and Tennessee from 1931 to 1950," Ph.D. diss., Univ. of Kentucky, 1950, pp. 2, 95; Carlos Clifton Erwin, "Economic Analysis of the Dark Tobacco Growers Cooperative Association of Western Kentucky and Tennessee," M.S. thesis, Univ. of Kentucky, 1948; Willard H. Minton, "A Study of the Dark Tobacco Cooperative Associations in Kentucky from 1931 to 1950 with Special Emphasis on Expectations, Accomplishments, and Member Relations," M.S. thesis, Univ. of Kentucky, 1950, pp. 38-39.

One result of the Bingham cooperative work was the enactment by the Kentucky legislature of the Bingham Cooperative Marketing Act, which made agricultural marketing organizations legal. This reform, however, did not insure the longevity of the burley or Black Patch cooperatives. See *Burley Tobacco Grower*, July 1922.

65. U.S. Department of Agriculture, *Tobaccos of the United States*, 6-7, 78-79.

Chapter 9. The Decline of the Countryside

1. Dewey W. Grantham, Jr., "Black Patch War: The Story of the Kentucky and Tennessee Night Riders, 1905-1909," *South Atlantic Quarterly* 59 (Spring 1960): 225; Theodore Saloutos, "The American Society of Equity in Kentucky: A Recent Attempt in Agrarian Reform," *Journal of Southern History* 5 (Aug. 1939): 363; Rick Gregory, "Robertson County and the Black Patch War, 1904-1909," *Tennessee Historical Quarterly* 39 (Fall 1980): 357.

2. *Appeal to Reason*, Oct. 8 and 15, 1910; *American Society of Equity News*, March 31, 1909; Clarksville *Leaf-Chronicle*, Oct. 2 and Nov. 7, 1905, and Feb. 15, 1909; *Black Patch Tobacco Journal*, Aug. 1907; Winchester *Democrat*, Dec. 7, 1906. For a general treatment of the impact that corporate capitalism had on American society at this time, see Alan Trachtenberg, *The Incorporation of America: Culture and Society in the Gilded Age* (New York: Hill and Wang, 1982).

3. E.P. Thompson, "The Moral Economy of the English Crowd in the Eighteenth Century," *Past and Present* 50 (Feb. 1971): 78-79; *Black Patch Tobacco Journal*, Aug. 1907.

4. Clarksville *Leaf-Chronicle*, Nov. 24, 1909.

5. *Black Patch Tobacco Journal*, Aug. 1907; Eric Foner, *Politics and Ideology in the Age of the Civil War* (New York: Oxford Univ. Press, 1980), 10, 58-59; idem, *Tom Paine and Revolutionary America* (New York: Oxford Univ. Press, 1976), 100-105, 124; Bruce Laurie, *Artisans into Workers: Labor in Nineteenth-Century America* (New York: Noonday Press, 1989), 49-52, 66-68, 109-10, 213; Steven Hahn, *The Roots of Southern Populism: Yeoman Farmers and the Transformation of the Georgia Upcountry, 1850-1890* (New York: Oxford Univ. Press, 1983), 2-3, 252-54, 286-87. See also Joyce Appleby, *Capitalism and a New Social Order: The Republican Vision of the 1790s* (New York: New York Univ. Press, 1984), 14, 42, 59, 86, 95-103. A crucial work that details the role of republicanism in the emergence of the American working class in the nineteenth century is Sean Wilentz, *Chants Democratic: New York City and the Rise of the American Working Class, 1788-1850* (New York: Oxford Univ. Press, 1984), 61-103, 157, 214-16, 238-47, 285-86, 302-5, 388. In "The Two Faces of Republicanism: Gender and Proslavery Politics in Antebellum South Carolina," *Journal of American History* 78 (March 1992): 1245-64, Stephanie McCurry challenges traditional historical views concerning republicanism by focusing on the rather undemocratic, private world where men "established their independence and status as citizens in the public sphere through the command of dependents in the households" (1246). McCurry argues that a "gendered approach" to historical analysis would broaden our customary male-dominated boundaries of political description. McCurry accurately portrays the private relations of personal domination as constituting "high politics." In this vein, the farmers involved in the Tobacco Wars employed agrarian republicanism in their quest to obtain greater control in their public, economic life while, at the same time, retaining the customary racial and gender hierarchies they controlled in their private lives.

6. The term *inherent ideologies* is taken from George Rudé, who used it to denote a "mother's milk" ideology that was based on experience and memory. This is distinct from "derived ideologies" or, "political, philosophical or religious ideas that, at varying stages of sophistication," Rudé says, "are absorbed in the more specifically popular culture." Derived ideologies, such as laissez-faire or the rights of man, can evolve into popular culture and soon constitute the new inherent ideology of the succeeding

generation. In Rudé's words, "There is no one-way traffic but constant interaction between the two." See Rudé, *Ideology and Popular Protest* (New York: Pantheon Books, 1980), 27-37.

7. *Black Patch Tobacco Journal,* Aug. 1907.

8. Clarksville *Leaf-Chronicle,* July 20, 1910.

9. Sara M. Evans and Harry C. Boyte, *Free Spaces: The Sources of Democratic Change in America* (New York: Harper and Row, 1986).

10. *Appeal to Reason,* Nov. 5, 1910.

11. Wendell Berry, *The Unsettling of America: Culture and Agriculture* (San Francisco: Sierra Club Books, 1977), 63. A provocative work that addresses the enduring power of the ideology of "progress," in spite of massive evidence that modern society clearly is not progressing in economic, social, and political terms, is Christopher Lasch, *The True and Only Heaven: Progress and Its Critics* (New York: Norton, 1991).

12. U.S. Bureau of the Census, *Statistical Abstract of the United States, 1989* (Washington, D.C., 1989), 626-29; *Statistical History of the United States: From Colonial Times to the Present* (New York: Basic Books, 1976), 457; Ingolf Vogeler, *The Myth of the Family Farm: Agribusiness Dominance of U.S. Agriculture* (Boulder, Colo.: Westview Press, 1981), 3-30, 67-85, 105-34, 217-45, 279.

13. An important but seldom-used portrait of modern agriculture is Jim Hightower, *Eat Your Heart Out: Food Profiteering in America* (New York: Crown Publishing Company, 1975).

14. For revealing journeys into the modern tobacco industry, see Elizabeth M. Whelan, *A Smoking Gun: How the Tobacco Industry Gets Away with Murder* (Philadelphia: George F. Stickley, 1984); Peter Taylor, *The Smoke Ring: Tobacco, Money, and Multinational Politics* (New York: Pantheon, 1984); and Bryan Burrough and John Helyar, *Barbarians at the Gate: The Fall of RJR Nabisco* (New York: Harper, Collins, 1990).

15. Daniel Zwerdling, "The Food Monsters: How They Gobble Up Each Other— And Us," *Progressive* 44 (March 1980): 19-21. Zwerdling adds that though the Procter and Gamble coffee campaign was expensive, "P&G didn't really lose money." The consumer financed the effort in paying inflated prices for other Proctor and Gamble products such as soap, toothpaste, and cake mix. In short, "the conglomerate merely shifted its profits to subsidize the coffee wars." The historical patterns of coffee production and marketing in many ways mirror those of tobacco. An introduction into the complex world of the South American coffee market is Marco Palacios, *Coffee in Colombia, 1850-1970: An Economic, Social and Political History* (Cambridge: Cambridge Univ. Press, 1980).

16. Vogeler, *Myth of the Family Farm,* 105-19; Hal Hamilton, "Organizing Rural Tobacco Farmers: Central Kentucky in Global Perspective," in *Communities in Economic Crisis: Appalachia and the South,* ed. John Gaventa, Barbara Ellen Smith, and Alex Willingham (Philadelphia: Temple Univ. Press, 1990), 76; Hightower, *Eat Your Heart Out,* 9-40.

17. Hamilton, "Organizing Rural Tobacco Farmers," 73-84; A. Frank Bordeaux and W. Wilson Hourigan, "Effects of Government Tobacco Programs," in *Social and Economic Issues Confronting the Tobacco Industry in the Seventies,* ed. A. Frank Bordeaux and Russell H. Brannon (Lexington: College of Agriculture and Center for Developmental Change, Univ. of Kentucky, 1972), 253-70.

18. Vogeler, *Myth of the Family Farm,* 105-19; Zwerdling, "Food Monsters," 16-26.

Zwerdling adds that in 1979 alone consumers paid an estimated fifteen billion dollars more than they would have if the food industry had not been so constrained.

19. Walter Goldschmidt, "A Tale of Two Towns," in *The People's Land: A Reader in Land Reform in the United States*, ed. Peter Barnes (Emmaus, Pa.: Rodale Press, 1975), 171-75. Goldschmidt's study was eventually published as *As You Sow: Three Studies in the Social Consequences of Agribusiness* (1947; Montclair, N.J.: Allanheld, Osmun, and Co., 1978). See Frances Moore Lappé and Joseph Collins, *Food First: Beyond the Myth of Scarcity* (New York: Ballentine Books, 1977), 265-66; and Frances Moore Lappé, "The Family Farm: Caught in the Contradictions of American Values," *Agriculture and Human Values* 2 (Spring 1985): 36-43. An excellent study that details the economic and social impact of industrialization on the southern Appalachian region and its small farming communities is Ronald D Eller, *Miners, Millhands, and Mountaineers: Industrialization of the Appalachian South, 1880-1930* (Knoxville: Univ. of Tennessee Press, 1982), 16-21, 123, 229-39. See also Mark Friedberger, *Farm Families and Change in Twentieth-Century America* (Lexington: Univ. Press of Kentucky, 1988), 46, 247.

20. *Black Patch Tobacco Journal*, Aug. 1907.

21. Richard Hofstadter, *The Age of Reform: From Bryan to FDR* (New York: Random House, 1955), 109-11; Morton Rothstein, "Farmer Movements and Organizations: Numbers, Gains, Losses," *Agricultural History* 62 (Summer 1988): 167.

22. Gilbert C. Fite, *Cotton Fields No More: Southern Agriculture, 1865-1980* (Lexington: Univ. Press of Kentucky, 1984), 49.

23. This approach is so pervasive that farming allies, in additional to critics, have often used the widely held stereotype. During the Tobacco Wars, for example, the Socialist newspaper *Appeal to Reason* noted, "American farmers, as a rule, are lethargic and slow to act" (Sept. 24, 1910). The American Society of Equity claimed, "The American farmer is a slow-thinking, lethargic individual" (*Wisconsin Equity News*, June 1, 1908). Sympathetic historians have also been guilty of this practice. Theodore Saloutos described the "slow, lethargic, and indifferent" farmer as a noteworthy impediment to agricultural organization; Saloutos, *Farmer Movements in the South, 1865-1933* (1960; Lincoln: Univ. of Nebraska Press, 1967), 174. Thomas D. Clark found even more deep-seated problems with "rural southerners," who, in Clark's estimation, lacked "any aesthetic taste. Both white and Negro were devoid of a sense of orderliness and beauty"; Clark, *The Emerging South*, 2d ed. (New York: Oxford Univ. Press, 1968), 95.

24. For some works on the Tobacco Wars that place the root cause of the conflict squarely within the realm of the overproduction thesis, see Dewey W. Grantham, Jr., *Southern Progressivism: The Reconciliation of Progress and Tradition* (Knoxville: Univ. of Tennessee Press, 1983), 324; Bill Cunningham, *On Bended Knees: The Night Rider Story* (Nashville: McClanahan Publishing House, 1983, 81; and Gregory, "Robertson County and the Black Patch War," 344.

A pathbreaking work that properly places overproduction of cotton within the context of seasonal indebtedness produced by economic conditions far beyond the control of farmers is Roger L. Ransom and Richard Sutch, "The 'Lock-In' Mechanism and Overproduction of Cotton in the Postbellum South," *Agricultural History* 49 (April 1975): 405-25. Overproduction is discussed within a populist context in Bruce Palmer, *"Man over Money": The Southern Populist Critique of American Capitalism* (Chapel Hill: Univ. of North Carolina Press, 1980), 117-21. See also Stephen J. DeCanio, "Cotton 'Overproduction' in Late Nineteenth-Century Southern Agriculture," 33 *Journal of Economic History* (Sept. 1973): 608-33.

25. I.A. Newby, *Plain Folk in the New South: Social Change and Cultural Persistence, 1880-1915* (Baton Rouge: Louisiana State Univ. Press, 1989), 9-14. Similar contradictory stereotypes have also been employed against African-Americans. As Lawrence W. Levine showed, "antithetical aphorisms such as 'to work like a nigger' and 'lazy as a nigger' had [blacks] conforming to a stereotype if they worked hard or if they did not. . . . Caught in the pinches of this dual image, if Negroes reacted to the American system with force they were living up to a stereotype, and if they did not they were also living up to a stereotype." See Levine, *Black Culture and Black Consciousness: Afro-American Folk Thought from Slavery to Freedom* (New York: Oxford Univ. Press, 1977), 336-37.

26. Fite, *Cotton Fields No More,* 71-72, 176-77, 183, 192. In 1910 editors of a Tennessee newspaper noted: "A lot of nonsense is being talked and written by the Republican newspapers about 'better agricultural methods.' When the people get sick of Republican politics and corrupt misrule, some smart aleck blames it on the farmers." Clarksville *Leaf-Chronicle,* Sept. 7, 1910.

27. Edward L. Schapsmeier and Frederick H. Schapsmeier, *Ezra Taft Benson and the Politics of Agriculture: The Eisenhower Years, 1953-1961* (Danville, Ill.: Interstate Printers and Publishers, 1975), 90-91; Vogeler, *Myth of the Family Farm,* 89-93; Nicolai quoted in Berry, *Unsettling of America,* 42.

28. USDA quoted in Hightower, *Eat Your Heart Out,* 132. Hightower adds that "Ralston Purina Company, which has had long experience as a corporate farmer, admits that they can offer no efficiency advantage. . . . an executive of the corporation said in 1973, 'the individual farmer . . . can meet, and many times surpass the efficiency of the large units that operate with hired management.' "

29. Lappé and Collins, *Food First,* 183-86; J. Patrick Madden, *Economies of Size in Farming: Theory, Analytical Procedures, and a Review of Selected Studies,* U.S. Department of Agriculture Economic Research Service, report no. 107 (Washington, D.C., 1967), 54; Vogeler, *Myth of the Family Farm,* 89-103; David Moberg, "Should We Save the Family Farm?" *Dissent* (Spring 1988): 203-4.

Bibliographical Essay

The crucial sources in locating the origins and subsequent development of both insurgent movements in the Tobacco Wars were local newspapers. In the burley region, I was dependent on the Lexington *Herald* and *Leader*, the Winchester *Democrat*, the *Farmers' Equity Journal*, the Woodford *Sun*, the Cincinnati *Enquirer*, and the *Burley Tobacco Grower*. In the Black Patch, the *Black Patch Tobacco Journal* and the Clarksville *Leaf-Chronicle* were indispensable, as were the Henderson *Daily-Gleaner*, the Madisonville *Semi-Weekly Hustler*, the Mayfield *Messenger*, and the Paducah *Sun*. National newspapers of various ideological strains, such as the *National Economist*, the *Appeal to Reason, Tobacco*, the *Western Tobacco Journal*, and the *Wisconsin Equity News*, proved very helpful.

I also consulted archival material from a variety of collections. The Burley Tobacco Cooperative Records, in the Special Collections Department of the M.I. King Library, University of Kentucky, Lexington, provided internal records of the Burley Tobacco Society, such as minutes of meetings and financial records. Such papers are rare in documenting insurgent organizations. The A.O. Stanley Papers at the University of Kentucky proved useful, as did the King Library's extensive collection of southern mercantile records, which provided a crucial insight into the nature of southern country stores and the debt system they supervised. Valuable also were the Tobacco Investigation Records, Bureau of Corporations, Record Group 122, National Archives, and the collection of Dun and Bradstreet reference books located in the Library of Congress. The Augustus Everett Willson Papers, Manuscript Department, Filson Club, Louisville, contained numerous sources related to the Tobacco Wars. Collections at the Tennessee State Library and Archives, Nashville, such as the Fort Family papers and the Washington Family Papers, also proved essential.

Government documents helped to document a wealth of social evidence. Most important was the *Report of the Commissioner of Corporations on the Tobaco Industry* (Washington, D.C., 1909). Also useful were *Bills for the Relief of Tobacco Growers*, 59th Cong., 2d sess., 1907, S. Doc. 372; *Hearings on the Relief of Tobacco Growers*, 60th Cong., 1st sess., 1903, S. Doc. 390; U.S. Department of Agriculture, Bureau of Agricultural Economics, *Tobaccos of the United States: Acreage, Yield per Acre, Production, Price, and Value, by States,*

1866-1945, and by Types and Classes, 1919-1945 (Washington, D.C., 1948). Court cases that proved vital were *United States* v. *American Tobacco Company*, 221 U.S. 106 (1911); and *Commonwealth of Kentucky* v. *Dr. David Amoss*, Hopkinsville, Ky., 1911.

Census material, at both the national and local levels, was heavily consulted. Vital was the Manuscript Census, Montgomery County, Tennessee, 1910 (microfilm), as well as the *Twelfth Census of the United States, 1900* and the *Thirteenth Census of the United States, 1910*, particularly the volumes titled *Agriculture*. I also utilized "Todd County, Kentucky, Tax List, 1906" and "Trigg County, Kentucky, Tax List, 1907," both on microfilm at the University of Kentucky.

The historical literature concerning the Tobacco Wars concentrates almost exclusively on the Black Patch War, thereby ignoring or dismissing the momentous events in the burley region. These works have also placed night riding at the center of their conceptual narratives, rather than the economic and organizational problems that produced vigilantism. See James O. Nall, *The Tobacco Night Riders of Kentucky and Tennessee, 1905-1909* (Louisville, 1939); John G. Miller, *The Black Patch War* (Chapel Hill, N.C., 1936); Dewey W. Grantham, Jr., "Black Patch War: The Story of the Kentucky and Tennessee Night Riders, 1905-1909," *South Atlantic Quarterly* 59 (Spring 1960); 215-25; Christopher Waldrep, "The Night Riders and the Law in Kentucky and Tennessee, 1870-1911," Ph.D. diss., Ohio State University, 1990; Rick Gregory, "Desperate Farmers: The Planters' Protective Association of Kentucky and Tennessee, 1904-1914," Ph.D. diss., Vanderbilt University, 1989. Suzanne Marshall Hall, "Breaking Trust: The Black Patch Tobacco Culture of Kentucky and Tennessee, 1900-1940," Ph.D. diss., Emory University, 1989, examines Black Patch farming at the social level. Books with a wider scope that discuss the burley movement are Theodore Saloutos, *Farmer Movements in the South, 1865-1933* (1960; Lincoln, Nebr., 1967); and Joseph G. Knapp, *The Rise of American Cooperative Enterprise, 1620-1920* (Danville, Ill., 1969).

Some contemporary articles were also important in understanding the wars: Anna Youngman, "Tobacco Pools of Kentucky and Tennessee," *Journal of Political Economy* 18 (Jan. 1910): 34-49; Eugene P. Lyle, Jr., "Night Riding—A Reign of Fear," *Hampton's Magazine* (June 1909): 461-74; and idem, "They That Ride by Night: The Story of Kentucky's Tobacco War," *Hampton's Magazine* (Feb. 1907): 175-87. See also Helen Morris Bleidt, "A History of the Development of Growers' Organizations and Tobacco Pools in the Burley District of Kentucky, 1902-1927," M.A. thesis, University of Kentucky, 1932; and Marie Taylor, "Night Riders in the Black Patch," M.A. thesis, University of Kentucky, 1934. The Black Patch War was the subject of Guthrie native Robert Penn Warren's first novel, *Night Rider* (New York, 1939).

The starting point for any discussion of the postwar South is C. Vann

Woodward, *Origins of the New South, 1877-1913* (Baton Rouge, La., 1951). Building on Woodward's pioneering work is Edward L. Ayers, *The Promise of the New South: Life After Reconstruction* (New York, 1992). The immediate effects of postwar economic decisions are treated in Robert P. Sharkey, *Money, Class, and Party: An Economic Study of Civil War and Reconstruction* (Baltimore, 1959); Irwin Unger, *The Greenback Era: A Social and Political History of American Finance, 1865-1879* (Princeton, N.J., 1964); Thomas D. Clark, "The Furnishing and Supply System in Southern Agriculture since 1865," *Journal of Southern History* 12 (Feb. 1946): 24-44; Walter T.K. Nugent, *Money and American Society, 1865-1880* (New York, 1968); Harold D. Woodman, *King Cotton and His Retainers: Financing and Marketing the Cotton Crop of the South, 1800-1925* (Lexington, Ky., 1968); and Roger L. Ransom and Richard Sutch, *One Kind of Freedom: The Economic Consequences of Emancipation* (Cambridge, Eng., 1977).

A vast literature has emerged concerning American agriculture. A sampling includes Gilbert C. Fite, *American Farmers: The New Minority* (Bloomington, Ind., 1981); Theodore Saloutos and John D. Hicks, *Twentieth-Century Populism: Agricultural Discontent in the Middle East, 1900-1939* (Lincoln, Nebr., 1951); and Stephen J. DeCanio, *Agriculture in the Postbellum South* (Cambridge, Mass., 1974). A provocative collection of essays is contained in Steven Hahn and Jonathan Prude, *The Countryside in the Age of Capitalist Transformation: Essays in the Social History of Rural America* (Chapel Hill, N.C., 1985). See also Pete Daniel, *Breaking the Land: The Transformation of Cotton, Tobacco, and Rice Culture since 1880* (Urbana, Ill., 1985).

Sources on the development of the American Tobacco Company are Robert F. Durden, *The Dukes of Durham, 1865-1929* (Durham, N.C., 1975); Patrick G. Porter, "Origins of the American Tobacco Company," *Business History Review* 43 (Spring 1969): 59-76; Nannie May Tilley, *The Bright-Tobacco Industry, 1860-1929* (Chapel Hill, N.C., 1948); and Jason Scott, "No Monopoly on Freedom: A Study of the American Tobacco Company from 1890 to 1911," senior thesis, Duke University, 1990. No recent biographies of James B. Duke exist. Important books on the larger contemporary development of monopoly capitalism are Hans B. Thorelli, *The Federal Antitrust Policy: Origination of an American Tradition* (Stockholm, 1954); Gabriel Kolko, *The Triumph of Conservatism: A Reinterpretation of American History, 1900-1916* (New York, 1963); and Alfred D. Chandler, Jr., *The Visible Hand: The Managerial Revolution in American Business* (Cambridge, Mass., 1977). A careful overview of the development of industry in North Carolina is Allen Tullos, *Habits of Industry: White Culture and the Transformation of the Carolina Piedmont* (Chapel Hill, N.C., 1989).

Social movements under way during the late 1800s are treated in Lawrence Goodwyn, *Democratic Promise: The Populist Moment in America* (New York, 1976); Steven Hahn, *The Roots of Southern Populism: Yeoman Farmers and the Transformation of the Georgia Upcountry, 1850-1890* (New York, 1983); and Bruce Palmer, *"Man over Money": The Southern Populist Critique of American Capitalism* (Chapel Hill, N.C., 1980). For Kentucky, a seldom-used but excellent review is Edward F. Prichard, Jr., "Popular Political Movements in Kentucky, 1875-1900," senior thesis, Princeton University, 1935. Particularly valuable is George C. Wright, *Racial Violence in Kentucky, 1865-1940: Lynchings, Mob Rule, and "Legal Lynchings"* (Baton Rouge, La., 1990). For Tennessee, see J.A. Sharp, "The Entrance of the Farmers' Alliance into Tennessee Politics," *East Tennessee Historical Society Publications* 9 (1937): 77-92; and Daniel M. Robison, *Bob Taylor and the Agrarian Revolt in Tennessee* (Chapel Hill, N.C., 1935).

Among numerous monographs on the decline of the family farm, a fine starting point is Ingolf Vogeler, *The Myth of the Family Farm: Agribusiness Dominance of U.S. Agriculture* (Boulder, Colo., 1981). The social consequences of the demise of family farms is authoritatively detailed in Walter Goldschmidt, *As You Sow: Three Studies in the Social Consequences of Agribusiness* (1947; Montclair, N.J., 1978). Also valuable are Roger Burbach and Patricia Flynn, *Agribusiness in the Americas* (New York, 1980); Frances Moore Lappé, "The Family Farm: Caught in the Contradictions of American Values," *Agriculture and Human Values* 2 (Spring 1985): 36-43; and David Moberg, "Should We Save the Family Farm?" *Dissent* (Spring 1988): 201-11. A sensitive and provocative work is Wendell Berry, *The Unsettling of America: Culture and Agriculture* (San Francisco, 1977).

The topic of republicanism as an insurgent ideology has given rise to a vast literature devoted to this subject. A pioneering work is J.G.A. Pocock, *The Machiavellian Moment: Florentine Political Thought and the Atlantic Republican Tradition* (Princeton, N.J., 1975). The debate is examined in Robert Shalhope, "Republicanism in Early America," *William and Mary Quarterly* 38 (1982): 334-56. See also Eric Foner, *Tom Paine and Revolutionary America* (New York, 1976); Joyce Appleby, *Capitalism and a New Social Order: The Republican Vision of the 1790s* (New York, 1984); idem, "Republicanism in Old and New Contexts," *William and Mary Quarterly* 37 (1985): 461-73; Sean Wilentz, *Chants Democratic: New York City and the Rise of the American Working Class, 1788-1850* (New York, 1984); Bruce Laurie, *Artisans into Workers: Labor in Nineteenth-Century America* (New York, 1989); and Christopher Lasch, *The True and Only Heaven: Progress and Its Critics* (New York, 1991).

Studies not specifically focused on either the Tobacco Wars or southern agriculture, but critical in delineating some conceptual matters, are E.P. Thompson, *The Making of the English Working Class* (New York, 1963); idem, "The Moral Economy of the English Crowd in the Eighteenth Century," *Past and Present* 50 (Feb. 1971): 76-136; William Greider, *Secrets of the Temple: How the Federal Reserve Runs the Country* (New York, 1987); John Gaventa, *Power and Powerlessness: Quiescence and Rebellion in an Appalachian Valley*

(Urbana, Ill., 1980); Theodore Rosengarten, *All God's Dangers: The Life of Nate Shaw* (New York, 1974); James C. Scott, *The Moral Economy of the Peasant: Rebellion and Subsistence in Southeast Asia* (New Haven, Conn., 1976); idem, *Weapons of the Weak: Everyday Forms of Peasant Resistance* (New Haven, Conn., 1985); George Rudé, *The Crowd in the French Revolution* (New York, 1959); Eric Hobsbawm and George Rudé, *Captain Swing: A Social History of the Great English Agricultural Uprising of 1830* (1968; New York, 1975); Sara M. Evans and Harry C. Boyte, *Free Spaces: The Sources of Democratic Change in America* (New York, 1986); Barbara S. Griffith, *The Crisis of American Labor: Operation Dixie and the Defeat of the CIO* (Philadelphia, 1988); David Thelen, *Paths of Resistance: Tradition and Dignity in Industrializing Missouri* (New York, 1986); Herbert G. Gutman, *Work, Culture, and Society in Industrializing America* (New York, 1977); Christopher Hill, *The World Turned Upside Down: Radical Ideas during the English Revolution* (New York, 1972); and Benjamin Barber, *Strong Democracy: Participatory Politics for a New Age* (Berkeley, Calif., 1984).

Index